Vacation
& Second Homes

THIRD EDITION

Published by Home Planners, LLC
Wholly owned by Hanley-Wood, LLC
Editorial and Corporate Offices:
3275 West Ina Road, Suite 110
Tucson, Arizona 85741
Distribution Center:
29333 Lorie Lane
Wixom, Michigan 48393

Jayne Fenton, President
Jennifer Pearce, Vice President, Group Content
Linda B. Bellamy, Executive Editor
Arlen Feldwick-Jones, Editorial Director
Vicki Frank, Managing Editor
Laura Hurst Brown, Project Editor
Tina Grijalva, Laura Moreno, Plans Editors
Peter Zullo, Graphic Designer
William Knight, Teralyn Morriss, Graphic Production Artists
Sara Lisa, Senior Production Manager
Fariba Crawford, Production Manager

Front cover:
Plan HPT700304 by ©Chatham Home Planning, Inc.
Photograph by Chris A. Little of Atlanta
To view floor plans, see page 323.
Back Cover:
Plan HPT700331 by ©Chatham Home Planning, Inc.
Photograph by Chris A. Little of Atlanta
To view floor plans, see page 350.

Book design by Peter Zullo
©1991, 1995
Third Edition, May 2002

10 9 8 7 6 5 4 3 2 1

Printed in the United States of America
Library of Congress Catalog Card Number: 2001094523
ISBN softcover: 1-881955-97-4

Contents

A sense of hospitality and a deep level of comfort fill these rooms, and outdoor living spaces offer an everyday getaway in this Southern retreat

Grand Getaway

This home, as shown in the photograph, may differ from the actual blueprints. For more detailed information, please check the floor plans carefully.

Rich with sleek notions of luxury, this coastal design offers comfort zones set off with a casual elegance. Even the formal spaces of this history house are light, bright and open in a rambling interior that's made for the ways we live today. Square columns and a simple balustrade enhance the façade—an inviting blend of Early American and modern seaside styles. Inside, a massive fireplace anchors the serene decor in the family room, the inviting heart of the home. French doors lead outside to a fabulous screened porch and a very cool wood deck with a *sunbathers wanted* attitude.

A galley-style kitchen features a walk-in pantry and a pass-through shared with the living room and breakfast area. Two sets of triple windows wrap the morning nook with sunlight that's filtered through classic vertical shutters. Nearby, the formal dining room provides tall windows that bring in a sense of nature and allow wide views.

To the left of the plan, the master wing provides an idyllic retreat for the homeowners. Privacy doors allow quiet conversation in the study yet the furnishings suggest a place for people to gather, laugh and have fun. Upstairs, two secondary bedrooms share a full bath. A spacious suite provides accommodations for a guest or converts to a bedroom for a teenager.

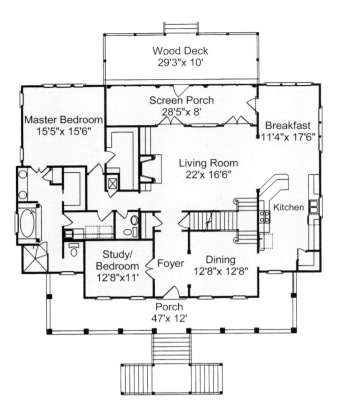

Wood Deck
29'3"x 10'

Screen Porch
28'5"x 8'

Master Bedroom
15'5"x 15'6"

Breakfast
11'4"x 17'6"

Living Room
22'x 16'6"

Kitchen

Study/
Bedroom
12'8"x11'

Foyer

Dining
12'8"x 12'8"

Porch
47'x 12'

PLAN HPT700419

First Floor: *2,036 square feet*
Second Floor: *1,230 square feet*
Total: *3,266 square feet*
Width: *57'-4"* **Depth:** *59'-0"*

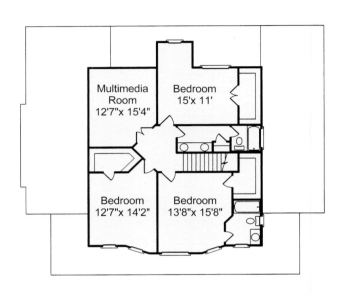

Multimedia
Room
12'7"x 15'4"

Bedroom
15'x 11'

Bedroom
12'7"x 14'2"

Bedroom
13'8"x 15'8"

Designer
©*Chatham Home Planning, Inc.*
Photographer
©*Chris A. Little, Atlanta, Georgia*

Rich vanilla cabinetry and honey hardwood floors are happy together in the gallery kitchen.

Above: Simple and serene, the dining room invites quiet events and crowd-size bashes.
Right: Rich with sleek notions of luxury, this coastal Country design offers much more than mere fashion.

Recognize the key elements that make a retreat different from a full-time house

Designer
©Chatham Home Planning, Inc.

Photographer
©Chris A. Little, Atlanta, Georgia

To view floor plans, see page 331.

Creating Your Own Retreat

by Jeanne Huber

When families dream of building a retreat, often the goal is to experience the pleasures of a simpler life. But when the time comes to actually build that retreat, they keep thinking of things to add. In no time, the retreat grows to look almost like a house. The result is two houses to keep up—and, unless you have loads of full-time help, there's nothing simple about that.

Here are some tips to make sure this doesn't happen to you.

✳ Take your cues from the site. Consider not only the view, but also the topography. How will wind and weather affect your cottage and your use of the land? On a windy site by the seashore, for example, you might be able to use the cottage as a windscreen, gaining a cozy patio on the inland side of the lot.

✳ Keep earth-moving to a minimum so that you preserve nature's landscaping. Often, native trees, bushes and wildflowers are what attract people to a particular lot. Remember, native plants provide the best habitat for wildlife—which can become a source of considerable entertainment—and they are well-adapted to survive on their own without weeding, watering or pruning. Somehow, native vegetation seems to look great all the time. Suburban-style landscaping needs to be continually tended or it looks like a mess.

✳ Keep the building small. It's that much less you'll need to clean and repair. Resist the temptation to add enough bedrooms for everyone in your extended family. For those rare family gatherings, you can always rent a nearby guest house or set up a tent in the yard. Or, build one large sleeping loft where cousins can spread out sleeping bags. It'll be more fun for them, and a lot saner for you.

✳ Splurge on space for a treasured hobby, preferably one you never seem to find time to enjoy at home: a darkroom, a woodcarving shop, an art studio, or simply a library with an overstuffed chair.

✳ Decorate with items you make while at the retreat. You'll enjoy the making and the memories. But don't over-decorate; you don't want to spend your cherished time straightening up.

✳ Design in ways that minimize the need for maintenance. Avoid gutters. Will there ever be a weekend when you would choose to be out on a ladder, keeping them clean? Instead, design the roof with broad overhangs and install an exterior drainage system to carry water away. Plantings or gravel at the roof's drip line can keep rainwater from splashing onto the siding and causing problems. Windows and other exterior features should be easy to maintain as well.

✳ Control costs—it's another way to give yourself more time to enjoy your retreat. Design rooms in four-foot increments so you use sheets of drywall or plywood efficiently. Specify stock-size doors and windows. And keep other details as simple as possible.

✳ Consider playing with materials a bit. It's a retreat, after all. In this seaside retreat, the architect used classic seaboard details and louver shutters. Other cottages gain style with unique furnishings. Shop for these not-quite antiques at secondhand stores, tag sales and country auctions.

Wild Mind
Wide Open Spaces

Where we go when it's time to get away is as important as where we live the rest of the year—yet we approach these places differently. How beautiful the land and how big the sky are as vital as the look of the neighborhood or the quality of the schools. Waking up to a view matters as much as whether the bedroom is up or down—and we want what we see through our windows to be as inspiring as the windows themselves.

The places we would most like to be come with a flavor—a look that has to do with *home*. Dreams of finding our way down to the ocean or up the side of a mountain go with spacious porticos, cozy alcoves, two-story walls and wide-open decks. Breezes harmonize with fireplaces, screened porches go with bare feet, and stars mingle with spa-style baths.

Here are fabulous retreats from 900 to 3,800 square feet that are ready for the most beautiful places on earth. Architecture rich with both history and a sense of the future invites flexibility and growth. Packed with amenities that provide a deep level of comfort, these homes also present cutting-edge exterior styles as striking as the scenery that will surround them.

We want what we see through our windows to be as inspiring as the windows themselves

This home, as shown in the photographs, may differ from the actual blueprints. For more detailed information, please check the floor plans on page 264 carefully.

Earth

great escapes and havens

Plan HPT700001

Square Footage: *2,227*
Width: *50'-0"* **Depth:** *71'-0"*

Here's a fun getaway with all of the comforts of home. An open arrangement of formal and casual spaces allows interior vistas that extend from the foyer to the rear porch. French doors open to a quiet den, which easily converts to a spare bedroom. To the rear of the plan, casual living space provides its own fireplace and access to the rear property. A vaulted ceiling lends an air of spaciousness to the kitchen. The breakfast nook takes in the scenery and invites casual meals. The sleeping wing includes a vaulted master suite with a box-bay window, a lavish bath and a walk-in closet.

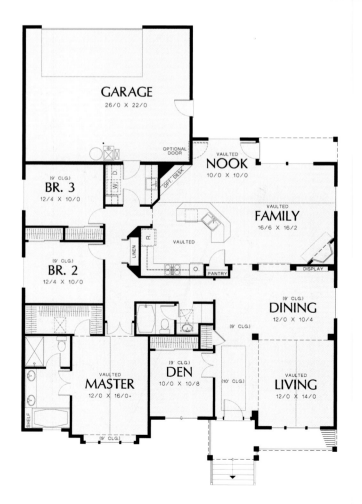

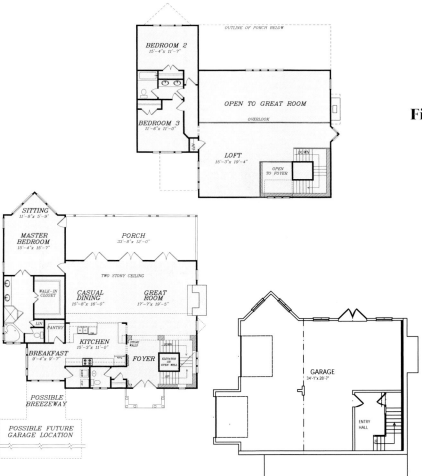

BEDROOM 2
15'-4"x 11'-7"

OUTLINE OF PORCH BELOW

OPEN TO GREAT ROOM

OVERLOOK

BEDROOM 3
11'-6"x 11'-0"

LOFT
15'-3"x 19'-4"

JOHN

OPEN
TO FOYER

SITTING
11'-8"x 5'-9"

MASTER
BEDROOM
15'-4"x 15'-7"

PORCH
33'-8"x 12'-0"

WALK-IN
CLOSET

TWO STORY CEILING

LIN

PANTRY

CASUAL
DINING
15'-8"x 16'-0"

GREAT
ROOM
17'-7"x 19'-5"

KITCHEN
15'-3"x 11'-0"

STONE
WALLS

JOHN

BREAKFAST
9'-4"x 9'-7"

FOYER

ELEVATOR
OR
OPEN WELL

POSSIBLE
BREEZEWAY

POSSIBLE FUTURE
GARAGE LOCATION

GARAGE
34'-1"x 28'-7"

ENTRY
HALL

Plan HPT700002

First Floor: *1,825 square feet*
Second Floor: *1,020 square feet*
Total: *2,845 square feet*
Finished Basement: *816 square feet*
Width: *49'-8"* **Depth:** *57'-0"*

A flagstone-decorated covered porch opens through French doors to a foyer where stone walls lead into the casual dining/great room area. This room is graced with a two-story ceiling and fireplace, as well as three sets of French doors opening to the rear porch. The kitchen leads into the breakfast area, which provides a door to the laundry room. The master bedroom includes a sitting area, walk-in closet, linen area and many other luxuries. Spacious family bedrooms share a full bath. A large loft is provided for a play area, bookshelves or whatever you desire. A balcony overlook allows views to the great room below, creating a sense of spaciousness.

Plan HPT700003

First Floor: *1,596 square feet*
Second Floor: *387 square feet*
Total: *1,983 square feet*
Width: *46'-6"* **Depth:** *65'-0"*

Front and rear covered porches add comfortable outdoor space to this fine three-bedroom home. A formal dining room is located near the entry. Nearby, a wall of windows and a warming fireplace characterize the comfortable great room. The island work area in the kitchen will make food preparation a breeze. A luxurious master suite contains a private dual-vanity bath with a garden tub and separate shower. The other two bedrooms each have a full bath. Note the extra storage space available off the rear porch. Please specify basement, crawlspace or slab foundation when ordering.

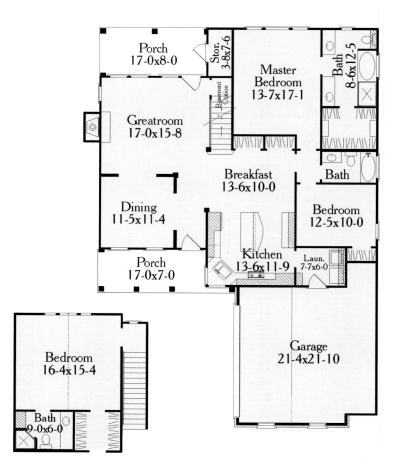

This Cape Cod design is enhanced with shingles, stone detailing and muntin windows. The entry is flanked on the left by a bedroom/den, perfect for overnight guests or a cozy place to relax. The hearth-warmed great room enjoys expansive views of the rear deck area. The dining room is nestled next to the island kitchen, which boasts plenty of counter space. The master bedroom is positioned at the rear of the home for privacy and has access to a private bath.

Plan HPT700004

Square Footage: *1,544*
Finished Basement: *1,018 square feet*
Width: *40'-0"* **Depth:** *60'-0"*

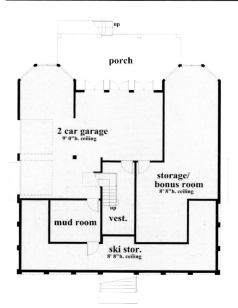

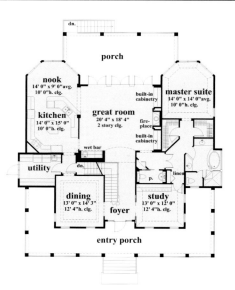

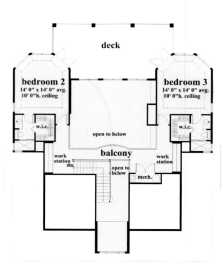

First floor plan labels:
porch
up
2 car garage
9' 0" ceiling
storage/
bonus room
8' 8" h. ceiling
up
vest.
mud room
ski stor.
8' 8" h. ceiling

Second floor plan labels:
dn.
porch
nook
14' 0" x 9' 0" avg.
10' 0" h. clg.
built-in
cabinetry
master suite
14' 0" x 14' 0" avg.
10' 0" h. clg.
kitchen
14' 0" x 15' 0"
10' 0" h. clg.
great room
20' 4" x 18' 4"
2 story clg.
fire-
place
built-in
cabinetry
wet bar
utility
dn.
p.
linen
dining
13' 0" x 14' 3"
12' 4" h. clg.
study
13' 0" x 12' 0"
12' 4" h. clg.
foyer
entry porch

Third floor plan labels:
deck
bedroom 2
14' 0" x 14' 0" avg.
10' 0" h. ceiling
bedroom 3
14' 0" x 14' 0" avg.
10' 0" h. ceiling
w.i.c.
open to below
w.i.c.
work
station
balcony
work
station
dn.
open to
below
mech.

Plan HPT700005

First Floor: *2,146 square feet*
Second Floor: *952 square feet*
Lower Level Entry: *187 square feet*
Total: *3,285 square feet*
Width: *52'-0"* **Depth:** *65'-4"*

Wild mountain breezes invigorate the senses in the great outdoor living areas of this sensational retreat. Tall windows wrap this noble exterior with dazzling details and allow plenty of natural light inside. A wraparound porch sets a casual but elegant pace for the home, with space for rockers and swings. Well-defined formal rooms are placed just off the foyer, which also leads to a wide-open great room. A host of French doors open this space to an entertainment veranda and, of course, inspiring views. Even formal meals take on the ease and comfort of a mountain region in the stunning, open dining room.

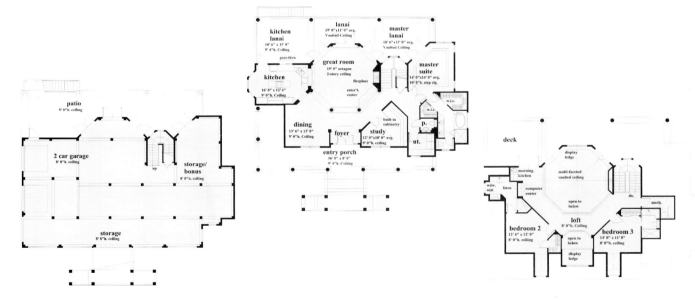

Plan HPT700006

First Floor: *1,855 square feet*
Second Floor: *901 square feet*
Total: *2,756 square feet*
Width: *66'-0"* **Depth:** *50'-0"*

This Southern tidewater cottage is the perfect vacation hideaway. An octagonal great room with a multi-faceted vaulted ceiling illuminates the interior. The island kitchen is brightened by a bumped-out window and a pass-through to the lanai. Two walk-in closets and a whirlpool bath await to indulge the homeowner in the master suite. A set of double doors opens to the vaulted master lanai for quiet comfort. The U-shaped staircase leads to a loft, which overlooks the great room and the foyer. Two additional family bedrooms are offered with private baths. A computer center and a morning kitchen complete the upstairs.

Plan HPT700007

First Floor: *1,642 square feet*
Second Floor: *1,205 square feet*
Total: *2,847 square feet*
Bonus Space: *340 square feet*
Width: *53'-7"* **Depth:** *72'-6"*

Arches, niches, detailed ceilings, multi-pane and specialty windows are strategically placed for the utmost in dramatic effects. A stepped ceiling highlights the formal dining room, which conveniently leads to a servery and pantry area in the gourmet kitchen. The gallery hall provides a powder room for guests. Three sets of French doors open the leisure room to spacious covered porch. The master suite features a tray ceiling, French doors and a rear deck. Walk-in closets, a whirlpool tub, a walk-in shower with shampoo niche, and separate vanities comprise the master bath.

Plan HPT700008

First Floor: *1,710 square feet*
Second Floor: *618 square feet*
Total: *2,328 square feet*
Width: *47'-0"* **Depth:** *50'-0"*

Here's a new American farm-house that's just right for any neighborhood—in town or far away. A perfect interior starts with an open foyer and interior vistas through a fabulous great room. A fireplace anchors the living space while a beamed, vaulted ceiling adds volume. Decorative columns open the central interior to the gourmet kitchen and breakfast area, which boasts a bay window. The master wing includes a study that easily converts to a home office. Upstairs, the secondary bedrooms feature built-in desks and walk-in closets.

Photo courtesy of Design Basics, Inc.

This home, as shown in the photograph, may differ from the actual blueprints. For more detailed information, please check the floor plans carefully.

Plan HPT700009

First Floor: *1,875 square feet*
Second Floor: *687 square feet*
Total: *2,562 square feet*
Width: *60'-0"* **Depth:** *59'-4"*

Two stunning elevations announce a well-planned interior with this design. French doors in the breakfast room open to a versatile office with a sloping ten-foot ceiling. A convenient utility area off the kitchen features access to the garage, a half bath and a generous laundry room complete with a folding table. A private entrance into the master suite reveals a pleasing interior. On the second floor, three large secondary bedrooms share a bath with dual sinks.

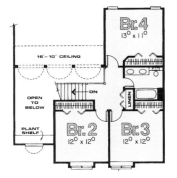

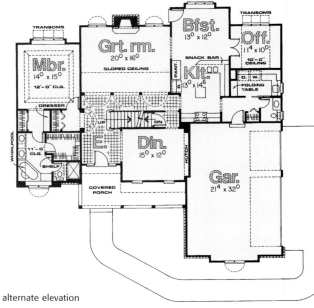

alternate elevation

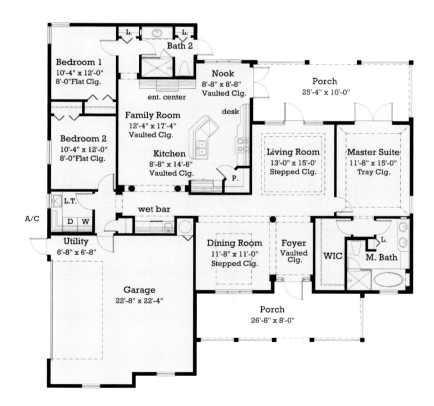

Plan HPT700010

Square Footage: *1,848*
Width: *58'-0"* **Depth:** *59'-6"*

Stucco and stone and striking country accents lend this home a unique flavor. A front covered porch leads to to a foyer opening to formal living and dining rooms. The master suite, living room and breakfast nook all access the rear porch. A wet bar, placed across from the kitchen, easily serves the formal areas and casual rooms nearby. A pantry and island workstation are found in the kitchen, overlooking the family room and nook. Bedrooms 2 and 3 utilize a hall bath found behind the family room.

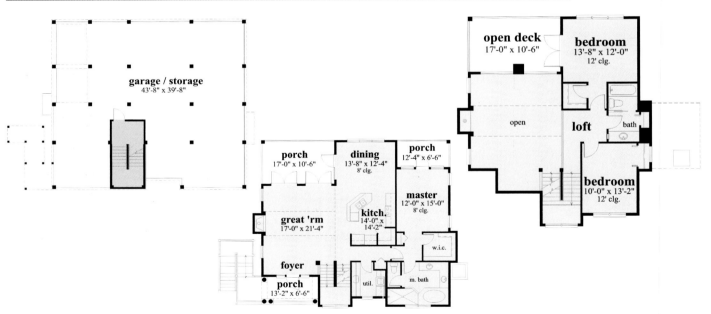

Plan HPT700011

First Floor: *1,342 square feet*
Second Floor: *511 square feet*
Total: *1,853 square feet*
Width: *44'-0"* **Depth:** *40'-0"*

Historic architectural details and timeless materials come together in this outrageously beautiful home. With a perfect Mediterranean spirit, arch-top windows create curb appeal and allow the beauty and warmth of nature within. An unrestrained interior blends formal and casual living spaces, with exceptional touches such as a row of French doors and lovely windows. To the rear of the plan, an elegant dining room easily flexes to serve traditional events as well as impromptu gatherings. An angled island counter accents the gourmet kitchen and permits wide interior vistas. The homeowner's retreat features a spacious bedroom that leads outside to a private porch—the best place in the world to count stars.

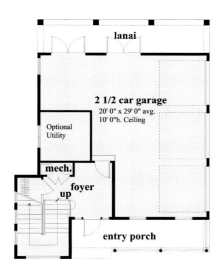

lanai

2 1/2 car garage
20' 0" x 29' 0" avg.
10' 0"h. Ceiling

Optional Utility

mech.

foyer
up

entry porch

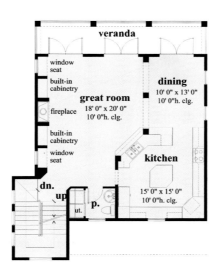

veranda

window seat

built-in cabinetry

fireplace

built-in cabinetry

window seat

great room
18' 0" x 20' 0"
10' 0"h. clg.

dining
10' 0" x 13' 0"
10' 0"h. clg.

dn.
up

p.

ut.

kitchen
15' 0" x 15' 0"
10' 0"h. clg.

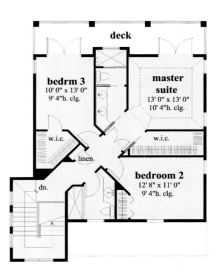

deck

bedrm 3
10' 0" x 13' 0"
9' 4"h. clg.

master suite
13' 0" x 13' 0"
10' 4"h. clg.

w.i.c.

w.i.c.

linen

dn.

bedroom 2
12' 8" x 11' 0"
9' 4"h. clg.

A stately tower adds a sense of grandeur to cool, contemporary high-pitched rooflines on this dreamy Mediterranean-style villa. Surrounded by outdoor views, the living space extends to a veranda through three sets of French doors. Decorative columns announce the dining area, which boasts a ten-foot ceiling and views of its own. Tall arch-top windows bathe a winding staircase with sunlight or moonlight. The upper-level sleeping quarters include a master retreat that offers a bedroom with views and access to the observation deck.

Plan HPT700420

First Floor: *874 square feet*
Second Floor: *880 square feet*
Lower Level Entry: *242 square feet*
Total: *1,996 square feet*
Width: *34'-0"* **Depth:** *43'-0"*

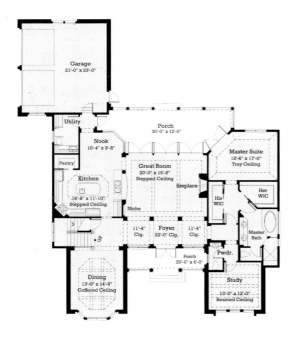

Plan HPT700012

First Floor: *2,073 square feet*
Second Floor: *682 square feet*
Total: *2,755 square feet*
Width: *64'-6"* **Depth:** *76'-8"*

The great room, central to the floor plan, adjoins a column-lined foyer and is set off by three sets of double French doors. A sweeping archway leads to the formal dining room, which has an impressive bay window. A planter box sets off the quiet study. The master suite fills the right wing and offers two walk-in closets, a dual-sink vanity, a whirlpool tub and a walk-in shower. Two secondary bedrooms share a dual-sink vanity upstairs. A loft provides space for computers and books.

Plan HPT700013

First Floor: *1,719 square feet*
Second Floor: *819 square feet*
Total: *2,538 square feet*
Width: *56'-0"* **Depth:** *51'-8"*

This gracious, four-bedroom, French country home has an appealing stone-and-brick and rough-hewn cedar exterior. A curving stairway in the entry leads to the family or guest bedrooms on the second floor. Downstairs, both the great room with fireplace and built-in entertainment center, and the master bedroom with a private bath and fitted walk-in closet face the large covered patio that extends across the back of the house. The formal dining room at the front is just a few steps from the island kitchen, with sloped ceilings and a bright breakfast area. A powder room and utility room are off the hall that leads to the two-car garage.

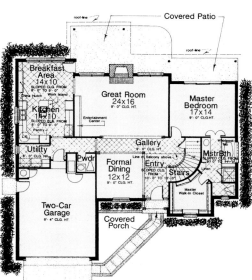

Plan HPT700014

Square Footage: *2,152*
Bonus Room: *453 square feet*
Width: *61'-8"* **Depth:** *69'-9"*

Stone, stucco and cedar shakes combine to create an enchanting exterior for this split-bedroom Craftsman bungalow. A tray ceiling adds elegance and definition to the open dining room, while the great room is enhanced by a cathedral ceiling and a fireplace flanked by built-ins. The spacious, efficiently designed kitchen features a useful center island and is open to both the breakfast bay and the great room.

©1999 Donald A. Gardner, Inc.

DECK

BRKFST.
13-4 x 10-2

BED RM.
15-0 x 14-8

KITCHEN
13-4 x 11-4

GREAT RM.
19-0 x 19-4

(cathedral ceiling)

MASTER
BED RM.
15-0 x 17-0

fireplace

walk-in
closet

walk-in
closet

railing   down

master bath

FOYER
7-8 x
9-2

DINING
13-4 x 12-0

UTILITY
10-0 x 8-0

PORCH

pd. rm.

GARAGE
21-0 x 23-2

storage

©1999 Donald A. Gardner, Inc.

PATIO

UNFIN. STORAGE/
MECHANICAL
28-4 x 18-8

FAMILY RM.
19-0 x 18-6

fireplace

BED RM.
14-6 x 15-0

bath

up

Plan HPT700015

Main Level: *2,068 square feet*
Lower Level: *930 square feet*
Total: *2,998 square feet*
Width: *72'-4"* **Depth:** *66'-0"*

This Craftsman-style home takes advantage of hillside views with its deck, patio and an abundance of rear windows. An open floor plan enhances the home's spaciousness. The great room features a cathedral ceiling, a fireplace with built-in cabinets and shelves, and access to the generous rear deck. Designed for ultimate efficiency, the kitchen serves the great room, dining room and breakfast area with equal ease. A tray ceiling lends elegance to the master bedroom, which features deck access, twin walk-in closets, and an extravagant bath.

rear view

29

Plan HPT700016

Main Level: *1,864 square feet*
Lower Level: *999 square feet*
Total: *2,863 square feet*
Bonus Room: *417 square feet*
Width: *60'-0"* **Depth:** *67'-2"*

Cedar shakes, siding and stone blend artfully together on the exterior of this attractive Craftsman-style home. Inside, a remarkably open floor plan separates the master suite from two family bedrooms for privacy. Optimizing family togetherness, the common areas of the home are pleasingly open with few interior walls to divide the rooms from one another. A tray ceiling adds definition to the dining room, while the great room is amplified by a cathe-dral ceiling. A tray ceiling also tops the master bedroom, which enjoys a lovely private bath with a walk-in closet. Two family bedrooms share a hall bath on the opposite side of the plan. ©1999 Donald A. Gardner, Inc.

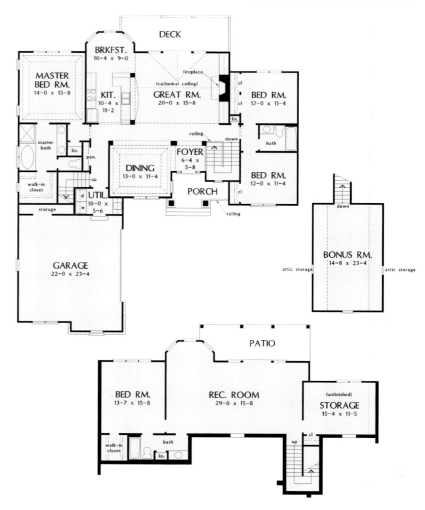

© 1999 Donald A. Gardner, Inc.

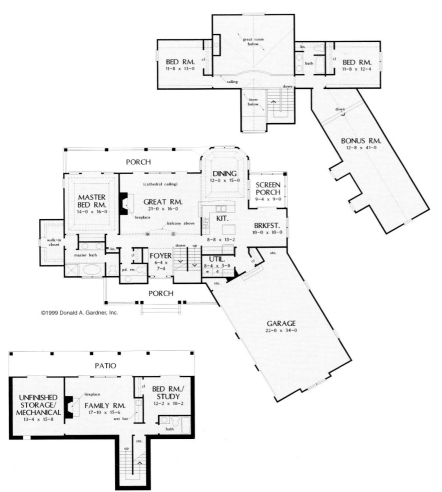

Upper Level

great room below

lin.

BED RM.
11-8 x 13-0

bath

cl

BED RM.
11-8 x 12-4

railing

down

foyer below

down

BONUS RM.
12-8 x 41-0

Main Level

PORCH

DINING
12-0 x 15-0

MASTER
BED RM.
14-0 x 16-0

(cathedral ceiling)

GREAT RM.
21-0 x 16-0

SCREEN
PORCH
9-4 x 9-0

fireplace

balcony above

KIT.

walk-in
closet

lin.

BRKFST.
8-8 x 13-2

master bath

cl

FOYER
6-4 x
7-4

down up

UTIL.
8-4 x 5-8

sto.

pd. rm.

w. d.

sto.

PORCH

GARAGE
22-0 x 34-0

©1999 Donald A. Gardner, Inc.

Lower Level

PATIO

UNFINISHED
STORAGE/
MECHANICAL
13-4 x 15-8

fireplace

FAMILY RM.
17-10 x 15-6

wet bar

cl

BED RM./
STUDY
12-2 x 10-2

bath

sto.

up

Plan HPT700017

Main Level: *1,662 square feet*
Upper Level: *585 square feet*
Lower Level: *706 square feet*
Total: *2,953 square feet*
Bonus Space: *575 square feet*
Width: *81'-4"* **Depth:** *68'-8"*

A stunning center dormer with an arched window embellishes the exterior of this Craftsman-style home. The dormer's arched window allows light into the foyer and built-in niche. The second-floor hall is a balcony that overlooks both the foyer and great room. A generous back porch extends the great room, which features an impressive vaulted ceiling and fireplace, while a tray ceiling adorns the formal dining room. The master suite, which includes a tray ceiling as well, enjoys back-porch access, a built-in cabinet, generous walk-in closet and private bath. Two more bedrooms are located upstairs, while a fourth can be found in the basement along with a family room.

©1991 Donald A. Gardner Architects, Inc.
Photography courtesy of Donald A. Gardner Architects, Inc.

This home, as shown in the photograph, may differ from the actual blueprints.
For more detailed information, please check the floor plans carefully.

Plan HPT700018

First Floor: *1,356 square feet*
Second Floor: *542 square feet*
Total: *1,898 square feet*
Bonus Room: *393 square feet*
Width: *59'-0"* **Depth:** *64'-0"*

The welcoming charm of this country farmhouse is expressed by its many windows and its covered, wraparound porch. A two-story entrance foyer is enhanced by a Palladian window in a clerestory dormer above to let in natural lighting. The first-floor master suite allows privacy and accessibility. The master bath includes a whirlpool tub, separate shower, double-bowl vanity and walk-in closet. The first floor features nine-foot ceilings throughout with the exception of the kitchen area, which sports an eight-foot ceiling. The second floor provides two additional bedrooms, a full bath and plenty of storage. ©1991 Donald A. Gardner Architects, Inc.

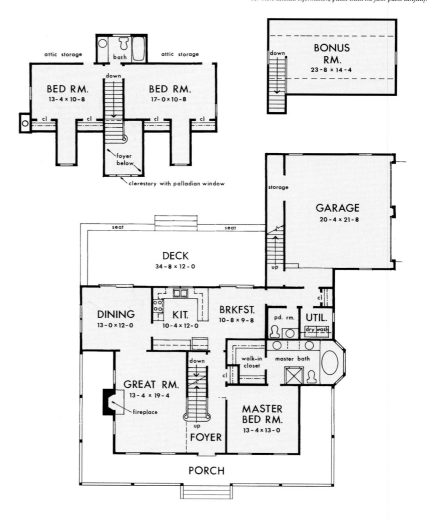

Prairies

ranch houses and haciendas

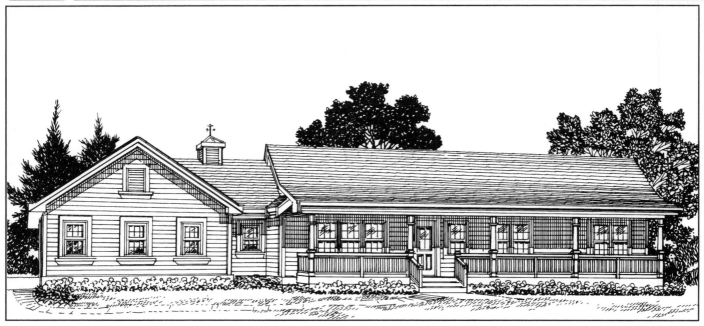

Plan HPT700019

Square Footage: *1,652*
Width: *78'-6"* **Depth:** *48'-0"*

QUOTE ONE®

Cost to build? See page 436
to order complete cost estimate
to build this house in your area!

This long, low ranch home has outdoor living on two porches—one to the front and one to the rear. Vaulted ceilings in the great room, kitchen and master bedroom add a dimension of extra space. A fireplace warms the great room, which opens to the country kitchen. The fine master suite also has doors to the rear porch and is graced by a walk-in closet, plus a full bath with a garden tub and dual vanity. The two-car garage contains space for a freezer and extra storage cabinets that are built in.

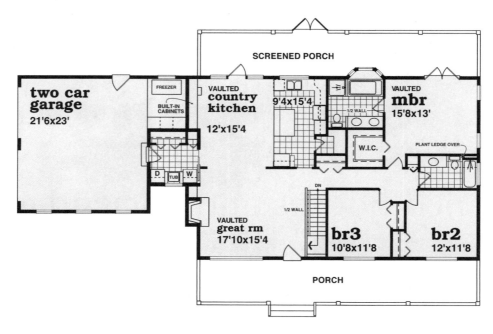

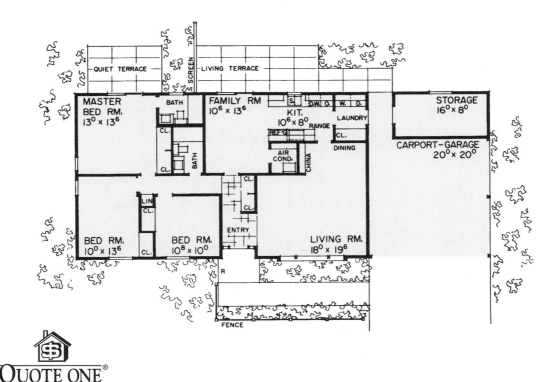

Plan HPT700020

Square Footage: *1,344*
Width: *68'-0"* **Depth:** *28'-0"*

L D

This charming Ranch-style home is perfect for empty-nesters or a small family. A study of the floor plan reveals fine livability. There are two full baths, a fine family room, an efficient work center, a formal dining area, bulk storage facilities and sliding glass doors to the quiet and living terraces. The laundry room is strategically located near the kitchen. Three bedrooms include a master bedroom with double closets and a full, private bath. Two secondary bedrooms share a full hall bath.

Plan HPT700021

Square Footage: *1,273*
Width: *54'-0"* **Depth:** *54'-0"*

Enjoy the feel of country in this classic three-bedroom brick-and-siding home. A roomy front porch awaits summer visitors or quiet contemplation of nature. Inside, the tiled entry introduces a faux-beamed living room. Curl up with a good book by the living-room fireplace or step out onto the side patio through the French door. Left of the living room, double doors open to the sleeping zone—two family bedrooms sharing a full hall bath and a master bedroom with a private bath. The kitchen opens to the dining room over a serving bar. Note the handy storage closet near the garage. Please specify crawlspace or slab foundation when ordering.

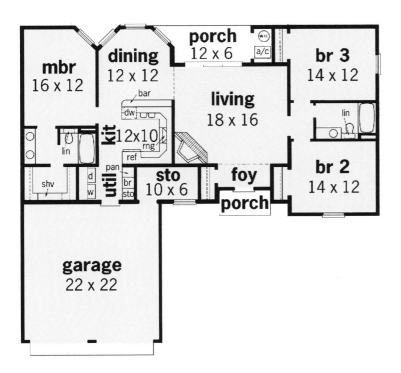

Plan HPT700022

Square Footage: *1,415*
Width: *56'-0"* **Depth:** *50'-0"*

Unusual window treatments and delicate wooden trim give this home an appealing exterior. A corner fireplace warms the living room, where a door opens to a back porch and patio. The U-shaped kitchen shares a snack bar with the bayed dining room. On the right side of the home a full hall bath links two secondary bedrooms. The master suite offers a full bath with a dual vanity and a walk-in closet with built-in shelves. The two-car garage includes a storage area. Please specify crawlspace or slab foundation when ordering.

Plan HPT700023

Square Footage: *1,356*
Width: *44'-0"* **Depth:** *37'-8"*

Charmingly compact, this easy-to-build design is ideal for first-time homeowners. The exterior is appealing with a brick facade, horizontal wood siding on the sides, a large brick chimney and a full-width covered veranda. The living room/dining room combination is warmed by a masonry fireplace and includes an optional spindle screen wall at the entry. A country kitchen has ample counter space, a U-shaped work area and dining space. Outdoor access can also be found here. Three bedrooms include a master suite with private bath and two family bedrooms sharing a full hall bath. Each bedroom has a roomy wall closet. Stairs to the basement are located in the kitchen area.

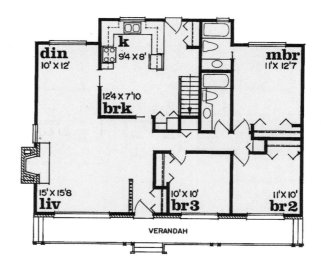

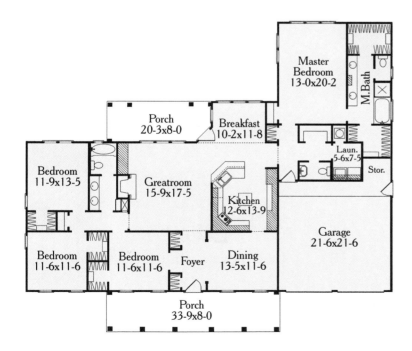

Master
Bedroom
13-0x20-2

M.Bath

Porch
20-3x8-0

Breakfast
10-2x11-8

Laun.
5-6x7-5

Stor.

Bedroom
11-9x13-5

Greatroom
15-9x17-5

Kitchen
12-6x13-9

Garage
21-6x21-6

Bedroom
11-6x11-6

Bedroom
11-6x11-6

Foyer

Dining
13-5x11-6

Porch
33-9x8-0

Laun.

Basement Stair
Location

Plan HPT700024

Square Footage: *2,267*
Width: *71'-2"* **Depth:** *62'-0"*

Six columns and a steeply pitched roof lend elegance to this four-bedroom home. To the right of the foyer, the dining area sits conveniently near the efficient island kitchen that enjoys plenty of work space. Natural light will flood the breakfast nook through a ribbon of windows facing the rear yard. Escape to the relaxing master bedroom, with its luxurious bath set between His and Hers walk-in closets. The great room is complete with a warming fireplace and built-ins. Three family bedrooms enjoy private walk-in closets and share a fully appointed bath. Please specify basement, crawlspace or slab foundation when ordering.

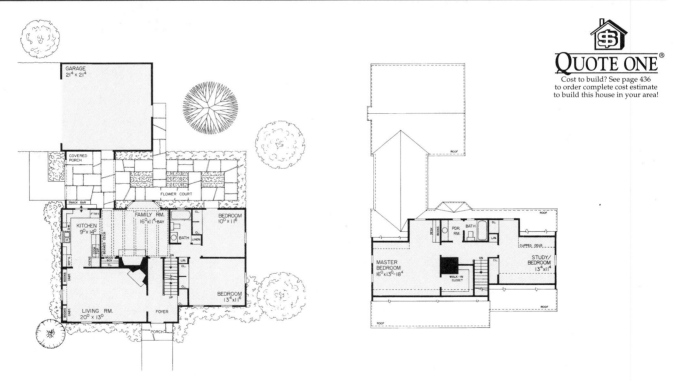

QUOTE ONE®
Cost to build? See page 436
to order complete cost estimate
to build this house in your area!

Plan HPT700025

First Floor: *1,182 square feet*
Second Floor: *708 square feet*
Total: *1,890 square feet*
Width: 44'-0" **Depth:** 64'-0"

L

This authentic adaptation is a half-house—with completion of the second floor, the growing family doubles their sleeping capacity. A fireplace warms the living room while a large hearth dominates the beam-ceiling family room. A deluxe master bedroom is located upstairs, away from the family bedrooms, and offers built-ins and a walk-in closet. A private study/bedroom also resides on the second floor. Take note of the covered porch leading to the garage and the flower court.

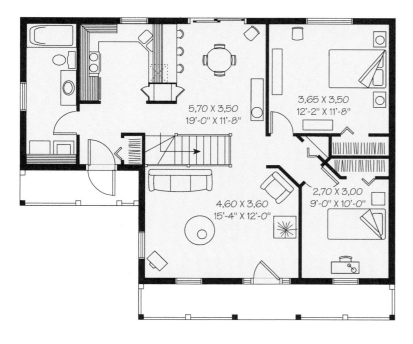

5,70 X 3,50
19'-0" X 11'-8"

3,65 X 3,50
12'-2" X 11'-8"

4,60 X 3,60
15'-4" X 12'-0"

2,70 X 3,00
9'-0" X 10'-0"

Plan HPT700026

Square Footage: *920*
Finished Basement: *920 square feet*
Width: *38'-0"* **Depth:** *28'-0"*

Compact yet comfortable, this country cottage has many appealing amenities. From a covered front porch that invites relaxed living, the entrance opens to the living room with access to the dining room and snack bar. Two bedrooms are secluded to the right of the plan; kitchen, bathroom and laundry facilities are located on the left side. A second porch off the kitchen provides room for more casual dining and quiet moments. This home is designed with a basement foundation.

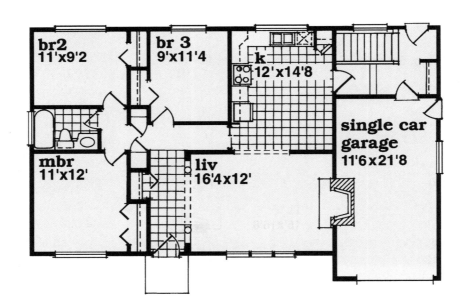

Plan HPT700028

Square Footage: *1,114*
Width: *48'-0"* **Depth:** *31'-0"*

For a starter home, this three-bedroom design retains plenty of style. Horizontal wood siding and shuttered windows bring a look of tradition to its facade. Inside, it holds a livable floor plan. The living room is introduced by columns and also has a fireplace and pocket doors that separate it from the large eat-in kitchen. A U-shaped work area in the kitchen is handy and efficient. The kitchen accesses a service area with a door to the single-car garage and stairs to the full basement—perfect for future expansion. Use all three bedrooms for sleeping space, or turn one bedroom into a home office or den.

PORCH

Plan HPT700029

Square Footage: *988*
Width: *38'-0"* **Depth:** *32'-0"*

This economical, compact home is the ultimate in efficient use of space. The central living room features a cozy fireplace and outdoor access to the front porch. A U-shaped kitchen serves a vaulted dining area, which offers access to the outdoors. The front entry is sheltered by a casual country porch, which also protects the living-room windows. The master bedroom has a walk-in closet and shares a full bath with the secondary bedrooms. A single or double garage may be built to the side or to the rear of the home.

QUOTE ONE®
Cost to build? See page 436
to order complete cost estimate
to build this house in your area!

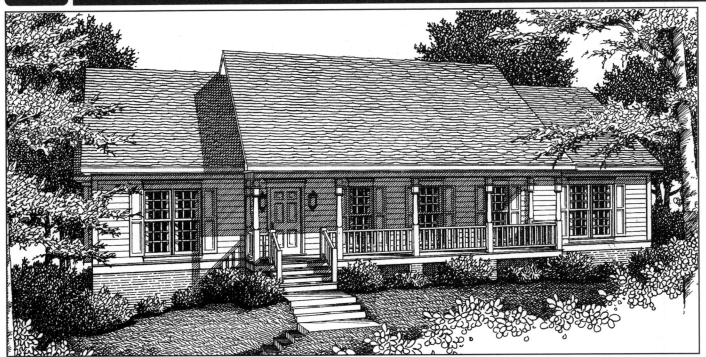

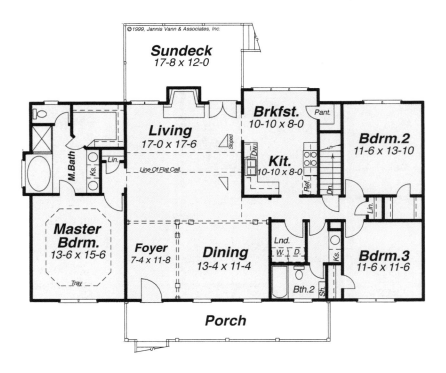

© 1999, Jannis Vann & Associates, Inc.

Sundeck 17-8 x 12-0

Brkfst. 10-10 x 8-0

Pant.

Living 17-0 x 17-6

Kit. 10-10 x 8-0

Bdrm.2 11-6 x 13-10

M.Bath

Lin.

Line Of Flat Ceil.

Dw.

Ref.

Dn.

Lin.

Master Bdrm. 13-6 x 15-6

Tray

Foyer 7-4 x 11-8

Dining 13-4 x 11-4

Lnd. W. D.

Ks.

Bdrm.3 11-6 x 11-6

Bth.2

Sh.

Porch

Plan HPT700030

Square Footage: *1,770*
Width: *59'-0"* **Depth:** *38'-0"*

This rambling ranch home has a heart of gold—with a volume ceiling, a fireplace and French-door access to the sun deck. An open dining room invites casual meals as well as dinner with guests. A gallery hall leads to the kitchen, which boasts a spacious breakfast area and a walk-in pantry. Split sleeping quarters include a master wing that provides a walk-in closet and a spacious bath with a garden tub and a knee-space vanity. Two secondary bedrooms share a full bath and a hall that leads to a laundry.

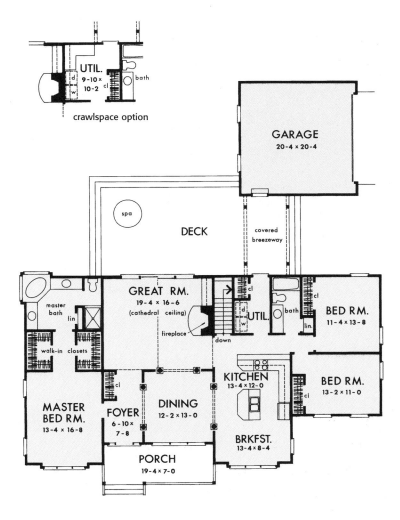

UTIL.
9-10 x
10-2

d
w

bath

crawlspace option

GARAGE
20-4 x 20-4

spa

DECK

covered
breezeway

GREAT RM.
19-4 × 16-6
(cathedral ceiling)

fireplace

down

cl

d
w

UTIL.

bath

lin.

BED RM.
11-4 × 13-8

master
bath

lin

walk-in closets

cl

BED RM.
13-2 × 11-0

KITCHEN
13-4 × 12-0

MASTER
BED RM.
13-4 × 16-8

FOYER
6-10 x
7-8

DINING
12-2 × 13-0

BRKFST.
13-4 × 8-4

PORCH
19-4 × 7-0

Plan HPT700031

Square Footage: *1,980*
Width: *63'-10"* **Depth:** *73'-4"*

Providing the utmost in flexible outdoor living, this home is graced with a covered front porch and generous rear deck. Inside is a floor plan that offers many amenities. The great room has a fireplace, cathedral ceiling and sliding glass doors with an arched window above to admit natural light. Impressive round columns promote a sense of elegance in the dining room. The master suite boasts two walk-in closets and a well-organized master bath with double-bowl vanity and a whirlpool tub. Two more bedrooms are located at the opposite end of the house for privacy. The garage is connected to the house with a breezeway. ©1992 Donald A. Gardner Architects, Inc.

Plan HPT700032

Square Footage: *1,550*
Width: *62'-9"* **Depth:** *36'-1"*

If you like the rustic appeal of ranch-style homes, you'll love this version. Both horizontal and vertical siding appear on the exterior and are complemented by a columned covered porch and a delightful cupola as accent. The entry opens to a huge open living/dining room combination. A fireplace in the living area is flanked by windows and doors to one of two rear decks. A vaulted ceiling runs the width of this area. The kitchen also accesses the deck and features counter space galore. Look for a private deck behind the master suite.

Plan HPT700033

Square Footage: *1,765*
Width: *58'-0"* **Depth:** *54'-0"*

This is a home for the growing family. A large great room shares an impressive space with the formal dining room for large family gatherings. The arrangement of the master suite on the quiet side of the house lends privacy to a generously sized suite with an even more generously designed bath. There's even a door from the bath outside, perfect for a hot tub retreat. Another practical feature of this home is the position of the den/Bedroom 4. Not only does it double as a guest room, but because it is accessible directly from the master bath, it would also make a perfect nursery.

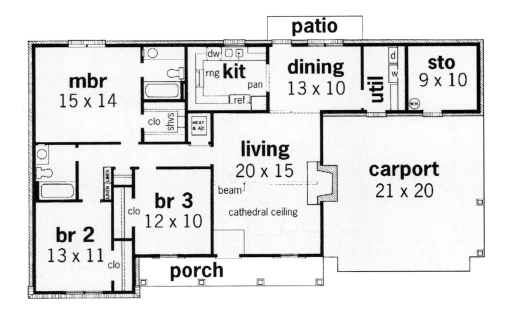

Plan HPT700034

Square Footage: *1,375*
Width: *61'-0"* **Depth:** *35'-0"*

A welcoming front porch opens to the vaulted living room and warming fireplace in this three-bedroom home. To the left of the living room is the sleeping zone. Two family bedrooms share a full bath. The master suite, shielded from any street noise by the secondary bedrooms, features a roomy walk-in closet and full bath. The U-shaped kitchen opens directly to the dining room and its patio access. A handy utility room opens from the dining room. Homeowners will appreciate the extra storage room off the carport, perfect for storing the family treasures. Please specify crawl-space or slab foundation when ordering.

Plan HPT700035

Square Footage: *1,400*
Width: *61'-0"* **Depth:** *44'-0"*

A brick-and-siding facade and charming cupola on the two-car garage roof introduces this three-bedroom home. The dining area opens from the entry and features built-in shelves and easy access to the U-shaped kitchen. A vaulted ceiling and warming fireplace adorn the living room, which includes patio access. Two family bedrooms share a bath to the left of the home, one includes a window seat. The master bedroom enjoys a private bath and walk-in closet. Homeowners will appreciate the additional storage closet in the garage. Please specify crawlspace or slab foundation when ordering.

Plan HPT700036

Square Footage: *1,383*
Finished Basement: *1,460 square feet*
Width: *50'-0"* **Depth:** *39'-0"*

Three attractive gables, arch-topped windows and a covered porch add tons of charm to this fine ranch home. Inside, a vaulted ceiling in the great room and high glass windows on the rear wall combine to create an open, spacious feel. An open dining room sits just off the great room. The ample kitchen layout features a built-in pantry and easy access to the dining room. A generous walk-in closet is found in the master suite, along with a pampering bath. Two secondary suites share a hall bath. Please specify basement, slab or crawlspace foundation when ordering.

Sundeck
10-0 x 10-0

M. Bath

Bedroom 2

Kitchen
8-0 x 10-0

Dining
10-4 x 10-0

Bath 2

OPT. PLANT SHELF
OPEN TO BDRM.

Ref.

W. D.

Master
Bedroom
11-6 x 14-6

Family Room
18-4 x 13-0

Cts.

Down

Entry

Bedroom 3
11-0 x 10-0

©1998, Jannis Vann & Associates, Inc.

Here is a rustic cottage that provides plenty of amenities. An open interior takes full advantage of outdoor views, and allows flexible space. The family room boasts a fireplace and vistas that extend to the rear property. The dining room features a double window and French-door access to the sundeck. Wrapping counters in the kitchen provide plenty of space for food preparation. The master suite provides a compartmented bath, front-property views and two wardrobes. The secondary bedrooms share a hall with linen storage.

Plan HPT700037

Square Footage: *1,208*
Width: *48'-0"* **Depth:** *29'-0"*

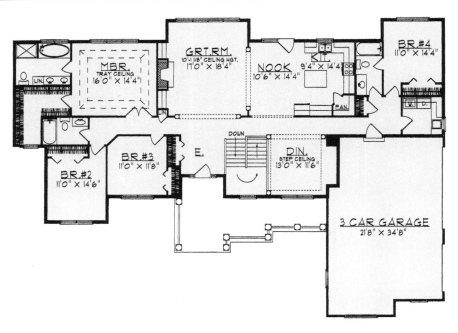

Plan HPT700038

Square Footage: *2,233*
Width: *82'-0"* **Depth:** *58'-0"*

This moderately sized farmhouse plan begins with a covered porch accented by columns. It opens to a foyer leading to the great room with ten-foot ceilings. A fireplace and built-in cabinets further adorn the great room. The kitchen and nook are nearby and contain an island workspace, pantry and access to the rear yard. The beautiful master suite is to the left of the foyer, along with two of the three family bedrooms. Graced by a tray ceiling and walk-in closet, the master bedroom is complemented by a delightful master bath. To the right of the foyer are stairs to the basement, the dining room and Bedroom 4. The laundry area sits in a service hall that leads to the three-car garage.

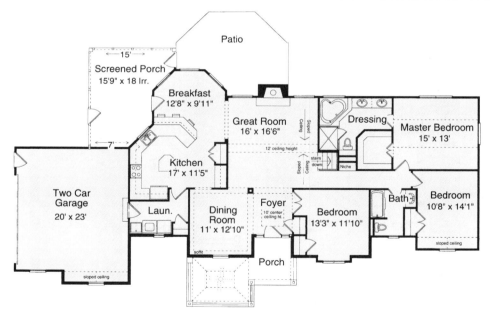

With its brick facade and gables, this home brings great curb appeal to any neighborhood. This one-story home features a great room with a cozy fireplace, a laundry room tucked away from the spacious kitchen, and a breakfast area accessing the screened porch. Completing this design are two family bedrooms and an elegant master bedroom suite featuring an ample walk-in closet accessed by double doors. A dressing area in the master bathroom is shared with a dual vanity and a step-up tub.

Plan HPT700039

Square Footage: *1,759*
Width: *82'-10"* **Depth:** *47'-5"*

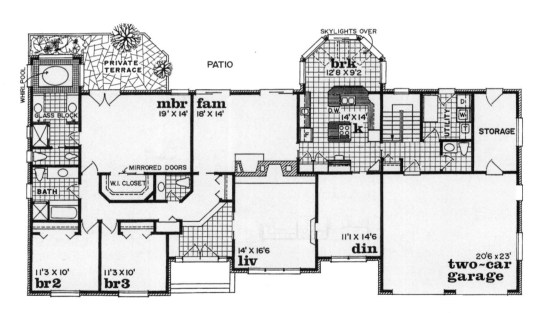

Plan HPT700040

Square Footage: *2,419*
Width: *85'-2"* **Depth:** *46'-8"*

Long and low, with brick siding and multi-pane shuttered windows, this ranch home is the picture of elegance. Enter through double doors to a sunken foyer and sunken living room with a fireplace. The dining room is beyond the living room and a step up. The family room, to the rear of the plan, features a fireplace and sliding glass doors to the rear patio. The kitchen provides a cooktop island and counter and cabinet space to suit any gourmet. The master bedroom enjoys a private terrace and bath with two vanities, a whirlpool tub and a separate shower. Two family bedrooms are to the front of the plan.

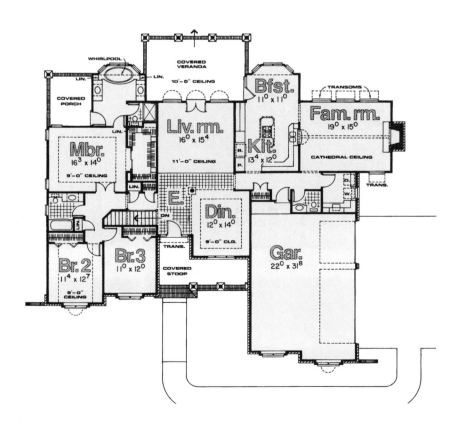

Plan HPT700041

Square Footage: *2,399*
Width: *72'-8"* **Depth:** *64'-6"*

nteresting window treatments and a charming porch extend the attention-getting nature of this brick ranch home. Beyond the covered porch, the entry showcases the formal dining room to the right and the multi-windowed living room straight ahead. The L-shaped kitchen features an island cooktop and blends with the bay-windowed breakfast room and welcoming family room to create a comfortable area for family gatherings. Located for privacy, the master suite includes a huge walk-in closet. A covered porch, accessed from the master bath, offers a wonderful outdoor retreat. The amenity-filled master bath contains twin vanities and an oval whirlpool tub. Two secondary bedrooms share a full bath.

Plan HPT700042

Square Footage: *2,362*
Width: *76'-0"* **Depth:** *49'-0"*

Delicate elongated windows add a lovely contrast to the rustic textures of this charming ranch home. The great room is sure to be a favorite living area. It features a wall of windows to the rear, a fireplace flanked by built-in cabinets, and archways to the hall and kitchen, where a large island and additional built-ins provide ample work space. Across the breakfast nook through double doors is a convenient and comfortable office with built-in cabinets.

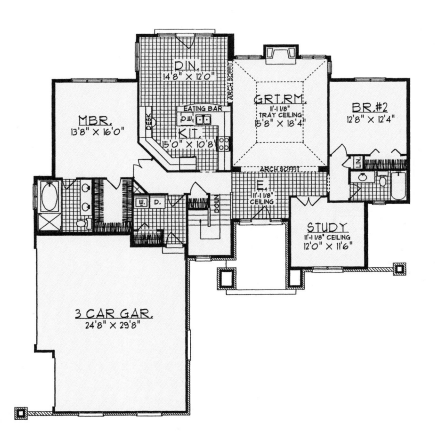

Plan HPT700043

Square Footage: *1,830*
Width: *62'-0"* **Depth:** *64'-0"*

This beautiful contemporary ranch-style home offers interesting windows and varied siding textures. The tiled entry opens to the great room with a tray ceiling, arched thresholds and a fireplace. The casual dining area opens to the kitchen with a bar and built-in desk. The master suite is accented by double doors, a walk-in closet and a bath with an oval tub and a separate shower. A secondary bedroom is on the opposite side of the house, and a study to the front might also be used as a den or third bedroom.

Plan HPT700044

Square Footage: *1,782*
Width: *52'-0"* **Depth:** *59'-4"*

Symmetrical gables offset a hip roof and arch-top windows and complement a stately brick exterior with this traditional design. Inside, the formal dining room opens from an elegant tiled entry and offers space for quiet, planned occasions as well as traditional festivities. The casual living area shares a three-sided fireplace with the breakfast area and hearth room, while the kitchen offers a convenient snack bar for easy meals. A nine-foot ceiling enhances the master suite, which features a whirlpool tub, twin vanities, an ample walk-in closet and a compartmented toilet. Split sleeping quarters offer privacy to both the master and the family bedrooms, which share a full bath.

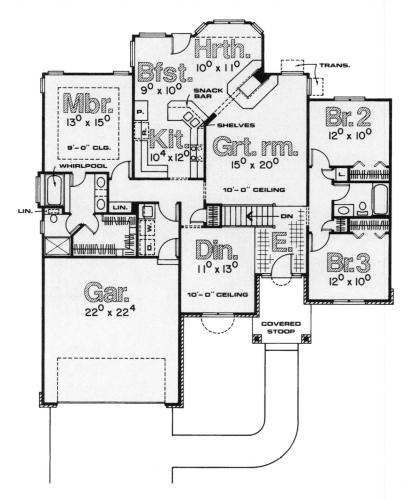

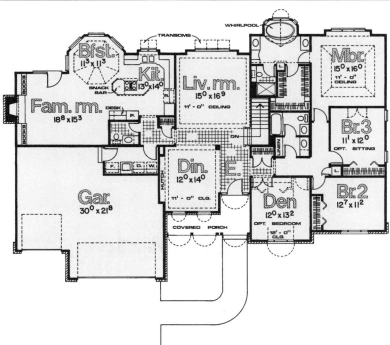

Elegant arches at the covered entry of this home announce an exqui-site floor plan with plenty of bays and niches. The tiled entry opens to the formal living and dining rooms, which enjoy open, soaring space defined by arches and a decorative column. A gourmet kitchen offers an island cooktop counter, and serves a bayed breakfast nook and a conven-ient snack bar. The sleeping wing includes a master suite with a whirlpool bath, a sizable walk-in closet, two vanities and a box-bay window. Two family bedrooms share a full bath nearby, while a secluded den offers the possi-bility of a fourth bedroom.

Plan HPT700045

Square Footage: *2,498*
Width: *76'-0"* **Depth:** *55'-4"*

G. MacDonald

Plan HPT700046

Square Footage: *1,604*
Width: *48'-8"* **Depth:** *48'-0"*

A thoughtful arrangement makes this uncomplicated three-bedroom plan comfortable. The living and working areas are grouped together for convenience—a great room with cathedral ceiling, dining room with wet bar pass-through and kitchen with breakfast room. The sleeping area features a spacious master suite with a skylit bath, whirlpool tub and large walk-in closet. Two smaller bedrooms accommodate the rest of the family.

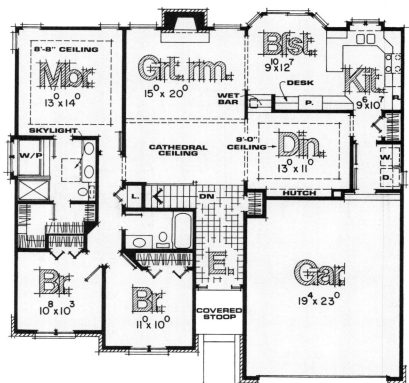

QUOTE ONE®
Cost to build? See page 436
to order complete cost estimate
to build this house in your area!

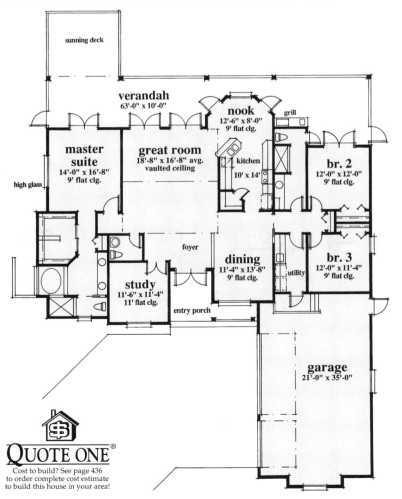

Plan HPT700047

Square Footage: *2,200*
Width: *63'-0"* **Depth:** *79'-0"*

L

A joyful marriage of indoor/outdoor living relationships endures in this spirited one-story home. All rooms to the rear offer access to a full-length veranda and a screened porch, perfect for enjoying cool breezes and beautiful sunsets. An airy, open feeling greets you with the combination of the formal dining room (divided from the foyer by a half-wall), the spacious great room and the charming kitchen, complete with a walk-in pantry and bayed breakfast nook. Split sleeping quarters contain the master wing to the left and two secondary bedrooms to the right. The secluded master suite is highlighted by a double walk-in closet, a relaxing garden tub with a privacy wall, a separate shower and a double-bowl vanity.

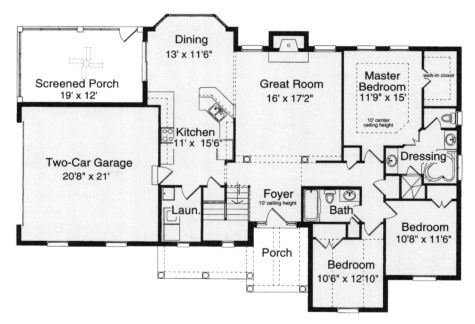

Plan HPT700048

Square Footage: *1,611*
Width: *67'-0"* **Depth:** *44'-0"*

This three-bedroom brick home pampers the homeowner with its charming exterior and efficient floor plan. A cozy front porch creates a delightful place to greet guests or to relax on warm summer days. Columns define the great room while dual windows and a gas fireplace on the rear wall offer an attractive first impression. The spacious kitchen and dining area with bar seating and a bayed window create an expansive yet comfortable center for preparing meals and for enjoying the formal as well as informal dining experience. Introducing a delightful screened porch are sliding doors from the dining area. Providing a luxurious retreat, the master bedroom showcases a tray ceiling and a lavishly equipped dressing room.

Plan HPT700049

Square Footage: *1,702*
Width: *55'-0"* **Depth:** *76'-4"*

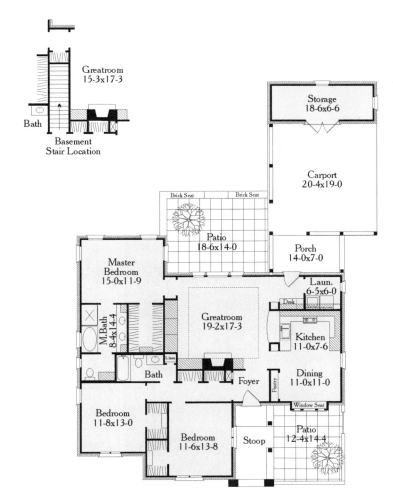

Greatroom
15-3x17-3

Bath

Basement
Stair Location

Storage
18-6x6-6

Carport
20-4x19-0

Brick Seat   Brick Seat

Patio
18-6x14-0

Porch
14-0x7-0

Master
Bedroom
15-0x11-9

M.Bath
8-4x14-4

Greatroom
19-2x17-3

Laun.
6-5x6-0

Desk

Kitchen
11-0x7-6

Linen

Bath

Foyer

Pantry

Dining
11-0x11-0

Bedroom
11-8x13-0

Bedroom
11-6x13-8

Stoop

Window Seat

Patio
12-4x14-4

Arched lintels, shutters and a covered entryway lend this home country charm. Inside, the foyer leads directly to the great room with a fireplace and built-ins along two walls. Nearby, the kitchen joins the dining area, which has a built-in pantry and window seat. Keeping household records organized will be easy with the built-in desk by the laundry room. The sleeping quarters reside on the left of this design. The master suite includes a lavish bath with a garden tub. Two secondary bedrooms share a bath. Homeowners will be pleased by the large storage area off the carport. Please specify basement, crawlspace or slab foundation when ordering.

Plan HPT700050

Square Footage: *2,012*
Width: *59'-0"* **Depth:** *67'-8"*

In this plan, a large tiled area extends from the entry foyer through to the breakfast nook and island kitchen. It unites the areas and helps to separate them from the massive great room. Look for a warming fireplace and abundant windows in this grand living area. The dining room is distinguished by soffits and columns, but is near to the kitchen for convenience. The master bedroom is exquisite with a tray-ceiling accent, walk-in closet and bath with double sinks, spa tub and separate shower. Two family bedrooms share the use of a full bath with double sinks. One of these bedrooms has a walk-in closet. A two-car garage sits to the front of the plan, but offers a side entry that does not detract from the beauty of the facade.

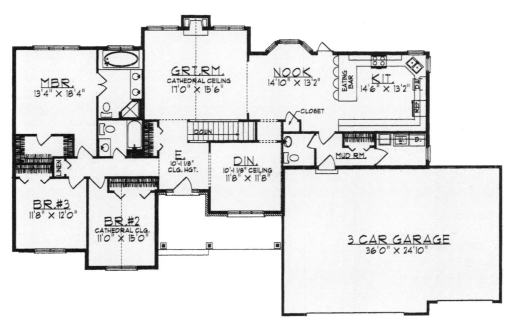

This traditional ranch meets the needs of a growing family. A ten-foot ceiling graces the foyer, which leads to the dining room, bedroom hallway, great room and stairs to the basement. To the right of the foyer is the dining room, with a ten-foot ceiling and a view of the front yard. The center hall directs you to three bedrooms: two family bedrooms and a master suite with a walk-in closet and a striking master bath. The great room, straight ahead from the entry foyer, enjoys a cathedral ceiling and a fireplace. The kitchen/nook area features a bay window and an eating bar. The handy mudroom leads to a three-car garage.

Plan HPT700051

Square Footage: *2,017*
Width: *81'-0"* **Depth:** *51'-4"*

Plan HPT700052

First Floor: *1,098 square feet*
Second Floor: *431 square feet*
Total: *1,529 square feet*
Width: *45'-0"* **Depth:** *53'-4"*

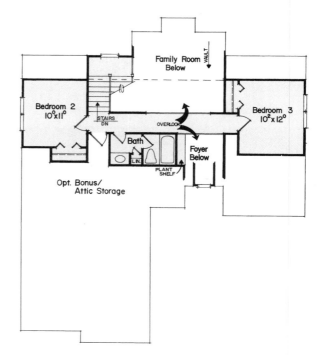

European detailing gives this house special appeal. Corner quoins, keystone lintels and multiple gables are just some of its exterior charms. Amenities abound inside with built-in plant shelves, niches and a tray ceiling in the master bedroom. The focal point of the vaulted great room is the fireplace, framed by a window and a French door. The galley kitchen leads to a well-lit breakfast area and convenient access to the garage. The split floor plan places two family bedrooms sharing a full bath to the left of the great room, and the master suite privately tucked at the right. The luxurious double-vanity master bath includes a garden tub set in a radius window. Please specify basement, crawlspace or slab foundation when ordering.

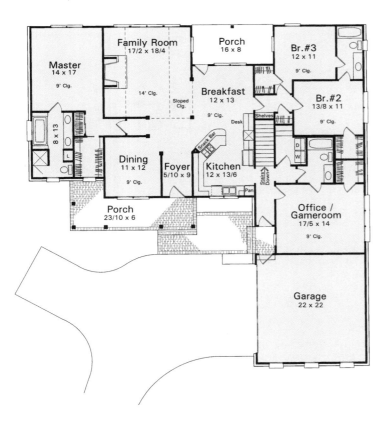

Plan HPT700053

Square Footage: *2,361*
Width: *66'-10"* **Depth:** *69'-5"*

A traditional with flexibility! It is complete with a number of amenities, such as a lavish master suite, a fireplace in the family room and front and rear covered porches. The formal dining room will please with no cross-room traffic. Both of the family bedrooms have walk-in closets and share a full bath. A flex room is located near the two-car garage and offers a walk-in closet as well as a full bath, making it perfect for use as a game room, home office or guest suite.

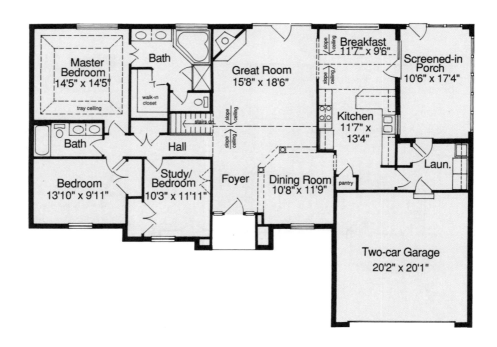

Plan HPT700054

Square Footage: *1,782*
Width: *67'-2"* **Depth:** *47'-0"*

Perfect for empty-nesters or young families, this transitional home is a charming addition to any neighborhood. Transforming the third bedroom into a home office or study opens the foyer and great room to an even larger visual area, creating a extraordinary layout. Note the big screened porch off the kitchen and breakfast area—great for refreshing family meals. The master suite features a private bath with a soaking tub and a large walk-in closet. An additional family bedroom across the hall is perfect for a guest suite or nursery. A full hall bath is located nearby.

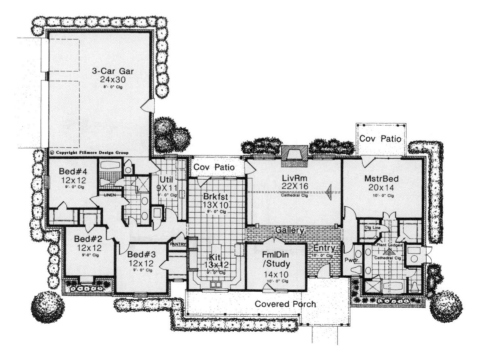

This one-story Victorian farmhouse features a covered porch, Palladian windows and decorative fish-scale shingles. A large kitchen and breakfast area provide plenty of room to maneuver for the cook of the family. A cathedral ceiling graces the spacious living room. The master bedroom is located on the right side of the plan, and includes a cathedral ceiling in the bath, plant ledges and a private covered patio. On the left side, three additional bedrooms share a full bath. A large utility area furnishes convenience and economy.

Plan HPT700055

Square Footage: *2,495*
Width: *87'-10"* **Depth:** *62'-7"*

KOIZUMI/BUTLER

Plan HPT700056

Square Footage: *2,415*
Width: *74'-0"* **Depth:** *54'-0"*

L D

This traditional design incorporates the perfect floor plan for a large family. Privacy is assured with three family bedrooms and a strategically placed laundry on the left side of the home, and a large master bedroom with a luxurious bath and spacious walk-in closet on the right side. The family room looks out to the covered porch and continues on to the efficient kitchen, with a writing desk, a large pantry and access to the dining room. The kitchen also features a snack bar that provides a perfect opportunity to chat with folks in the large gathering room with its warming fireplace and access to the backyard terrace.

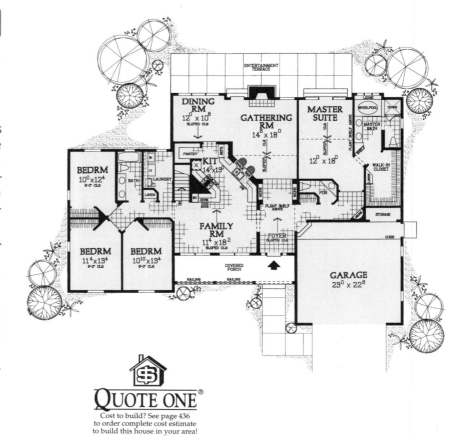

Quote One®
Cost to build? See page 436
to order complete cost estimate
to build this house in your area!

Plan HPT700057

Square Footage: *1,835*
Width: *71'-0"* **Depth:** *43'-5"*

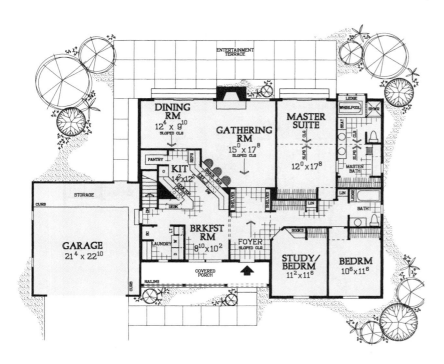

Quote One®

Cost to build? See page 436
to order complete cost estimate
to build this house in your area!

Country living is the focus of this charming design. A cozy covered porch invites you into the foyer with the sleeping area on the right and the living area straight ahead. From the windowed front-facing breakfast room, enter the efficient kitchen with its corner laundry room, large pantry, snack-bar pass-through to the gathering room, and passage to the dining room. The massive gathering room and dining room feature sloped ceilings, an impressive fireplace and access to the rear terrace. Terrace access is also available from the master bedroom with its sloped ceiling and a master bath that includes a whirlpool tub, a separate shower and a separate vanity area. A study at the front of the house can also be converted into a third bedroom.

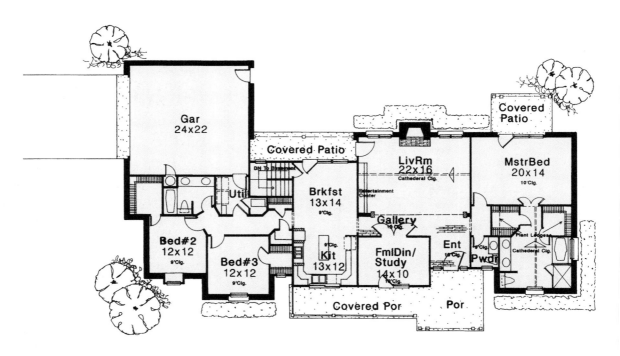

Plan HPT700027

Square Footage: *2,277*
Width: *87'-10"* **Depth:** *46'-10"*

This Victorian farmhouse exterior features siding, brick and a long front porch to enjoy long summer evenings. The large brick entry leads into a huge living room with a fireplace and built-ins. A formal dining room or study has doors leading to the front porch. Doors off the breakfast room open to a covered patio to the rear of the plan. All bedrooms feature walk-in closets with the master suite enjoying His and Hers walk-in closets, plus a large bath with a garden tub and a stall shower.

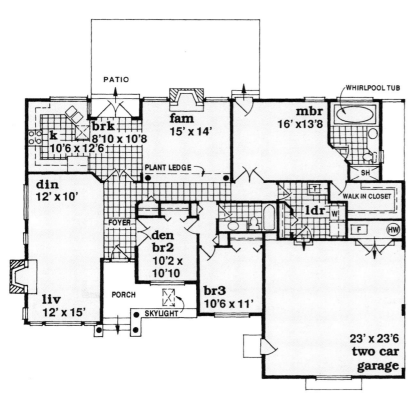

PATIO

WHIRLPOOL TUB

brk
8'10 x 10'8

fam
15' x 14'

mbr
16' x13'8

k
10'6 x 12'6

SH

PLANT LEDGE

din
12' x 10'

WALK IN CLOSET

FOYER

ldr
W

F

HW

den
br2
10'2 x
10'10

liv
12' x 15'

PORCH

br3
10'6 x 11'

23' x 23'6
two car
garage

SKYLIGHT

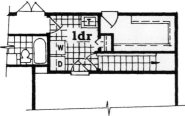

ldr
W
D
T

Plan HPT700058

Square Footage: *1,883*
Width: *64'-0"* **Depth:** *48'-0"*

The interior relies on a great floor plan. From a skylit, covered porch, the plan begins with a large entry opening to the living room with a fireplace and den—or Bedroom 2—which can be accessed through double doors in the entry or a single door in the hall. Decorative columns line the hall and define the family-room space. A fireplace, flanked by windows, is a focal point in this casual living area. The nearby breakfast room opens to the patio and connects the family room to the U-shaped kitchen. The master suite is huge and amenity-filled. It also has patio access and features a bath with a whirlpool tub and separate shower. An additional bedroom is served by a full bath. A large laundry room connects the two-car garage to the main house.

Plan HPT700059

Square Footage: *2,093*
Width: *71'-2"* **Depth:** *56'-4"*

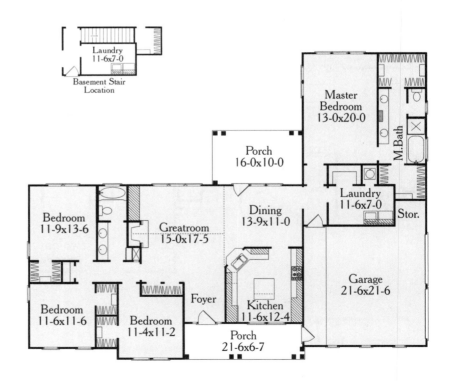

Laundry
11-6x7-0

Basement Stair
Location

Master
Bedroom
13-0x20-0

M.Bath

Porch
16-0x10-0

Laundry
11-6x7-0

Stor.

Bedroom
11-9x13-6

Greatroom
15-0x17-5

Dining
13-9x11-0

Bedroom
11-6x11-6

Bedroom
11-4x11-2

Foyer

Kitchen
11-6x12-4

Garage
21-6x21-6

Porch
21-6x6-7

Welcome your family home to this wonderful four-bedroom cottage. Step through the entry door with its transom and sidelights to a well-lit foyer. A ribbon of windows greets the eye in the great room, and a warming fireplace spreads comfort. A pass-through window to the kitchen is an added convenience. The master suite enjoys a private wing, luxurious bath and His and Hers walk-in closets. On the opposite side of the plan, three secondary bedrooms—all with walk-in closets!—share a full bath. Please specify basement, crawlspace or slab foundation when ordering.

Plan HPT700060

Square Footage: *1,557*
Width: *50'-0"* **Depth:** *50'-0"*

Here's a grand retreat with a pretty facade and an open interior. A wraparound porch leads to a gallery foyer defined by decorative columns and views of the outdoors. A fireplace warms the open great room, capped by a vaulted ceiling. The dining space is highlighted by a plant shelf and offers sliding-glass door ac-cess to the rear porch. Wrapping counters in the kitchen allow plenty of space for food preparation. Other kitchen amenities include a snack counter, planning desk and a pantry. To the right of the plan, the vaulted master suite provides a wardrobe large enough for two. Nearby, a flex room easily converts from a den to an additional bedroom.

Plan HPT700061

Square Footage: *1,475*
Width: *44'-0"* **Depth:** *43'-0"*

A railed veranda and turned posts complement a lovely Palladian window on the exterior of this home. The foyer is brightly lit by a skylight, and leads to the living room with a vaulted ceiling, fireplace and bookshelves. The dining room overlooks a covered veranda that opens from the breakfast room. A well-organized kitchen features a butcher-block island. Sleeping quarters include a master suite and two family bedrooms that share a full double-vanity bath.

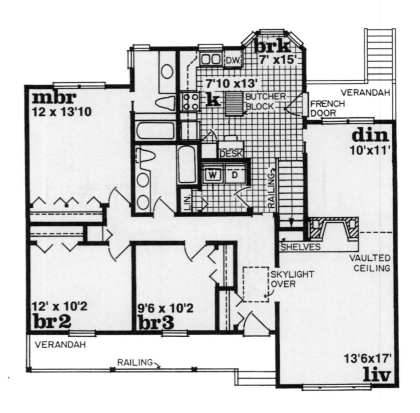

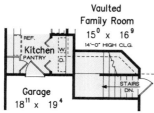

Vaulted
Family Room
15⁰ x 16⁹
14'-0" HIGH CLG.

REF.
Kitchen
PANTRY
W.
D.

Garage
18¹¹ x 19⁴

STAIRS
DN.

Plan HPT700062

Square Footage: *1,222*
Width: *40'-0"* **Depth:** *49'-2"*

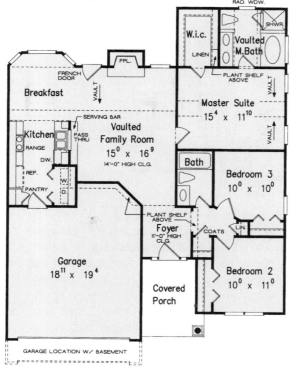

RAD. WDW.

W.i.c.

Vaulted
M.Bath
SHWR.

LINEN

FPL.

Breakfast

FRENCH
DOOR

VAULT

PLANT SHELF
ABOVE

VAULT

VAULT

Master Suite
15⁴ x 11¹⁰

SERVING BAR

Kitchen

PASS
THRU

RANGE

DW.

Vaulted
Family Room
15⁰ x 16⁹
14'-0" HIGH CLG.

Bath

REF.

W.
D.

PANTRY

PLANT SHELF
ABOVE

Bedroom 3
10⁰ x 10⁰

Foyer
11'-0" HIGH
CLG.

COATS

LIN.

Garage
18¹¹ x 19⁴

Bedroom 2
10⁰ x 11⁰

Covered
Porch

GARAGE LOCATION W/ BASEMENT

This traditional one-story family house allows plant lovers to bring nature close to home. The facade features window boxes off of the bedroom and above the garage—perfect for geraniums! Inside, you'll find two plant shelves—one in the foyer and one in the master suite. The bayed breakfast nook lets the sun shine on morning meals. Vaulted ceilings in the family room and master bedroom lend spaciousness to the plan. Two family bedrooms are located near the front of the home, secluding the master suite at the rear. A large walk-in closet and luxurious bath with both a garden tub and shower will spoil any homeowner. Please specify basement or crawlspace foundation when ordering.

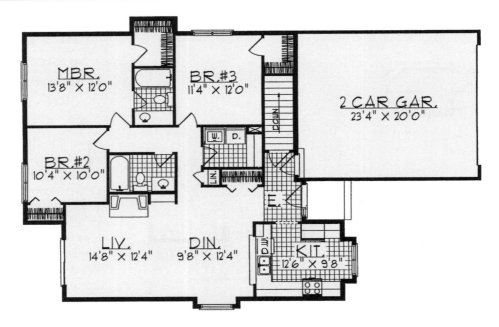

Plan HPT700063

Square Footage: *1,342*
Width: *37'-0"* **Depth:** *59'-4"*

uild on a narrow lot with this plan—it's only thirty-seven feet wide. But that doesn't affect the classic floor plan at all. The recessed entry opens to a tiled hall with a stairway to the basement at one end and kitchen at the other. Straight ahead are the living and dining areas which combine to form one large, open space. A warm hearth is the focus at one end. Bedrooms are just down a short hallway. Bedroom 3 has a walk-in closet and shares a full bath with Bedroom 2. The master bedroom also contains a walk-in closet but has its own private bath. A laundry room with space for a washer and dryer and a utility closet sits close to the bedrooms for convenience. The two-car garage accesses the main house at the entry hall.

Plan HPT700064

Square Footage: *1,467*
Width: *49'-0"* **Depth:** *43'-0"*

Vaulted ceilings across the rooms at the rear of this home add spaciousness to the dining room, living room and master bedroom. The kitchen is open to the dining area and has an island cooktop and corner sink. A service entry leads to the two-car garage and holds the laundry alcove and a storage closet. The master suite is as gracious as those found in much larger homes, with a walk-in closet and a bath with spa tub, separate shower and double sinks.

Plan HPT700065

Square Footage: *2,058*
Width: *61'-10"* **Depth:** *50'-4"*

This floor plan is designed to maximize the view to the rear of the lot. Double doors off the foyer open to a vaulted den or study. The gallery hall introduces the vaulted living and dining rooms. The country kitchen offers a masonry fireplace, breakfast bay, preparation island with television nook. A spacious master bedroom features both coffered and vaulted ceilings; the walk-in wardrobe opens to a lavish ensuite with His and Hers vanity and whirlpool spa. Two additional bedrooms, one with a vaulted ceiling, share a main bathroom with twin vanities and a soaking tub.

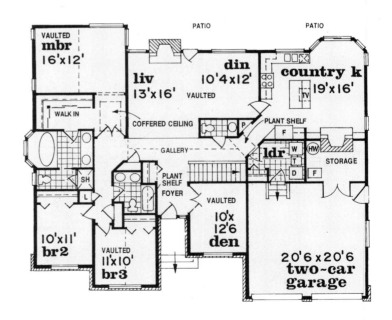

Plan HPT700066

Square Footage: *1,462*
Width: *52'-0"* **Depth:** *46'-0"*

Simple yet elegant describes this ranch-style home. Amenities of this home include a welcoming foyer and a spacious great room with marvelous cathedral ceilings, not to mention a gas fireplace. Just down the hallway are two additional bedrooms, a full bath and a master suite. The master suite features two closets with ample storage space. The kitchen is open to the great room and offers a breakfast bar and dining area. Off the kitchen is a laundry room with an additional storage closet.

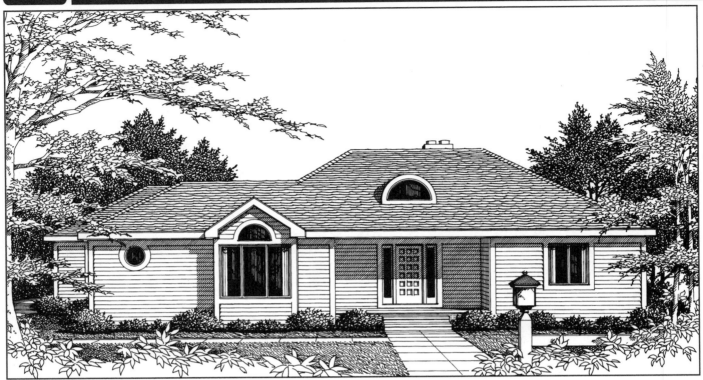

Plan HPT700067

Square Footage: *1,658*
Width: *70'-6"* **Depth:** *48'-6"*

With clean, contemporary accents, the exterior of this home features circle and half-circle windows, sidelights at the entry and horizontal wood siding. The wide front porch is set up a few steps and leads to a foyer opening to the great room. Here you'll enjoy a corner fireplace and built-in bench. The dinette also opens to this terrace and connects to the U-shaped kitchen. The master suite includes a box-bay window and walk-in closet in the bedroom and separate shower and whirl-pool tub in the bath. Family bedrooms are to the right of the foyer and share a full bath with double sinks.

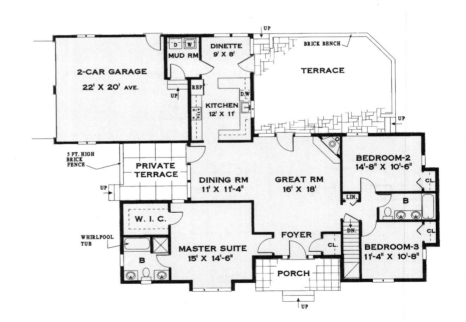

Plan HPT700068

Square Footage: *1,999*
Width: *60'-0"* **Depth:** *55'-0"*

L

Small families will appreciate the layout of this traditional ranch home. The foyer opens to the gathering room with a fireplace and sloped ceiling. The dining room, in turn, leads to the gathering room for entertaining ease and offers sliding glass doors to a rear terrace. The breakfast room also provides access to a covered porch for dining outdoors. The media room to the left of the home offers a bay window and a wet bar.

Plan HPT700069

First Floor: *1,423 square feet*
Second Floor: *871 square feet*
Total: *2,294 square feet*
Width: *47'-0"* **Depth:** *57'-0"*

This delightful design blends the dormers, gables and shuttered windows of a farmhouse with the delicate porch trim and elegant oval window of a Victorian home. The foyer opens to the formal dining room, adjacent to a large island kitchen with ample counter space. The great room includes a fireplace flanked by double doors opening to the backyard and borders a sunlit breakfast area. The master suite provides a full bath with a corner garden tub and a large walk-in closet. Upstairs, each of three bedrooms has special features—one offers a walk-in closet and a private bath, another enjoys a dormer alcove, and the third provides both a walk-in closet and a dormer alcove.

Plan HPT700070

Square Footage: *1,594*
Width: *52'-8"* **Depth:** *55'-5"*

This home boasts transitional trends with its charming exterior. The entrance foyer with columns introduces the formal dining room and leads to the massive great room with a sloped ceiling and cozy fireplace. On the right, you will find French doors leading to a library/bedroom featuring built-in bookcases—another set of French doors accesses the rear deck. A family bedroom nearby shares a full bath. The gourmet kitchen enjoys an angled sink counter and a breakfast area with a bay window and built-in bench. The secluded master bedroom includes a walk-in closet, a full bath with dual vanities, and private access to the laundry room. This plan includes an optional layout for a third bedroom.

Deck

Master Bedroom
11' x 13'

Breakfast
13' x 9'4"

built in bench

Library/
Bedroom
11'8" x 12'10"

Great Room
15' x 16'4"

built-in bookcases

walk-in closet

Kitchen
13' x 12'3"

Bath

Sloped ceiling

Bath

Laun.

stairs down

Dining Room
10'4" x 11'

Foyer

Bedroom
11'8" x 10'

stairs up

Two Car Garage
21'3" x 23'8"

Porch

Bedroom
11'8" x 10'5"

Optional 3rd Bedroom

Plan HPT700071

Square Footage: *1,439*
Width: *49'-0"* **Depth:** *54'-10"*

Reminiscent of Cape Cod styling, this cozy home boasts a siding and brick exterior, a front porch and two front-facing dormers. The foyer is flanked on the left by the dining room, complete with decorative entrance columns. The vaulted great room enjoys a French door to the rear property and a fireplace. The bayed breakfast room flows into the kitchen—pantry included. The right side of the plan is home to two family bedrooms, which share a full bath. The master suite is on the other end of the home for maximum privacy. A whirlpool tub, dual vanities, plant shelf, compartmented toilet, walk-in closet and separate shower enhance the master bath. Please specify basement or crawlspace foundation when ordering.

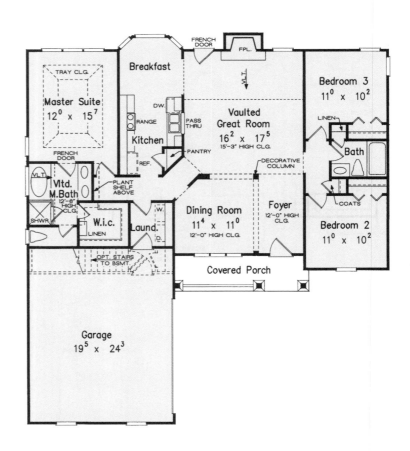

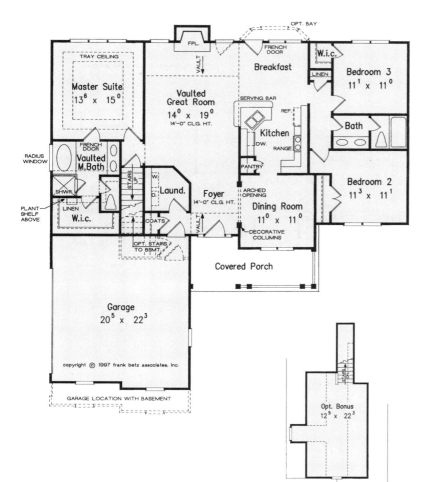

TRAY CEILING

Master Suite
13⁶ x 15⁰

Vaulted
M.Bath

RADIUS
WINDOW

FRENCH
DOOR

SHWR.

PLANT
SHELF
ABOVE

LINEN

W.i.c.

STAIRS

W.
D.

Laund.

COATS

OPT. STAIRS
TO BSMT.

Garage
20⁵ x 22³

copyright © 1997 frank betz associates, inc.

GARAGE LOCATION WITH BASEMENT

FPL.

VAULT

OPT. BAY

FRENCH
DOOR

Breakfast

W.i.c.

LINEN

Bedroom 3
11¹ x 11⁰

Vaulted
Great Room
14⁰ x 19⁰
14'-0" CLG. HT.

SERVING BAR

REF.

Kitchen

DW.

RANGE

Bath

PANTRY

Foyer
14'-0" CLG. HT.

ARCHED
OPENING

Dining Room
11⁰ x 11⁰

DECORATIVE
COLUMNS

VAULT

Bedroom 2
11³ x 11¹

Covered Porch

Opt. Bonus
12⁵ x 22³

STAIRS

Plan HPT700072

Square Footage: *1,571*
Bonus Space: *334 square feet*
Width: *53'-6"* **Depth:** *55'-10"*

Stone trim enhances the siding exterior of this three-bedroom country home. Decorative columns define the dining room, to the right of the vaulted foyer. Entertaining will be easy from the centrally located kitchen with its serving bar, pantry and efficient use of space. The nearby breakfast nook enjoys French-door access to the backyard—or choose an optional bay window for more natural light. A warming fireplace adorns the vaulted great room. Privately located off the great room, the master suite features high quality amenities, including a tray ceiling, vaulted bathroom, plant shelf, radius window, separate shower and soaking tub.

Plan HPT700073

Square Footage: *2,232*
Bonus Space: *384 square feet*
Width: *79'-8"* **Depth:** *58'-2"*

With a rambling, open interior, this lovely ranch home features a spacious living area with French doors that open to the rear property. A fireplace warms the heart of the home. A well-organized kitchen boasts wrapping counters, a double sink and a snack counter. Triple-window views highlight the formal dining room. To the left of the foyer, a quiet sitting area invites reading and conversation. Nearby, two secondary bedrooms share a full bath with a dual vanity. A secluded master suite boasts a garden tub and a walk-in closet. This home is designed with a basement foundation.

©1993 Donald A. Gardner Architects, Inc.

B. NATHAN

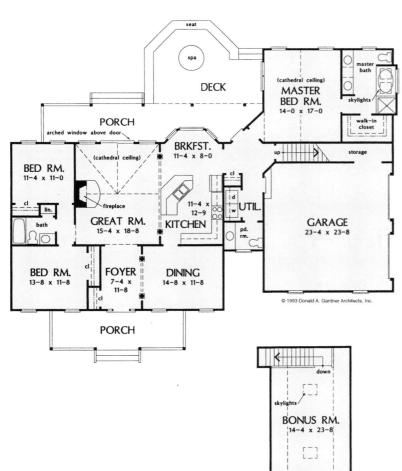

seat

spa

DECK

PORCH

(cathedral ceiling)
MASTER
BED RM.
14-0 x 17-0

master
bath

skylights

walk-in
closet

arched window above door

(cathedral ceiling)

BRKFST.
11-4 x 8-0

up

storage

BED RM.
11-4 x 11-0

cl

11-4 x
12-9

d
w

UTIL.

GARAGE
23-4 x 23-8

cl

lin.

fireplace

bath

GREAT RM.
15-4 x 18-8

KITCHEN

pd.
rm.

BED RM.
13-8 x 11-8

cl

FOYER
7-4 x
11-8

DINING
14-8 x 11-8

cl

PORCH

© 1993 Donald A. Gardner Architects, Inc.

down

skylights

BONUS RM.
14-4 x 23-8

Plan HPT700074

Square Footage: *1,864*
Bonus Space: *420 square feet*
Width: *70'-4"* **Depth:** *56'-4"*

Quaint and cozy on the outside with porches front and back, this three-bedroom country home surprises with an open floor plan featuring a large great room with a cathedral ceiling. A central kitchen with an angled counter opens to the breakfast and great rooms for easy entertaining. The privately located master bedroom has a cathedral ceiling and access to the deck. Two secondary bedrooms share a full hall bath. A bonus room makes expanding easy.

Cost to build? See page 436 to order complete cost estimate to build this house in your area!

89

Plan HPT700075

Square Footage: *1,289*
Width: *46'-0"* **Depth:** *52'-4"*

The multiple gables, arched picture window and shutters give this charming home great curb appeal. The foyer leads directly into the vaulted great room which contains a warming fireplace framed by a window and a door to the backyard. Air flow is at a maximum in the main living area, with a low kitchen wall and open ceiling between the dining room, great room, kitchen and breakfast area. The galley kitchen has plenty of counter space. A private master suite with tray ceiling has a luxurious bath—complete with a garden tub, shower and large walk-in closet. On the opposite side of the house are Bedrooms 2 and 3, which share a full bath. Please specify basement, crawlspace or slab foundation when ordering.

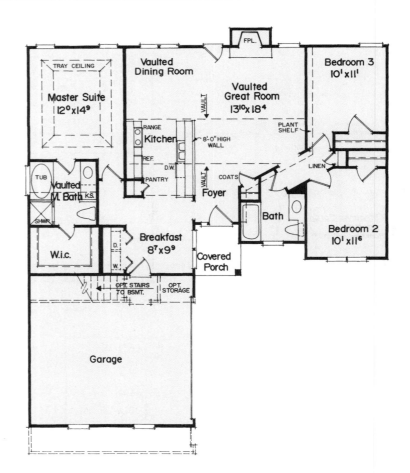

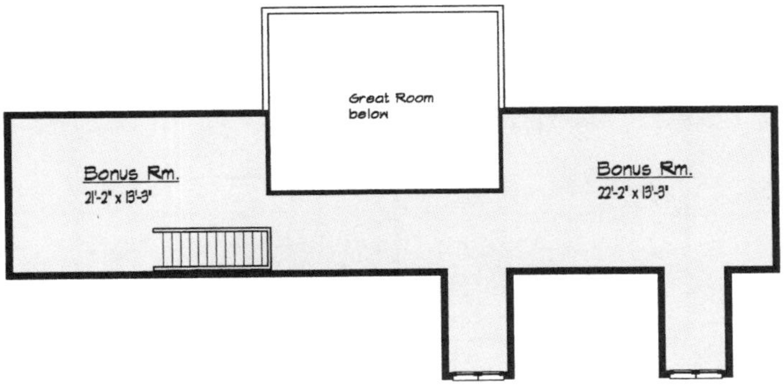

Plan HPT700076

Square Footage: *1,736 square feet*
Bonus Space: *890 square feet*
Width: *64'-0"* **Depth:** *57'-0"*

This is a delightful little design, with a low-slung profile, yet sporting a volume roofline. It is this volume roof that gives shape to the cathedral ceiling in the great room, providing a sense of spaciousness. The covered porch beyond the great room is connected to a screened porch just off the island kitchen—alfresco dining in any weather! The master suite, with a walk-in closet, is complemented by two family bedrooms sharing a full bath. Make one bedroom a den or home office, if you choose. A stairway, just at the entry, leads to the second floor, ready for completion at a future date. The two-car garage connects to the main house via the utility room. Please specify basement or crawlspace foundation when ordering.

Floor plan labels:

Great Room below

Bonus Rm. 21'-2" x 13'-3"
Bonus Rm. 22'-2" x 13'-3"

Screened Porch 21'-0" x 13'-6" (cathedral clg.)
Kitchen 21'-6" x 13'-0"
Great Room 19'-6" x 15'-5" (cathedral clg.)
Porch 41'-2" x 8'-0"
Master Bedroom 12'-6" x 15'-5"
Pantry
Utility
Balcony above
Foyer 8'-6" x 6'-0"
Bedroom 11'-4" x 12'-1"
Bedroom 13'-0" x 12'-1"
Garage 21'-2" x 23'-4"

Plan HPT700077

First Floor: *1,501 square feet*
Second Floor: *631 square feet*
Total: *2,132 square feet*
Width: *76'-0"* **Depth:** *48'-4"*

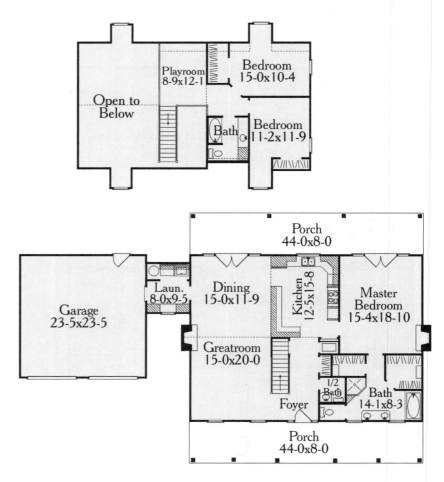

This home reveals its rustic charm with a metal roof, dormers and exposed column rafters. The full-length porch is an invitation to comfortable living inside. The great room shares a fireplace with the spacious dining room that has rear-porch access. The kitchen is this home's focus, with plenty of counter and cabinet space, a window sink and an open layout. The first-floor master suite features two walk-in closets and a grand bath. Two family bedrooms and a playroom reside on the second floor. Please specify basement, crawlspace or slab foundation when ordering.

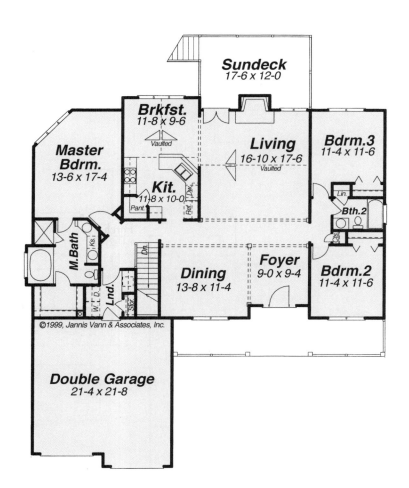

Sundeck
17-6 x 12-0

Brkfst.
11-8 x 9-6

Vaulted

Master
Bdrm.
13-6 x 17-4

Kit.
11-8 x 10-0

Pant.

Living
16-10 x 17-6
Vaulted

Bdrm.3
11-4 x 11-6

Lin.

Bth.2

M. Bath

Dn.

Dining
13-8 x 11-4

Foyer
9-0 x 9-4

Bdrm.2
11-4 x 11-6

Lnd.

W.T.D.

©1999, Jannis Vann & Associates, Inc.

Double Garage
21-4 x 21-8

Plan HPT700078

Square Footage: *1,865*
Width: *56'-0"* **Depth:** *58'-0"*

Three dormers and a warming covered front porch would make anyone feel welcome in this country/ranch home. The vaulted ceiling in the living room definitely gives you a feeling of spaciousness along with the cozy fireplace. The elaborate kitchen features lots of counter space, a pantry and a breakfast area. On the far left side of the home, the master bedroom enjoys privacy. The home is completed with a double garage.

Plan HPT700079

Square Footage: *1,882*
Bonus Room: *363 square feet*
Width: *61'-4"* **Depth:** *55'-0"*

An arched window in a center front-facing gable lends style and beauty to the facade of this three-bedroom home. An open common area features a great room with a cathedral ceiling, a formal dining room with a tray ceiling, a functional kitchen and an informal breakfast area. The area separates the master suite from the secondary bedrooms for privacy. The master suite provides a dramatic vaulted ceiling, access to the back porch and abundant closet space. Access to a versatile bonus room is near the master bedroom.

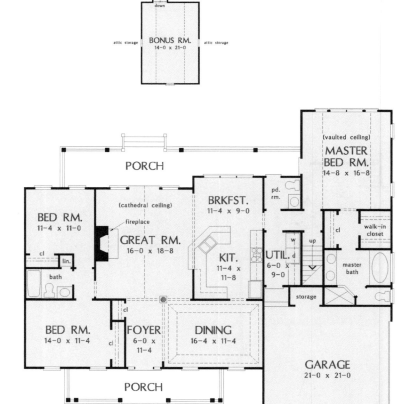

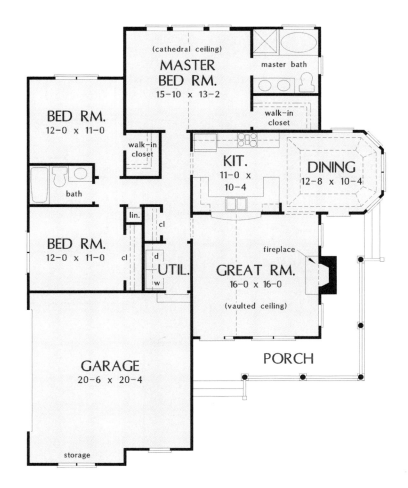

© 1999 Donald A. Gardner, Inc.

(cathedral ceiling)

MASTER BED RM.
15-10 x 13-2

master bath

BED RM.
12-0 x 11-0

walk-in closet

walk-in closet

bath

KIT.
11-0 x 10-4

DINING
12-8 x 10-4

lin.

cl

BED RM.
12-0 x 11-0

cl

d

w

UTIL.

fireplace

GREAT RM.
16-0 x 16-0

(vaulted ceiling)

GARAGE
20-6 x 20-4

PORCH

storage

Plan HPT700080

Square Footage: *1,422*
Width: *45'-6"* **Depth:** *57'-8"*

Multiple gables, an arched picture window and an L-shaped front porch add size and style to this charming home. An open floor plan enhances spaciousness in the common areas of this compact home, where a vaulted ceiling in the great room and a bay window and tray ceiling in the dining room create volume and elegance. A pass-through from the kitchen to the great room adds to the plan's openness. The master bedroom boasts a cathedral ceiling and a trio of windows. The master bath features a dual-sink vanity and a separate tub and shower. ©1999 Donald A. Gardner, Inc..

Plan HPT700081

Square Footage: *1,652*
Bonus Room: *367 square feet*
Width: *64'-4"* **Depth:** *51'-0"*

A classic country exterior enriches the appearance of this economical home, while its front porch and two skylit back porches encourage weekend relaxation. The great room features a cathedral ceiling and a fireplace with adjacent built-ins. The master suite enjoys a double-door entry, back-porch access and a tray ceiling. The master bath has a garden tub set in the corner, a separate shower, twin vanities and a skylight. Loads of storage, an open floor plan and walls of windows make this three-bedroom plan very livable.

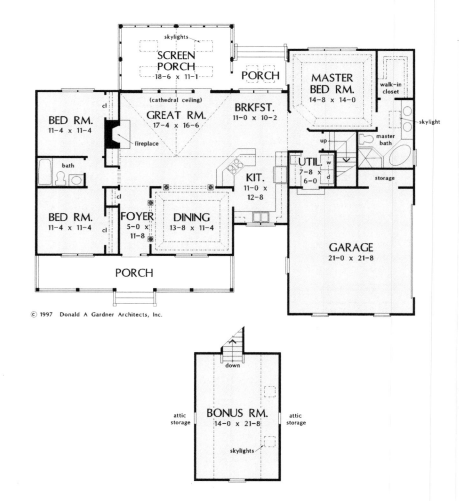

© 1997 Donald A. Gardner Architects, Inc.

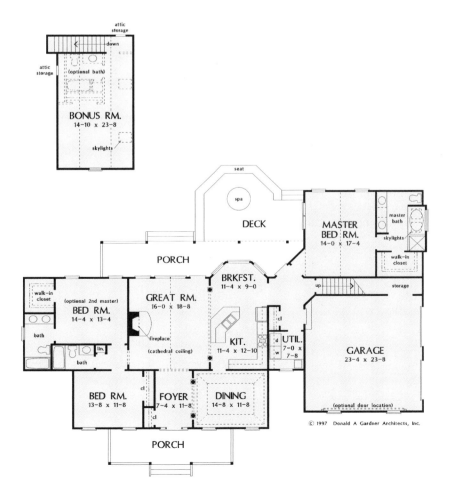

attic
storage

down

attic
storage

(optional bath)

BONUS RM.
14-10 x 23-8

skylights

seat

spa

DECK

PORCH

BRKFST.
11-4 x 9-0

MASTER
BED RM.
14-0 x 17-4

master
bath

skylights

walk-in
closet

up

storage

walk-in
closet

(optional 2nd master)
BED RM.
14-4 x 13-4

GREAT RM.
16-0 x 18-8

KIT.
11-4 x 12-10

UTIL.
7-0 x
7-8

GARAGE
23-4 x 23-8

bath

fireplace

(cathedral ceiling)

lin.

bath

BED RM.
13-8 x 11-8

cl

FOYER
7-4 x 11-8

DINING
14-8 x 11-8

cl

PORCH

(optional door location)

© 1997 Donald A Gardner Architects, Inc.

Plan HPT700082

Square Footage: *2,057*
Bonus Room: *444 square feet*
Width: *80'-10"* **Depth:** *61'-6"*

With its clean lines and symmetry, this home radiates grace and style. Inside, cathedral and tray ceilings add volume and elegance. The L-shaped kitchen includes an angled snack bar to the breakfast bay and great room. Secluded at the back of the house, the vaulted master suite includes a skylit bath. Of the two secondary bedrooms, one acts as a "second" master suite with its own private bath, and an alternate bath design creates a wheelchair-accessible option. The bonus room makes a great craft room, playroom, office or optional fourth bedroom with a bath. The two-car garage loads to the side.

©1999 Donald A. Gardner, Inc.

B. NATHAN

Plan HPT700083

First Floor: *1,830 square feet*
Second Floor: *679 square feet*
Total: *2,509 square feet*
Bonus Room: *346 square feet*
Width: *81'-2"* **Depth:** *48'-0"*

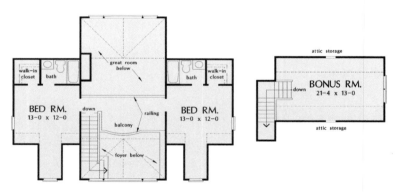

An expansive, wrapping front porch creates a charming facade for this gracious home. The vaulted foyer receives light from the center clerestory dormer, while an overlooking balcony adds height and drama to the breathtaking entry. A vaulted ceiling heightens the great room. The master bedroom features a tray ceiling for added elegance and a private bath. Both upstairs bedrooms enjoy dormer windows, walk-in closets and private baths. A bonus room above the garage easily converts to a home office or guest suite.

©1999 Donald A. Gardner, Inc.

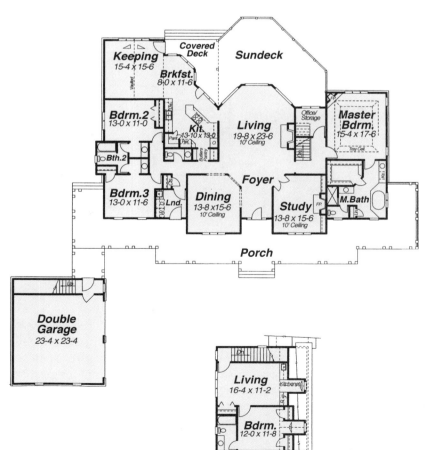

Covered Deck

Sundeck

Keeping
15-4 x 15-6

Brkfst.
8-0 x 11-6

Bdrm.2
13-0 x 11-0

Kit.
13-10 x 13-0

Living
19-8 x 23-6
10' Ceiling

Office/ Storage

Master Bdrm.
15-4 x 17-6

Bth.2

Tray Ceil.

Bdrm.3
13-0 x 11-6

Lnd.

Dining
13-8 x15-6
10' Ceiling

Foyer

Study
13-8 x 15-6
10' Ceiling

M.Bath

FP

Porch

Double Garage
23-4 x 23-4

Living
16-4 x 11-2

Bdrm.
12-0 x 11-8

Room Above Garage

Plan HPT700084

Square Footage: *2,911*
Width: *90'-0"* **Depth:** *100'-0"*

Gracious porches span the entire front of this charming country ranch accented by second-floor dormers. The detached garage is connected by a covered extension of the porch, allowing access to the laundry room, which leads conveniently to the kitchen. A dramatic bayed living room is the focal point of the house as you enter the foyer. The foyer is flanked by the dining room and a study, which features built-in shelving and a direct-vent fireplace. Open stairs leading to the lower level are located in the vestibule of the master suite. A small office sits behind the stairs. This home is ideal for a pristine view of a lake or mountains.

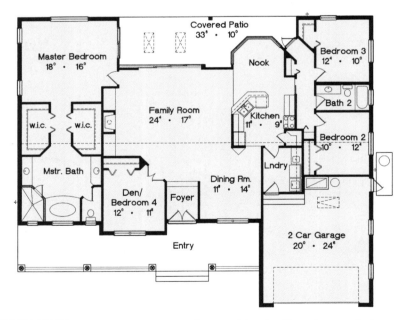

Plan HPT700085

Square Footage: *2,308*
Width: *67'-0"* **Depth:** *56'-8"*

Corner quoins combined with arch-top windows and a columned entry lend an exciting facade to this four-bedroom home. The foyer is entered through double doors and introduces the open dining and family room area. The master suite occupies the left side of the plan and enjoys a sun-strewn sitting room, two walk-in closets and a luxurious bath complete with a garden tub and separate shower. The kitchen sits conveniently near the dining room and features a pantry, desk and view through the breakfast-nook windows. Two family bedrooms, sharing a full bath, reside near the kitchen. A third bedroom or guest suite is located by the family room.

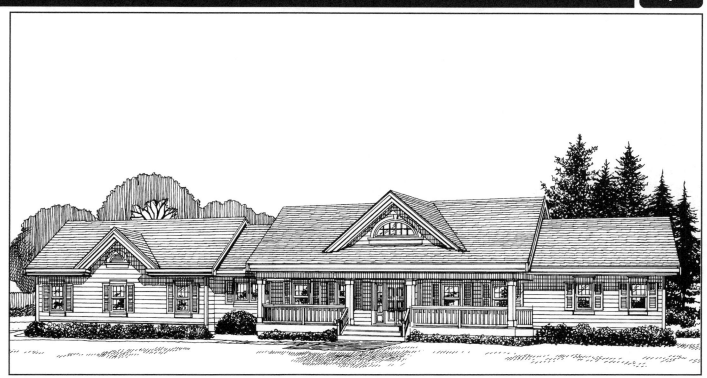

VAULTED
great rm
15'6x18'4

brk
11'6x10'

PANTRY

FREEZER

two car garage
21'x23'

RECYCLING BINS

k
11'6x11'

ARCH

din
12'x11'

BUILT-IN CABINETS

RAILING

DN

W.I.C.

VAULTED
mbr
12'x17'8

PLANT LEDGE OVER

VAULTED ENTRY

br3
12'x11'

VAULTED
br2
12'x11'

PLANT LEDGE OVER

PORCH

$S
QUOTE ONE®
Cost to build? See page 436
to order complete cost estimate
to build this house in your area!

This wide, wonderful ranch has it all: three bedrooms, full basement or crawlspace, formal dining room and a breakfast room in the country kitchen. All of this revolves around a central great room with a gas fireplace and media wall. The vaulted entry with plant ledges and a stunning window creates immediate impact. The master bedroom features a walk-in closet, soaking tub and separate shower. Both the master bedroom and Bedroom 2 present vaulted ceilings. The garage entry contains washer/dryer space and a walk-in pantry.

Plan HPT700086
Square Footage: *1,880*
Width: *88'-0"* **Depth:** *42'-0"*

Photo by Chris A. Little, courtesy of Chatham Home Planning, Inc.

This home, as shown in the photograph, may differ from the actual blueprints. For more detailed information, please check the floor plans carefully.

Plan HPT700087

Square Footage: *2,471*
Width: *62'-10"* **Depth:** *75'-3"*

Old World elements adorn this home, including quoins, keystone arches, a Palladian window and keystone lintels. Just to the left of the foyer is the dining room, which leads to the island kitchen. The kitchen enjoys close proximity to the well-lit breakfast room and a convenient utility room. The hearth-warmed living room looks to a rear porch. The right side of the plan is devoted to the sleeping quarters. The master bedroom is situated at the rear and boasts a private bath with many amenities. Three family bedrooms and another full bath complete this plan.

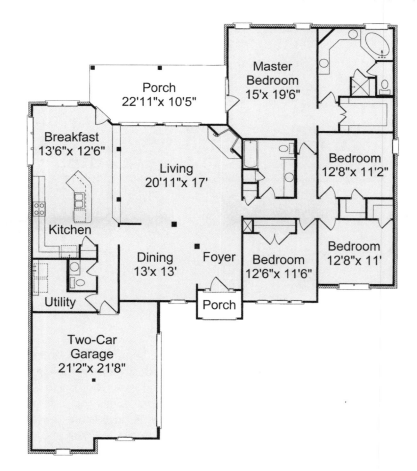

Lakes

waterfront cabins and chalets

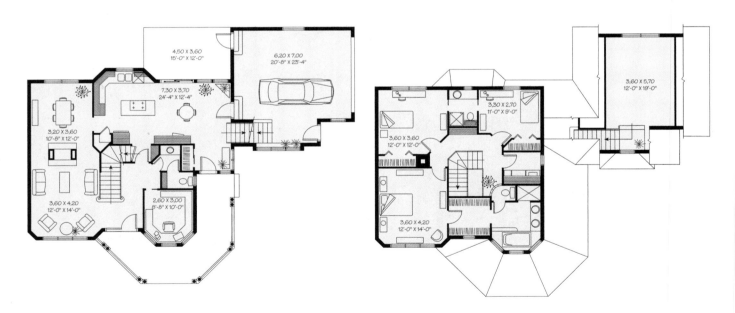

Plan HPT700088

First Floor: *1,044 square feet*
Second Floor: *894 square feet*
Total: *1,938 square feet*
Bonus Room: *228 square feet*
Width: *58'-0"* **Depth:** *43'-6"*

This charming country traditional home provides a well-lit home office, harbored in a beautiful bay with three windows. The second-floor bay brightens the master bath, which has a double-bowl vanity, a step-up tub and a dressing area. The living and dining rooms share a two-sided fireplace. The gourmet kitchen has a cooktop island counter and enjoys outdoor views through sliding glass doors in the breakfast area. A sizable bonus room above the two-car garage can be developed into hobby space or a recreation room. This home is designed with a basement foundation.

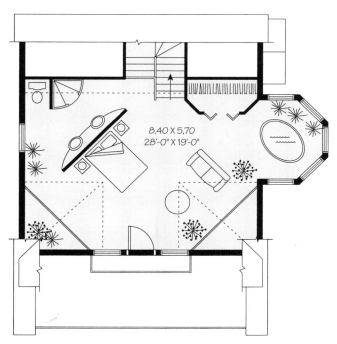

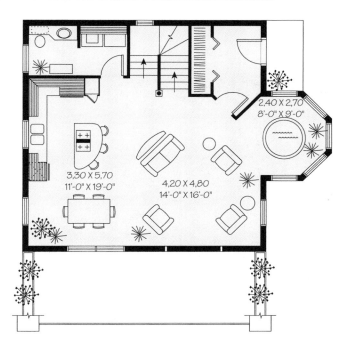

8,40 X 5,70
28'-0" X 19'-0"

3,30 X 5,70
11'-0" X 19'-0"

4,20 X 4,80
14'-0" X 16'-0"

2,40 X 2,70
8'-0" X 9'-0"

This home is absolutely full of windows, and a large deck enhances the outdoor living possibilities. Picture the wall of windows facing the seashore, with the sound of waves lulling you into a calm, comfortable feeling. Inside, an open floor plan includes a family/dining room, an L-shaped kitchen with a snack bar, and a full bath with laundry facilities. A special treat is the bumped-out hot tub room, almost entirely surrounded by windows. Upstairs, choose either the one- or two-bedroom plan. This home is designed with a basement foundation.

Plan HPT700089

First Floor: *737 square feet*
Second Floor: *587 square feet*
Total: *1,324 square feet*
Width: *33'-0"* **Depth:** *26'-0"*

Plan HPT700090

Square Footage: 2,385
Lower–Level Entry: 109 square feet
Width: 60'-0" **Depth:** 52'-0"

Cottage accommodations are provided with this seaside vacation dream home. Southern enchantment and Key West style intertwine to create an alluring facade decked in horizontal siding. Once inside, the foyer steps lead up to the formal living areas on the main floor. To the left, a study is enhanced by a vaulted ceiling and double doors that open onto a front balcony. This room makes a perfect home office for quiet escapes. Vaulted ceilings create a lofty feel throughout the home, especially in the central great room, which overlooks the rear deck—perfect for summertime entertainment. The island kitchen is open to an adjacent breakfast nook. Guest quarters reside on the right side of the plan—one boasts a private bath.

porch

master suite
12'-8" x 17'-8"
10'-0" tray clg.

open to below

w.i.c.

overlook

dn

master bath

dn

porch

2 car garage

bonus/ storage

storage

Plan HPT700091

First Floor: *1,383 square feet*
Second Floor: *595 square feet*
Total: *1,978 square feet*
Width: *48'-0"* **Depth:** *42'-0"*

deck

covered porch

porch

dining
11'-0" x 12'-8"
11'-0" tray clg.

fireplace

great room
15'-0" x 19'-6"
vaulted clg.

br. 3
11'-6" x 12'-0"
10'-0"h. clg.

porch

built ins

kitchen
11'-0" x 12'-0"

br. 2
12'-10" x 12'-0"
10'-0"h. clg.

up

stor.

util.

up
foyer

entry

This fabulous Key West home blends interior space with the great outdoors. Designed for a balmy climate, this home boasts expansive porches and decks—with outside access from every area of the home. A sun-dappled foyer leads via a stately mid-level staircase to a splendid great room, which features a warming fireplace tucked in beside beautiful built-in cabinetry. Highlighted by a wall of glass that opens to the rear porch, this two-story living space opens to the formal dining room and a well-appointed kitchen. Spacious secondary bedrooms on the main level open to outside spaces and share a full bath. Upstairs, a ten-foot tray ceiling highlights a private master suite, which provides French doors to an upper-level porch.

Plan HPT700092

First Floor: *2,151 square feet*
Second Floor: *734 square feet*
Total: *2,885 square feet*
Bonus Room: *522 square feet*
Width: *99'-0"* **Depth:** *56'-0"*

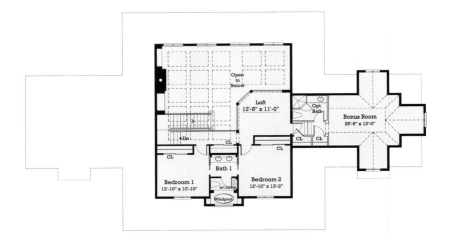

Wraparound front and rear porches provide plenty of outdoor livability in this distinctive Victorian farmhouse. Clapboard siding, louvered shutters, accents of standing-seam metal roofs and multi-pane windows provide just the right touch to this waterfront home. Specialty ceilings, interior columns, a fireplace, a loft, a unique bonus room with optional bath, island kitchen workstation and double French doors top the list of the home's indoor amenities. Access the coffered-ceiling study through pocket doors off the foyer that borders a stepped-ceiling formal dining room. The master suite features a projected whirlpool tub augmented by a decorative dormer that sheds natural light into the deluxe master bath. Please specify basement or crawlspace foundation when ordering.

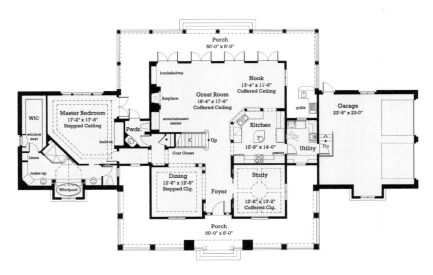

br. 3
11'-4" x 13'-0"
vaulted clg.

deck

open to below

sitting

overlook

open

master
suite
16'-0" x 14'-0"
vaulted clg.

dn

dn

master
bath

w.i.c.

Plan HPT700093

First Floor: *1,542 square feet*
Second Floor: *971 square feet*
Total: *2,513 square feet*
Width: *46'-0"* **Depth:** *51'-0"*

br. 2
11'-4" x 13'-0"
10'-0"h. clg.

covered porch

built ins

great room
19'-0" x 18'-0"
2-story clg.

fireplace

built ins

dining
12'-0" x 14'-0"
10'-0" h. clg.

up

up

foyer

kitchen
10'-8" x 13'-6"

butler pantry

util.

built ins

study
13'-4" x 12'-0"
vaulted clg.

entry porch

bonus/ storage/

2 car garage

storage

storage

Arches, columns and French doors pay homage to a captivating Key West style that's light, airy and fully au courant. A contemporary, high-pitched hip roof tops a chic compendium of gables, turrets and dormers—the perfect complement to an elegant and breezy entry porch. French doors lead to a quiet study or parlor, which features a wall of built-in shelves and a view of the front property through an arch-topped window. Built-ins frame the fireplace in the great room too, providing an anchor for a wall of glass that brings in a sense of the outdoors. The main level includes a secluded secondary bedroom, or guest quarters. Upstairs, a balcony hall allows interior vistas of the living area below, and connects a secondary bedroom and bath with the master suite.

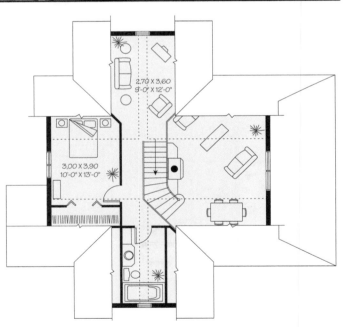

Plan HPT700094

First Floor: *1,024 square feet*
Second Floor: *456 square feet*
Total: *1,480 square feet*
Width: *32'-0"* **Depth:** *40'-0"*

Pillars, a large rear porch and plenty of window views lend a classic feel to this lovely country cottage. Inside, the entry room has a roomy closet and an interior entry door to eliminate drafts. The light-filled L-shaped kitchen lies conveniently near the entrance. A large room adjacent to the kitchen serves as a dining, living and viewing area. A fireplace adds warmth to the entire living space. A master suite boasts a walk-in closet and full bath. On the second floor, a second bedroom and full bath provide privacy to guests or family. This home is designed with a basement foundation.

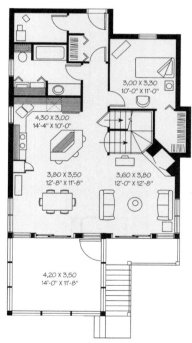

3,00 X 3,30
10'-0" X 11'-0"

4,30 X 3,00
14'-4" X 10'-0"

3,80 X 3,50
12'-8" X 11'-8"

3,60 X 3,80
12'-0" X 12'-8"

4,20 X 3,50
14'-0" X 11'-8"

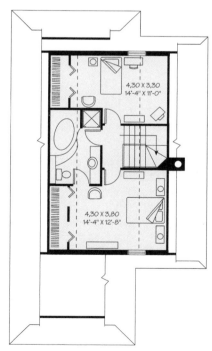

4,30 X 3,30
14'-4" X 11'-0"

4,30 X 3,80
14'-4" X 12'-8"

This vacation home enjoys a screened porch and sits on stilts to avoid any water damage. Truly a free-flowing plan, the dining room, living room and kitchen share a common space, with no walls separating them. An island snack counter in the kitchen provides plenty of space for food preparation. A family bedroom and full bath complete the first level. Upstairs, two additional bedrooms—with ample closet space—share a lavish bath, which includes a whirlpool tub and separate shower. This home is designed with a basement foundation.

Plan HPT700095

First Floor: *895 square feet*
Second Floor: *576 square feet*
Total: *1,471 square feet*
Width: *26'-0"* **Depth:** *36'-0"*

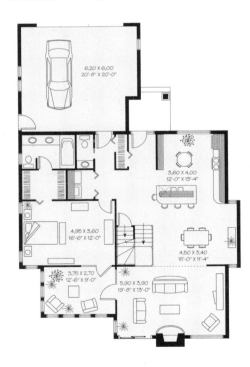

Plan HPT700096

First Floor: *1,431 square feet*
Second Floor: *1,054 square feet*
Total: *2,485 square feet*
Width: *40'-0"* **Depth:** *60'-0"*

Whether your views are mountain, water, woodland or desert, this contemporary home allows you to incorporate them into your decor through its large windows. The main-level master suite has private access to a sun room, while for those who want a direct dose of the elements there is a large open deck. The main living area is open, so that a fireplace in the living room can be seen from the dining room and kitchen. Three bedrooms, two bathrooms and a powder room complete the plan. This home is designed with a basement foundation.

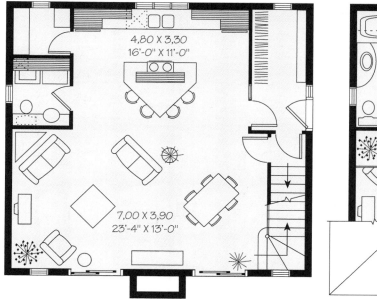

4,80 X 3,30
16'-0" X 11'-0"

7,00 X 3,90
23'-4" X 13'-0"

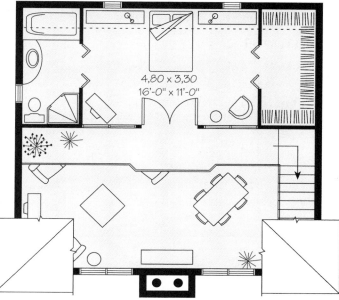

4,80 x 3,30
16'-0" X 11'-0"

This stunning country cottage has a heart of gold, with plenty of windows to bring in a wealth of natural light. Open planning allows the first-floor living and dining room to share the wide views of the outdoors. Glass doors frame the fireplace and open to the rear deck. A second-floor mezzanine enjoys an overlook to the living area and leads to a generous master suite with a walk-in closet and a sitting area. This home is designed with a basement foundation.

Plan HPT700097

First Floor: *728 square feet*
Second Floor: *420 square feet*
Total: *1,148 square feet*
Width: *28'-0"* **Depth:** *26'-0"*

Plan HPT700098

First Floor: *448 square feet*
Second Floor: *448 square feet*
Total: *896 square feet*
Width: *16'-0"* **Depth:** *41'-6"*

Perfect for a lakeside, vacation or starter home, this two-story design is sure to be a favorite. A large railed porch on the first floor and the covered balcony on the second floor are available for watching the sunrise. On the first floor, the spacious living room is convenient to the kitchen and dining area. A powder room finishes off this level. Upstairs, the sleeping zone consists of two bedrooms, each with roomy closets, and a full hall bath with a linen closet. The front bedroom accesses the balcony.

BEDROOM 2
13'-0" x 9'-0"

LINEN

DN

BATH

BEDROOM 1
13'-0" x 11'-4"

COVERED
BALCONY
16'-0" x 10'-0"

KITCHEN
15'-2" x 9'-0"

W/D

DINE

HVAC

UP

PR

LIVING ROOM
15'-2" x 11'-3"

PORCH
16'-0" x 10'-0"

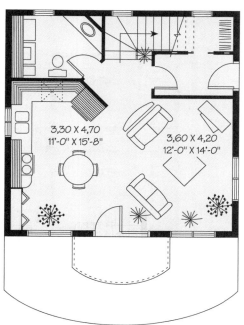

3,30 X 4,70
11'-0" X 15'-8"

3,60 X 4,20
12'-0" X 14'-0"

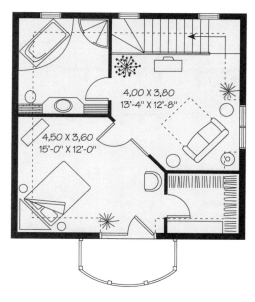

4,00 X 3,80
13'-4" X 12'-8"

4,50 X 3,60
15'-0" X 12'-0"

Plan HPT700099

First Floor: *576 square feet*
Second Floor: *576 square feet*
Total: *1,152 square feet*
Width: *24'-0"* **Depth:** *24'-0"*

This cozy lakefront vacation home is great for the small family or retired couple. Double doors open into a combined kitchen/dining/living room area, large enough for family gatherings. A powder room is located at the rear of the plan, where a staircase leads to the second floor. Upstairs, a loft/sitting area easily converts to additional sleeping quarters just outside of the master suite. This large master bedroom provides a roomy walk-in closet and private access to a petite front balcony with spacious views. The sitting area and master bedroom share access to a second-floor full bath with a corner soaking tub and separate shower. This home is designed with a basement foundation.

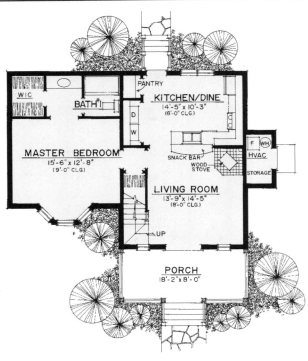

Plan HPT700100

First Floor: *836 square feet*
Second Floor: *481 square feet*
Total: *1,317 square feet*
Width: *38'-2"* **Depth:** *34'-0"*

This sweet lakeside cottage is sure to please with its quaint charm and convenient floor plan. A covered porch greets family and friends and offers a place to sit and enjoy the summer breezes. Inside, the living room—with its warming fireplace—flows nicely into the kitchen/dining area. A snack bar, pantry and plenty of cabinet and counter space are just some of the features found here. The first-floor master suite includes a bay window, walk-in closet and private bath. Upstairs, two bedrooms share a bath and linen closet.

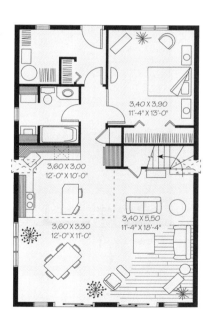

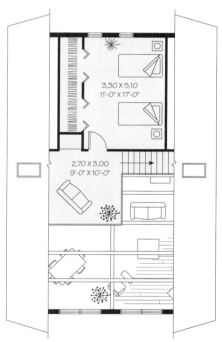

This home is an ideal retreat for empty-nesters, with a room for the grandkids when they visit. Sleep under the eaves away from the main living area in a delightful upstairs bedroom with a loft feel. This charming chalet offers two bedrooms, one bathroom and an all-in-one living area with a kitchen, dining room and family room coexisting compatibly. A fireplace keeps this home cozy in the winter, and the open patio beckons on warmer days. The laundry room downstairs is large and can be used for storage and extra closet space. Please specify basement or crawlspace foundation when ordering..

Plan HPT700101

First Floor: *945 square feet*
Second Floor: *335 square feet*
Total: *1,280 square feet*
Width: *24'-8"* **Depth:** *38'-4"*

Plan HPT700102

First Floor: *858 square feet*
Second Floor: *502 square feet*
Total: *1,360 square feet*
Width: *35'-0"* **Depth:** *29'-8"*

This fine brick home features a bay-windowed sun room, perfect for admiring the view. Inside this open floor plan, a family room features a fireplace and a spacious eat-in kitchen with access to the sun room. A bedroom, full bath, and laundry facilities complete this floor. Upstairs there are two more bedrooms sharing a compartmented bath, as well as an overlook to the family room below. Please specify basement or crawl-space foundation when ordering.

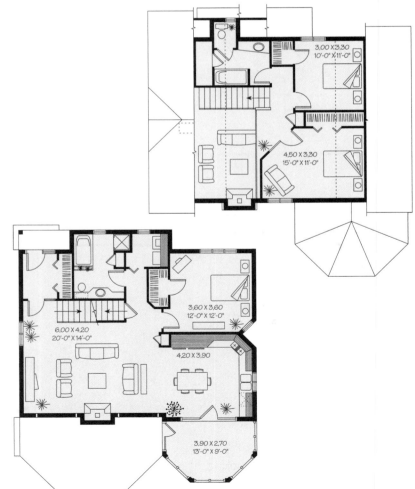

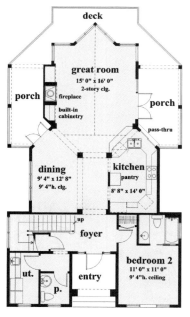

deck

great room
15' 0" x 16' 0"
2-story clg.

porch

fireplace

built-in
cabinetry

porch

pass-thru

dining
9' 4" x 12' 8"
9' 4"h. clg.

kitchen
8' 8" x 14' 0"

pantry

up

foyer

ut.

p.

entry

bedroom 2
11' 0" x 11' 0"
9' 4" ceiling

deck

vaulted ceiling

deck

open to below

overlook

loft

clg. slope

master suite
11' 6" x 17' 8"
vaulted clg.

clg. slope

dn.

m. bath
vaulted clg.

mech.

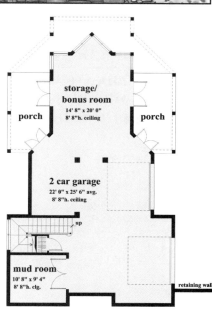

storage/ bonus room
14' 8" x 20' 0"
8' 8"h. ceiling

porch

porch

2 car garage
22' 0" x 25' 6" avg.
8' 8"h. ceiling

up

mud room
10' 8" x 9' 4"
8' 8"h. clg.

retaining wall

This traditional country cabin is a vacationer's dream. Stone and vertical wood siding rustically camouflage the exterior, while the inside pampers in lavish style. An elegant entryway extends into the foyer, where straight ahead, the two-story great room visually expands the lofty interior. This room provides a warming fireplace and offers built-in cabinetry. Double doors open to a fresh veranda, which wraps around to the rear deck—a perfect place to enjoy the outdoors. Upstairs, a vaulted ceiling enhances the master suite and its private bath. A private deck from the master suite can be accessed through a set of double doors. The loft area overlooking the great room accesses a second deck. The basement level hosts a bonus room, storage area and a two-car garage.

Plan HPT700103
First Floor: *1,143 square feet*
Second Floor: *651 square feet*
Total: *2,445 square feet*
Width: *32'-0"* **Depth:** *57'-0"*

Plan HPT700104

Square Footage: *680*
Loft: *419 square feet*
Width: *26'-6"* **Depth:** *28'-0"*

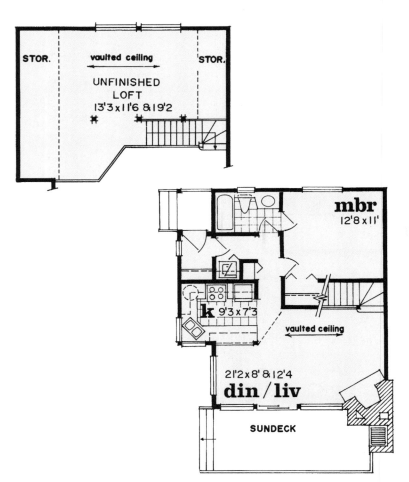

Full window walls provide the living and dining rooms of this rustic vacation home with natural light. A full sun deck with a built-in barbecue sits just outside the living area and is accessed by sliding glass doors. The entire living space has a vaulted ceiling to gain spaciousness and to allow for the full-height windows. The efficient U-shaped kitchen has a pass-through counter to the dining area and a corner sink with windows overhead. A master bedroom is on the first floor and has the use of a full bath. A loft overlooking the living room provides an additional 419 square feet not included in the total.

Plan HPT700105

First Floor: *1,157 square feet*
Second Floor: *638 square feet*
Total: *1,795 square feet*
Width: *36'-0"* **Depth:** *40'-0"*

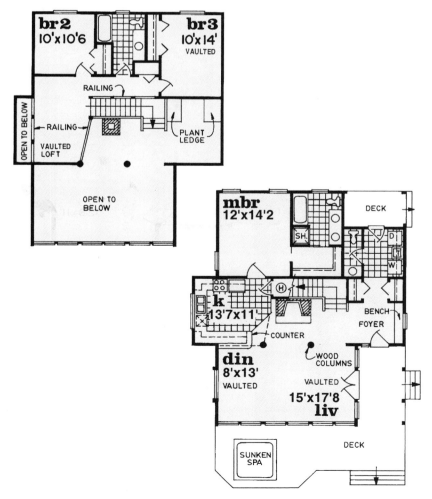

This leisure home is perfect for outdoor living, with French doors opening to a large sun deck and sunken spa. The open-beam, vaulted ceiling and high window wall provide views for the living and dining rooms, which are decorated with wood columns and warmed by a fireplace. The step-saving U-shaped kitchen has ample counter space and a bar counter to the dining room. The master suite on the first floor features a walk-in closet and a private bath. A convenient mudroom with an adjoining laundry room accesses a rear deck. Two bedrooms on the second floor share a full bath.

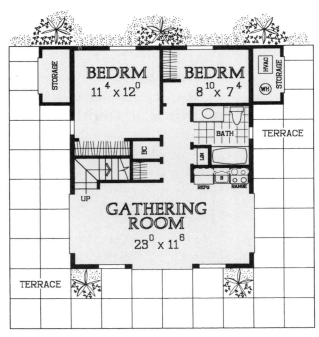

QUOTE ONE®

Cost to build? See page 436
to order complete cost estimate
to build this house in your area!

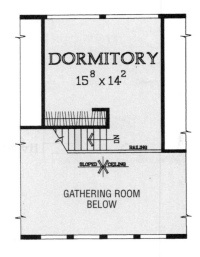

Plan HPT700106

First Floor: *784 square feet*
Second Floor: *275 square feet*
Total: *1,059 square feet*
Width: *32'-0"* **Depth:** *30'-0"*

This chalet-type vacation home, with its steep, overhanging roof, will catch the eye of even the most casual onlooker. It is designed to be completely livable whether it's the season for swimming or skiing. The dormitory on the upper level will sleep many vacationers, while the two bedrooms on the first floor provide the more convenient and conventional sleeping facilities. With a wraparound terrace and plenty of storage space, this is a perfect design.

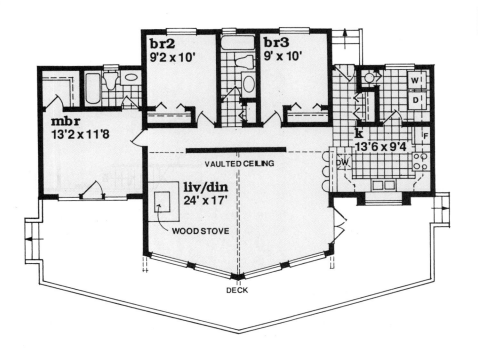

Plan HPT700107

Square Footage: *1,292*
Width: *52'-0"* **Depth:** *34'-0"*

The casual living space of this cozy home offers room to kick off your shoes or put on a bash, and is highlighted by a wood stove and a vaulted ceiling. A wraparound deck provides space to enjoy the great outdoors, while tall windows bring plenty of natural light inside. A tile kitchen offers plenty of counter space and a snack counter. The master suite nestles to the left of the living area, and boasts a walk-in closet. Two secondary bedrooms allow space for guests and family members.

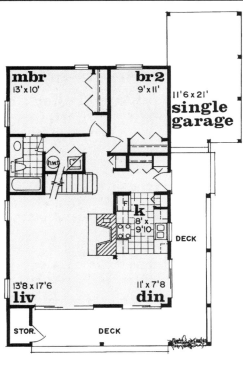

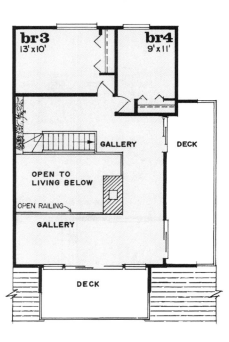

Plan HPT700108

First Floor: *986*
Second Floor: *722 square feet*
Total: *1,708 square feet*
Width: *36'-6"* **Depth:** *53'-6"*

This charming four-bedroom home is dramatic on the outside and comfortable on the inside. Large glass sliding doors and floor-to-ceiling windows flood the interior with natural light. A vaulted living room features an oversized fireplace and connects to the dining area. A galley kitchen features a sink overlooking the deck. The master bedroom and a secondary bedroom to the rear share the use of a full bath. The second floor holds two additional bedrooms and a gallery area with front and side decks. Use this area as a playroom or studio.

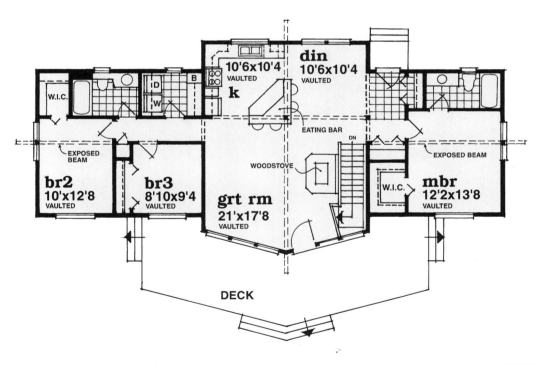

This three-bedroom leisure home is perfect for the family that spends casual time out of doors. An expansive wall of glass gives a spectacular view to the great room and accentuates the high vaulted ceilings throughout the design. The great room is also warmed by a wood stove and is open to the dining room and L-shaped kitchen. A triangular snack bar graces the kitchen and provides space for casual meals. Bedrooms are split, with the master bedroom on the right side of the plan and family bedrooms on the left.

Plan HPT700109

Square Footage: *1,405*
Width: *62'-0"* **Depth:** *29'-0"*

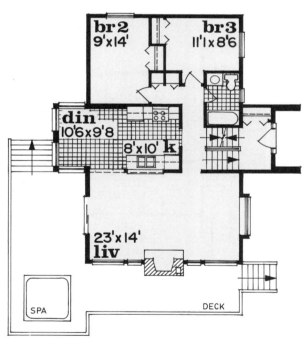

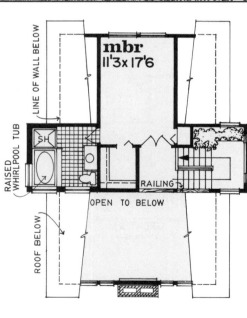

Plan HPT700110

Main Level: *1,070 square feet*
Second Level: *552 square feet*
Total: *1,622 square feet*
Width: *38'-0"* **Depth:** *40'-0"*

An expansive wall of glass, rising to the roof's peak, adds architectural interest and gives the living room of this home a spectacular view. The living room also boasts a vaulted ceiling, an oversized masonry fireplace and has access to a deck with a wonderful spa tub. The dining room is nearby, directly across from the galley-style kitchen. Two bedrooms sit to the rear of the plan and share a full bath. The second-level master suite caters to comfort with a walk-in closet, spa tub and separate shower.

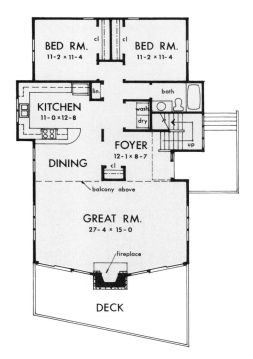

BED RM.
11-2 × 11-4

BED RM.
11-2 × 11-4

cl   cl

lin.

bath

KITCHEN
11-0 ×12-8

wash.
dry

FOYER
12-1 × 8-7

up

DINING

cl

balcony above

GREAT RM.
27-4 × 15-0

fireplace

DECK

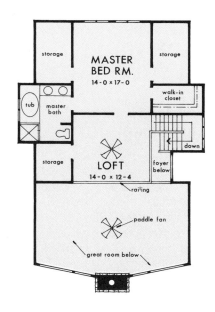

storage

MASTER
BED RM.
14-0 × 17-0

storage

walk-in
closet

tub

master
bath

down

LOFT
14-0 × 12-4

foyer
below

railing

paddle fan

great room below

This rustic three-bedroom vacation home allows for casual living both inside and out. The two-story great room offers dramatic space for entertaining with windows stretching clear to the roof, maximizing the outdoor view. A stone fireplace is the focal point of this room. Two family bedrooms on the first floor share a full hall bath. The second floor holds the master bedroom with a spacious master bath and a walk-in closet. A large loft area overlooks the great room and entrance foyer. ©1989 Donald A. Gardner Architects, Inc.

Plan HPT700111

First Floor: *1,374 square feet*
Second Floor: *608 square feet*
Total: *1,982 square feet*
Width: *40'-0"* **Depth:** *60'-8"*

Plan HPT700112

First Floor: *936 square feet*
Loft: *358 square feet*
Total: *1,294 square feet*
Width: *30'-0"* **Depth:** *32'-0"*

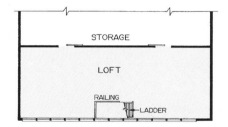

This space-efficient leisure home offers many extras. Adding the optional carport adds an extra 12 feet to the width of the home. The sun deck wraps around two sides and features a built-in barbecue and hot tub. The living room boasts a soaring vaulted ceiling, a large fireplace and sliding glass doors to the sun deck. The galley-style kitchen has a breakfast bar that connects it to the living area. Two bedrooms on the first level share the use of a full bath. A ladder to the second level reaches to a loft area that works as additional bedroom space.

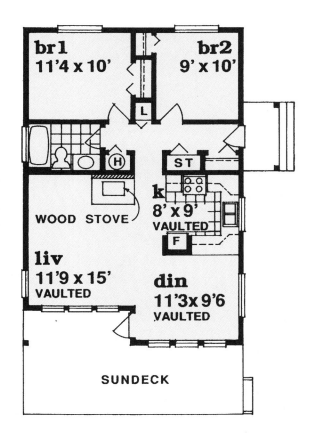

br1
11'4 x 10'

br2
9' x 10'

L

WOOD STOVE

ST

k
8' x 9'
VAULTED

F

liv
11'9 x 15'
VAULTED

din
11'3x 9'6
VAULTED

SUNDECK

Plan HPT700113

Square Footage: *817*
Width: *24'-0"* **Depth:** *36'-0"*

This compact, economical cottage is perfect as a getaway retreat or a cozy retirement home. Abundant windows overlook the sun deck and capture the views beyond for panoramic enjoyment. Vaulted ceilings and an open floor plan throughout the living and dining rooms enhance the feeling of spaciousness on the inside. For colder months, there is a wood stove in the living room. The kitchen is also vaulted and features a U-shaped workspace and countertop open to the dining area. Two bedrooms are to the rear; each has a wall closet. They share a full bath and a linen closet.

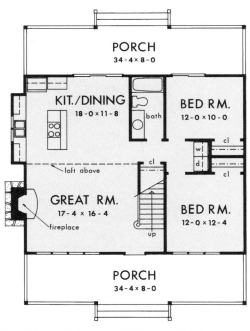

PORCH
34-4 × 8-0

KIT./DINING
18-0 × 11-8

bath

BED RM.
12-0 × 10-0

w
d

cl

cl

loft above

cl

GREAT RM.
17-4 × 16-4

fireplace

BED RM.
12-0 × 12-4

up

PORCH
34-4 × 8-0

LOFT/
STUDY
11-4 × 13-8

STO.
3-4 ×
6-4

walk-in
closet

master
bath

railing

down

MASTER
BED RM.
12-0 × 14-0

great room below

QUOTE ONE®
Cost to build? See page 436
to order complete cost estimate
to build this house in your area!

Plan HPT700114

First Floor: *1,027 square feet*
Second Floor: *580 square feet*
Total: *1,607 square feet*
Width: *37'-4"* **Depth:** *44'-8"*

This economical, rustic three-bedroom plan sports a relaxing country image with both front and back covered porches. The openness of the great room to the kitchen/dining areas and the loft/study area is reinforced with a shared cathedral ceiling. An abundance of windows in the great room, sliding glass doors in the kitchen and an over-the-sink window fill this open space with natural light and usher in the beauty of the outdoors. The first floor allows for two bedrooms, a full bath and a utility area. The master suite on the second floor has a walk-in closet and a private bath. ©1992 Donald A. Gardner Architects, Inc.

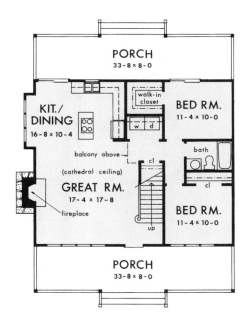

PORCH
33-8 × 8-0

KIT./
DINING
16-8 × 10-4

walk-in
closet

BED RM.
11-4 × 10-0

w d

balcony above

(cathedral ceiling)

cl

bath

GREAT RM.
17-4 × 17-8

fireplace

cl

up

BED RM.
11-4 × 10-0

PORCH
33-8 × 8-0

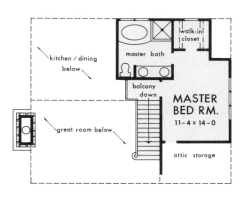

kitchen / dining
below

walk-in
closet

master bath

balcony
down

great room below

MASTER
BED RM.
11-4 × 14-0

attic storage

A mountain retreat, this rustic home features covered porches at the front and rear. Enjoy open living in the great room and kitchen/dining room combination. Here, a fireplace provides the focal point and a warm welcome that continues into the L-shaped island kitchen. A cathedral ceiling graces the great room and gives an open, inviting sense of space. Two bedrooms—one with a walk-in closet—and a full bath on the first level are complemented by a master bedroom on the second floor. This suite includes a walk-in closet and deluxe bath. Attic storage is available on the second floor. ©1991 Donald A. Gardner Architects, Inc.

Plan HPT700115

First Floor: *1,002 square feet*
Second Floor: *336 square feet*
Total: *1,338 square feet*
Width: *36'-8"* **Depth:** *44'-8"*

Plan HPT700116

Square Footage: *1,838*
Finished Basement: *1558 square feet*
Width: *61'-8"* **Depth:** *60'-8"*

Thoughtful use of space was employed in this design. The result—functional living spaces with options. The main level consists of the gathering room with balcony access that shares a through-fireplace with the study or optional bedroom. The dining room and kitchen are open areas. Note the convenient island range and amount of counter area for the gourmet. A laundry room (plenty of counter room here, too!) and powder room complete the main level. The lower level is equally well-planned with a large activity room, two bedrooms with sliding glass doors onto a terrace, and a full bath.

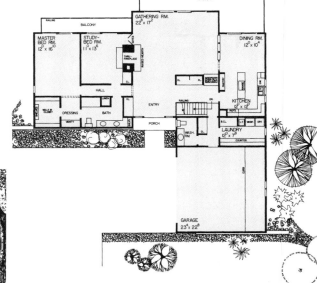

rear view

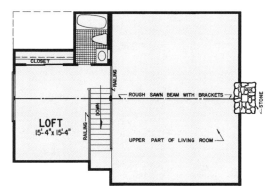

LOFT
15'-4" x 15'-4"

CLOSET

ROUGH SAWN BEAM WITH BRACKETS

STONE

DOWN

RAILING

RAILING

UPPER PART OF LIVING ROOM

Plan HPT700117

First Floor: *1,036 square feet*
Second Floor: *273 square feet*
Total: *1,309 square feet*
Width: *39'-0"* **Depth:** *38'-0"*

D

WASH TUB DRY

LAUNDRY ROOM

CLOSET

SHOWER BATH

D.W. RANGE

KITCHEN & DINING
20'-0" x 8'-0"

SINK

REFRIG.

FIREPLACE

STONE

CLOSET CLOSET

BEDROOM
11'-8" x 13'-0"

STORAGE

WH

RAILING

COATS

LIVING ROOM
20'-0" x 19'-0"

UP

DN.

PORCH
36'-0" x 10'-0"

WOOD POSTS & RAILING

QUOTE ONE®
Cost to build? See page 436
to order complete cost estimate
to build this house in your area!

This charming farmhouse design will be economical to build and a pleasure to occupy. Like most vacation homes, this design features an open plan. The large living area includes a living room, a dining room and a massive stone fireplace. A partition separates the kitchen from the living room. The first floor also holds a bedroom, a full bath and a laundry room. Upstairs, a spacious sleeping loft overlooks the living room. Don't miss the large front porch—this will be a favorite spot for relaxing.

© Design Traditions

Plan HPT700118

Square Footage: *2,721*
Width: *69'-3"* **Depth:** *79'-3"*

In this design, equally at home in the country or at the coast, classic elements play against a rustic shingle-and-stone exterior. Porch columns provide the elegance, while banks of cottage-style windows let in lots of natural light. The symmetrical layout of the foyer and formal dining room blend easily with the cozy great room. Here, a fireplace creates a welcome atmosphere that invites you to select a novel from one of the built-in bookcases and curl up in your favorite easy chair. The adjacent U-shaped kitchen combines with a sunny breakfast room that opens to a rear porch, making casual meals a pleasure. This home is designed with a walkout basement foundation.

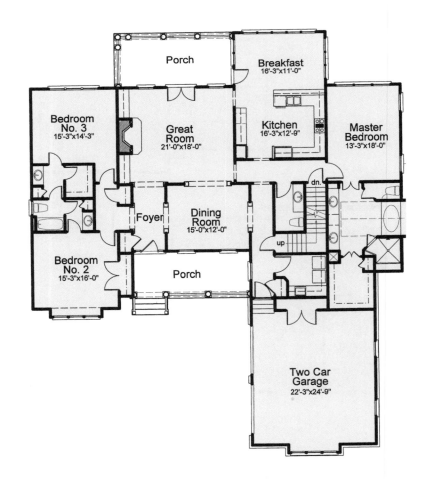

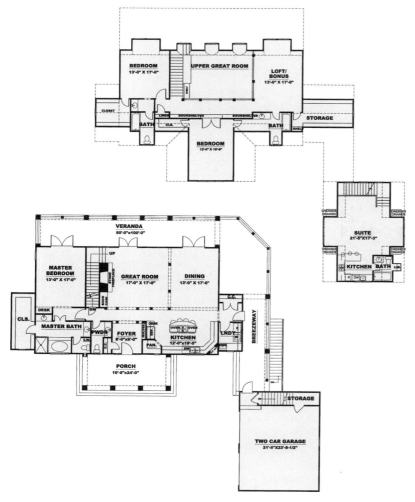

Plan HPT700119

First Floor: *1,708 square feet*
Second Floor: *1,049 square feet*
Total: *2,757 square feet*
Guest Suite: *478 square feet*
Bonus Room: *208 square feet*
Width: *84'-0"* **Depth:** *76'-7"*

This relaxing retreat focuses on outdoor views and indoor comfort zones. The entry leads to an open interior and views that extend from the foyer to the rear veranda. French doors invite gentle breezes and fresh air to mingle with the warmth of the fireplace in the heart of the home. The central gallery hall connects a spacious master suite with the casual living and dining areas. A gourmet kitchen shares interior vistas with the dining room, and boasts a cooktop island and snack counter. A walk-in pantry and planning desk provide convenience for the homeowners. Upstairs, two secondary suites share a balcony hall that leads to a bonus loft.

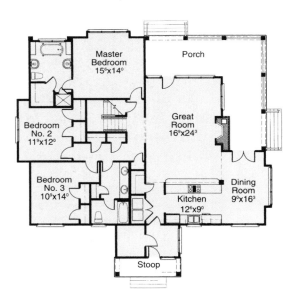

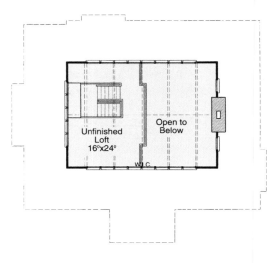

Plan HPT700120

Square Footage: *2,019*
Unfinished Loft: *384 square feet*
Width: *56'-0"* **Depth:** *56'-3"*

This design takes inspiration from the casual fishing cabins of the Pacific Northwest and interprets it for modern livability. It offers three options for a main entrance. One door opens to a mud porch, where a small hall leads to a galley kitchen and the vaulted great room. Two French doors on the side porch open to the dining room. Another porch entrance opens directly into the great room, which is centered around a massive stone fireplace and accented with a wall of windows. The secluded master bedroom features a bath with a claw-foot tub and twin pedestal sinks, as well as a separate shower and walk-in closet. Two more bedrooms share a bath. An unfinished loft looks over the great room.

rear view

Plan HPT700121

Square Footage: *1,426*
Width: *67'-6"* **Depth:** *47'-8"*

Rustic charm abounds in this amenity-filled, three-bedroom plan. From the central living area with its cathedral ceiling and fireplace to the sumptuous master suite, there are few features omitted. Be sure to notice the large walk-in closet in the master bedroom, the pampering whirlpool tub and the separate toilet compartment. Two other bedrooms have a connecting bath with a vanity for each. The house wraps around a screened porch with skylights—a grand place for eating and entertaining. The spacious rear deck has plenty of room for a hot tub. ©1987 Donald A. Gardner Architects, Inc.

DECK
29-8 x 9-0

hot tub

down

skylights

SCREENED   PORCH
29-0 x 10-0

clerestory above

BED RM.
10-8 x 11-0

lin.

bath

cl

BED RM.
10-8 x 11-0

fireplace

KIT.
8-10 x 11-8

MASTER BED RM.
13-4 x 17-0

walk in closet

GREAT RM.
20-0 x 21-6
(cathedral ceiling)

cl

pd. rm.

master bath

tub

dry wash

FOYER

PORCH
27-6 x 6-0

down

Plan HPT700122

Square Footage: *1,680*
Unfinished Basement: *1,653 square feet*
Width: *62'-8"* **Depth:** *59'-10"*

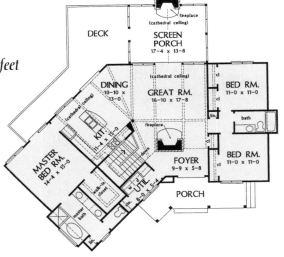

This rustic retreat is updated with contemporary angles and packs a lot of living into a small space. The great room features a fireplace, a wall of windows and access to the screened porch (with its own fireplace!), and adjoins the dining area. A highly efficient island kitchen is sure to please with a cathedral ceiling, access to the rear deck and tons of counter and cabinet space. Two family bedrooms, sharing a full bath are arranged to the right, while the master suite is secluded to the opposite side of the plan.
©1997 Donald A. Gardner Architects, Inc.

rear view

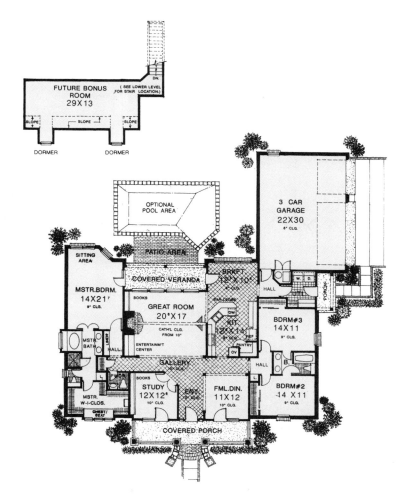

Plan HPT700123

Square Footage: *2,387 square feet*
Bonus Room: *377 square feet*
Width: *69'-6"* **Depth:** *68'-11"*

This three-bedroom home brings the past to life with Tuscan columns, dormers and fanlight windows. The entrance is flanked by the dining room and study. The great room boasts cathedral ceilings and a fireplace. The spacious kitchen adjoins a breakfast nook and accesses the rear covered veranda. The master bedroom enjoys a sitting area, access to the covered veranda, a spacious bathroom with a bumped-out tub, and a walk-in closet. This home is complete with two family bedrooms.

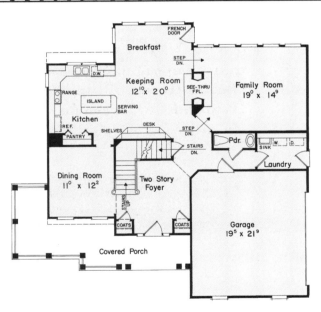

Plan HPT700124

First Floor: *1,223 square feet*
Second Floor: *1,163 square feet*
Total: *2,386 square feet*
Bonus Room: *204 square feet*
Width: *50'-0"* **Depth:** *46'-0"*

Classic capstones and arched windows complement rectangular shutters and pillars on this traditional facade. The family room offsets a formal dining room and shares a see-through fireplace with the keeping room. A gourmet kitchen boasts a food-preparation island with a serving bar, a generous pantry and French-door access to the rear property. Upstairs, a sensational master suite with a tray ceiling opens from a gallery hall with a balcony overlook and features a vaulted bath with a plant shelf, whirlpool spa and walk-in closet. Bonus space offers the possibility of an adjoining sitting room. Three additional bedrooms share a full bath. Please specify basement or crawlspace foundation when ordering.

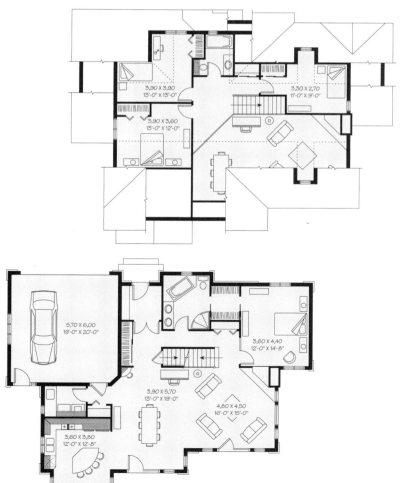

Plan HPT700125

First Floor: *1,324 square feet*
Second Floor: *688 square feet*
Total: *2,012 square feet*
Width: *55'-0"* **Depth:** *41'-0"*

Perfect for waterfront property, this home boasts windows everywhere. Inside, open planning can be found in the living room, which offers a corner fireplace for cool evenings and blends beautifully into the dining and kitchen areas. All areas enjoy windowed views. A laundry room is conveniently nestled between the kitchen and the two-car garage. The master suite features a walk-through closet and sumptuous bath. Upstairs, three uniquely shaped bedrooms share a full bath. This home is designed with a basement foundation.

Plan HPT700126

Square Footage: *1,858*
Bonus Room: *365 square feet*
Width: *55'-8"* **Depth:** *64'-10"*

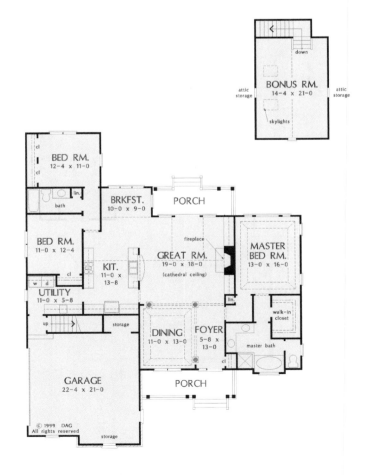

A smart combination of stone and siding, multiple gables and eye-catching windows contributes to the warm Craftsman style of this three-bedroom home. A tray ceiling and interior columns highlight the formal dining room, while the great room and kitchen enjoy a soaring cathedral ceiling. Built-in bookshelves border the fireplace in the great room, where a clerestory dormer brings in an abundance of natural light. A split-bedroom design places two family bedrooms and a bath with a linen closet on one side of the home and the master suite with a walk-in closet and private bath on the other.

DECK

SCREEN PORCH
10-0 x 14-0

DINING
12-0 x 14-0

GREAT RM.
16-0 x 20-2
(cathedral ceiling)

fireplace

DECK

MASTER BED RM.
14-0 x 16-0

BRKFST.
10-0 x 12-0

KITCHEN
14-4 x 12-0

FOYER
9-8 x 12-0

cl

walk-in closet

bath

walk-in closet

walk-in closet

storage

UTILITY
10-0 x 6-0

d   w

BED RM./ STUDY
12-0 x 12-2

PORCH

master bath

GARAGE
22-4 x 20-0

storage

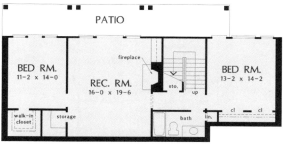

PATIO

BED RM.
11-2 x 14-0

REC. RM.
16-0 x 19-6

fireplace

sto.

up

BED RM.
13-2 x 14-2

walk-in closet

storage

bath

cl   cl

lin.

Plan HPT700127

Main Level: *1,901 square feet*
Lower Level: *1,075 square feet*
Total: *2,976 square feet*
Width: *64'-0"* **Depth:** *62'-4"*

The vaulted foyer receives light from two clerestory dormer windows and includes a niche for displaying collectibles. The generous great room enjoys a dramatic cathedral ceiling, a rear wall of windows, access to two rear decks, a fireplace and built-in bookshelves. A recreation room is located on the basement level. Two bedrooms can be found on the main floor, while two more flank the rec room downstairs. The master suite boasts an elegant tray ceiling, His and Hers walk-in closets and a luxurious bath with dual vanities, a garden tub and separate shower.

Plan HPT700128

First Floor: *1,369 square feet*
Second Floor: *1,239 square feet*
Total: *2,608 square feet*
Width: 49'-0" **Depth:** 46'-4"

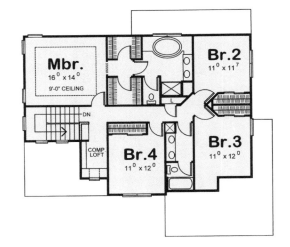

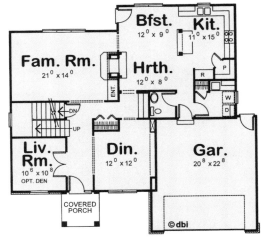

Matchstick trim and shutters provide rich embellishments and add a Tudor flavor to this European facade. A thoroughly modern interior begins with a gallery foyer that opens to a formal dining room and a flex room that converts to a den. The spacious family room provides a built-in entertainment center and shares a through-fireplace with a hearth room. A gourmet kitchen features a food-preparation island, a walk-in pantry and wrapping counters. Upstairs, the master suite offers a dressing area framed by walk-in closets. Three secondary bedrooms are connected by a hall that provides additional linen storage.

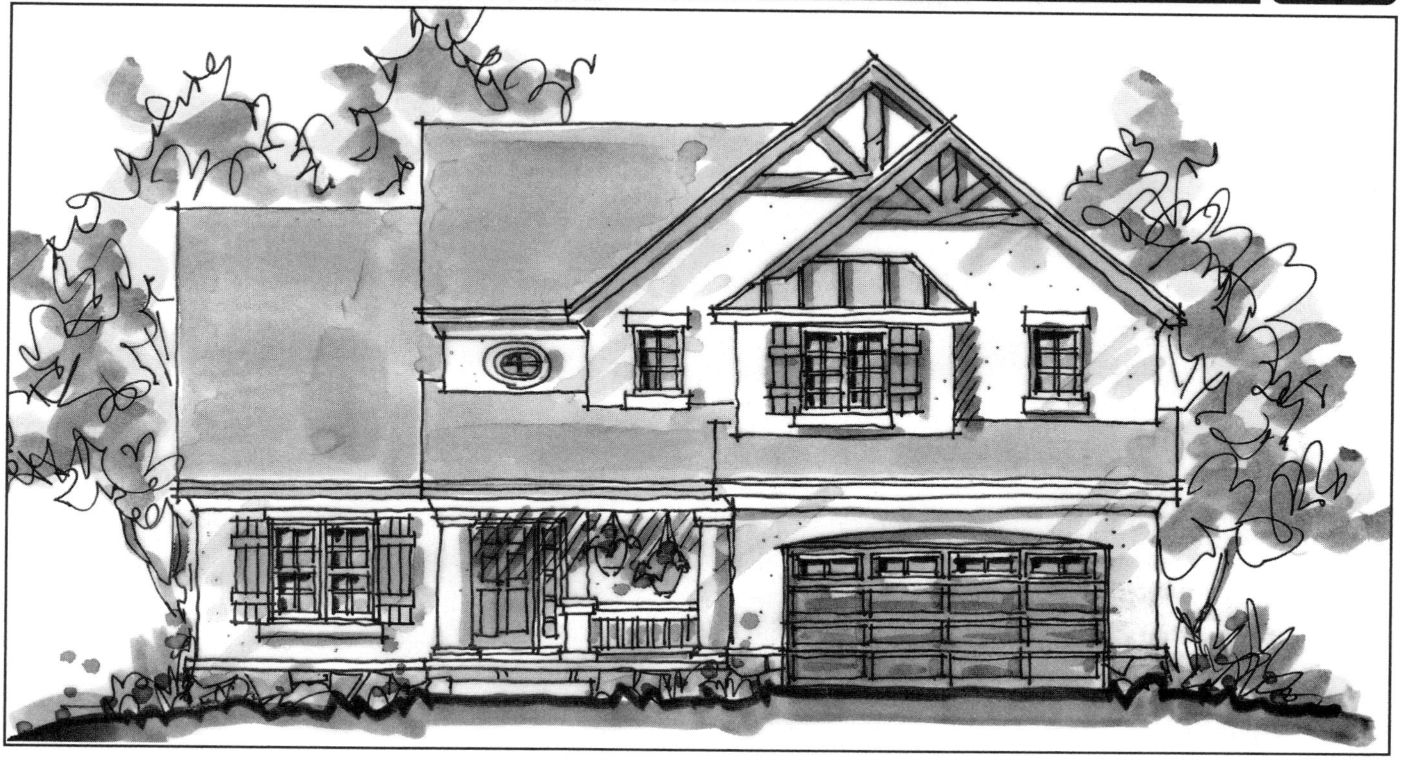

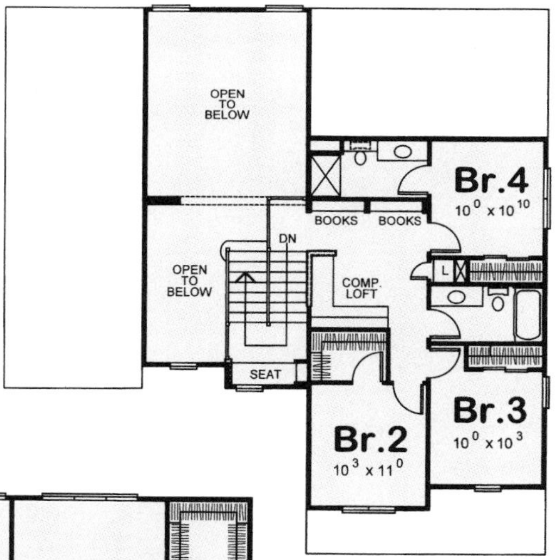
OPEN TO BELOW
Br.4
$10^{0} \times 10^{10}$
BOOKS
BOOKS
DN
OPEN TO BELOW
COMP. LOFT
L
SEAT
Br.2
$10^{3} \times 11^{0}$
Br.3
$10^{0} \times 10^{3}$

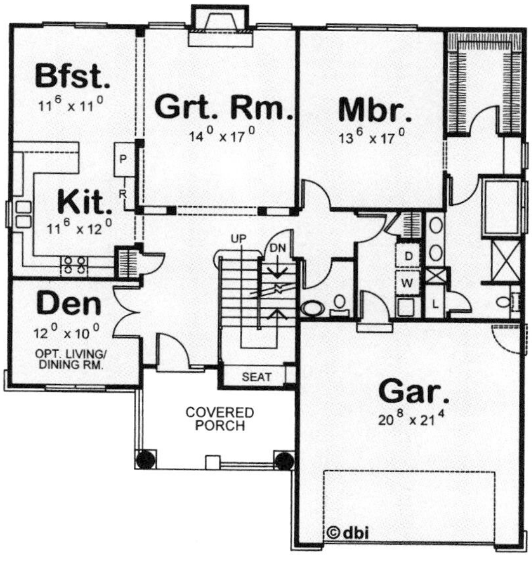
Bfst.
$11^{6} \times 11^{0}$
Grt. Rm.
$14^{0} \times 17^{0}$
Mbr.
$13^{6} \times 17^{0}$
P
R
Kit.
$11^{6} \times 12^{0}$
UP
DN
D
W
L
Den
$12^{0} \times 10^{0}$
OPT. LIVING/ DINING RM.
SEAT
COVERED PORCH
Gar.
$20^{8} \times 21^{4}$
©dbi

Plan HPT700129

First Floor: *1,538 square feet*
Second Floor: *727 square feet*
Total: *2,265 square feet*
Width: *48'-4"* **Depth:** *50'-0"*

Here's a sumptuous retreat with plenty of space for family members as well as guests—introduced by a very charming facade. At the heart of the home, a spacious great room boasts a fireplace framed by tall windows that allow great views. Decorative columns define an open arrangement of the foyer, living area and breakfast nook. A charming window seat resides in the landing. Second-floor sleeping quarters include three secondary bedrooms, one of which is a suite with a shower bath. The upper hall leads to an overlook of the foyer and offers a computer loft with built-in shelves.

© 1997 Donald A. Gardner Architects, Inc.

Plan HPT700130

First Floor: *2,067 square feet*
Second Floor: *615 square feet*
Total: *2,682 square feet*
Bonus Room: *394 square feet*
Width: *73'-0"* **Depth:** *60'-6"*

Multiple gables, columns and a balustrade add stature to the facade of this four-bedroom traditional home. Both the foyer and great room have impressive two-story ceilings and clerestory windows. The great room is highlighted by built-in bookshelves and French doors that lead to the back porch. The breakfast bay features a rear staircase to the upstairs bedrooms and the bonus room. Downstairs, the master suite enjoys an indulgent bath with a large walk-in closet, while a nearby bedroom/study offers flexibility. ©1997 Donald A. Gardner Architects, Inc.

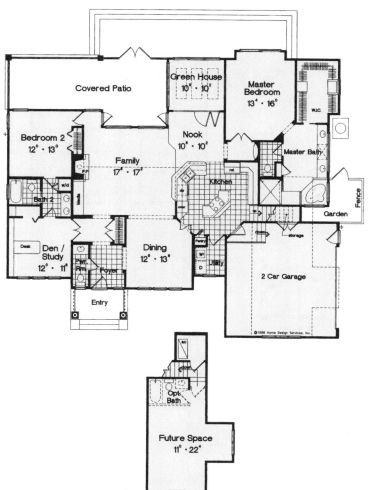

Plan HPT700131

Square Footage: *1,997*
Greenhouse: *123 square feet*
Bonus Room: *310 square feet*
Width: 64'-4" **Depth:** 63'-0"

The center of the hub of this charming plan is the spacious kitchen with an island and serving bar. The nearby breakfast nook accesses the greenhouse with its wall of windows and three large skylights. A built-in media center beside a warming fireplace is the focal point of the family room. Bedroom 2 shares a full bath with the den/study, which might also be a third bedroom. The master suite features large His and Hers vanity sinks, a corner tub with an open walk-in shower, and a super-sized walk-in closet. Future space over the garage can expand the living space as your family grows. Please specify basement, crawlspace or slab foundation when ordering.

Plan HPT700132

First Floor: *1,031 square feet*
Second Floor: *1,122 square feet*
Total: *2,153 square feet*
Width: *40'-0"* **Depth:** *63'-0"*

This home features the symmetrical facade and front gable of a Folk Victorian design. The front door opens directly to the great room, which offers a fireplace and access to a rear covered porch. The formal dining room, on the other side of the central staircase, adjoins an efficient kitchen. The breakfast room opens to the backyard. Upstairs, the sleeping quarters consist of three bedrooms, one a master suite with a walk-in closet and a full bath with double vanities and an oval garden tub. Two additional bedrooms, also with walk-in closets, share a full hall bath and a linen closet.

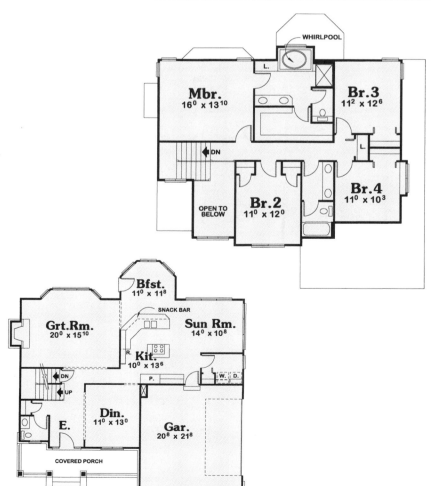

Plan HPT700133

First Floor: *1,256 square feet*
Second Floor: *1,108 square feet*
Total: *2,364 square feet*
Width: *46'-0"* **Depth:** *48'-0"*

This delightful design with its many windows provides a cheerful, sunlit retreat. On the first floor, a great room with a warming fireplace presents a place to relax. The kitchen, with a cooktop island and snack bar, offers easy access to the dining room and connects to the breakfast room and sun room. A powder room, two closets for extra storage and a handy laundry room complete the first floor. Upstairs, the master suite features a private bath with a spacious walk-in closet and a whirlpool tub. Three secondary bedrooms share another full bath.

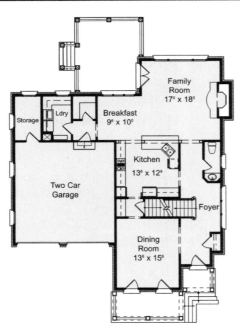

Plan HPT700134

First Floor: *1,278 square feet*
Second Floor: *1,277 square feet*
Total: *2,555 square feet*
Bonus Room: *322 square feet*
Width: *47'-0"* **Depth:** *58'-4"*

This traditional Jeffersonian-style home offers brick gables, classic details, horizontal siding, Doric columns and Chippendale railings. From the front porch, French doors open into the dining room. The grand foyer provides a powder room and leads to the family room, which is warmed by a massive hearth. A well-organized kitchen serves the formal dining room through a convenient butler's pantry. Double doors open to the rear porch from the family room. Upstairs, the master suite features a whirlpool bath and walk-in closet. Two additional bedrooms share a bath. This home is designed with a walkout basement foundation.

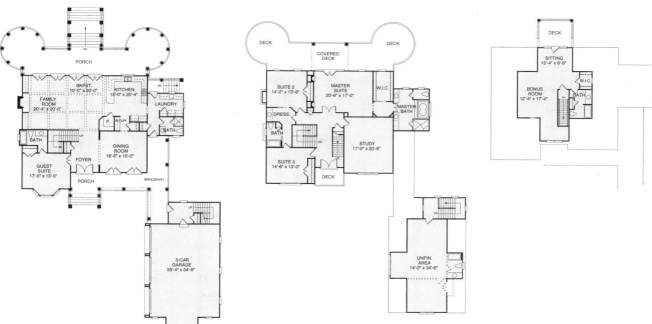

This grand waterfront home extends livability outside with its front and back porches and elevated deck—perfect for watching sunsets and catching ocean or lakeside breezes. The first floor flows from the open family room and breakfast nook to the kitchen with U-shaped counters. The dining room opens to the kitchen and the foyer. In the front a guest suite contains a private bath. Upstairs, the spacious master bedroom has a walk-in closet and access to the deck. The family bedrooms share a bath with the study. Attached to the main house by a breezeway, the garage includes an unfinished area that can be converted to an apartment above. The full bath is already installed.

Plan HPT700135

First Floor: *2,030 square feet*
Second Floor: *1,967 square feet*
Total: *3,997 square feet*
Bonus Space: *688 square feet*
Width: *80'-8"* **Depth:** *111'-8"*

Plan HPT700136

First Floor: *1,326 square feet*
Second Floor: *1,257 square feet*
Total: *2,583 square feet*
Width: *30'-0"* **Depth:** *78'-0"*

The steeply pitched pavilion roof is a distinctive feature that identifies this house as a classic French design. Inside, a long foyer ushers visitors into a generous great room, which is separated from the kitchen by a wide cased opening. An L-shaped breakfast bar provides a place for a quick snack. A lavish master suite offers separate His and Hers walk-in closets and an oversized shower. Please specify basement or crawlspace foundation when ordering.

GARAGE
20-4 x 23-0

LAUN.

GREAT ROOM
17-8 x 21-10

UP

COMP./
OFFICE

DINING ROOM
11-0 x 13-0

GUEST
11-4 x 12-0

MASTER
BEDROOM
12-10 x 16-2

BEDROOM
11-0 x 12-4

DOWN

BEDROOM
11-0 x 12-4

BEDROOM
10-8 x 12-0

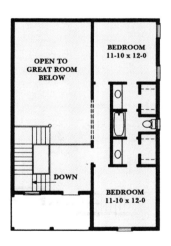

BEDROOM
11-10 x 12-0

OPEN TO
GREAT ROOM
BELOW

DOWN

BEDROOM
11-10 x 12-0

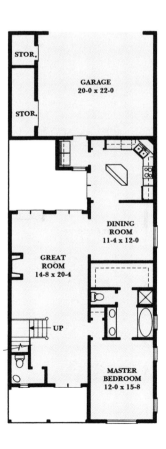

STOR.

GARAGE
20-0 x 22-0

STOR.

DINING
ROOM
11-4 x 12-0

GREAT
ROOM
14-8 x 20-4

UP

MASTER
BEDROOM
12-0 x 15-8

Plan HPT700137

First Floor: *1,270 square feet*
Second Floor: *630 square feet*
Total: *1,900 square feet*
Width: *28'-0"* **Depth:** *76'-0"*

Possessing an irresistible charm, this electric French design will elicit accolades from all who pass by. The double front porch provides a shady spot for a cool drink and a moment of relaxation. A spacious foyer, ample enough for a cherished antique, greets those who enter. Just beyond, the great room with its soaring ceiling gives additional flair to this open and inviting plan. An open-railed stairwell leads to a dramatic landing that overlooks the great room below. Access the second-floor porch easily from this landing. Two spacious bedrooms share a compartmented bath; each has a separate vanity and a walk-in closet.

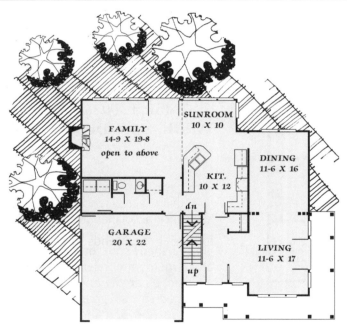

FAMILY
14-9 X 19-8
open to above

SUNROOM
10 X 10

KIT.
10 X 12

DINING
11-6 X 16

GARAGE
20 X 22

dn

up

LIVING
11-6 X 17

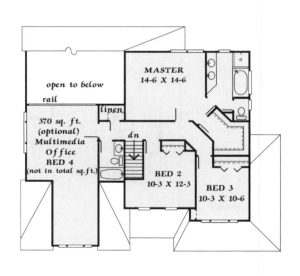

open to below

rail

MASTER
14-6 X 14-6

370 sq. ft.
(optional)
Multimedia
Office
BED 4
(not in total sq.ft.)

linen

dn

BED 2
10-3 X 12-3

BED 3
10-3 X 10-6

Plan HPT700138

First Floor: *1,299 square feet*
Second Floor: *937 square feet*
Total: *2,236 square feet*
Bonus Space: *370 square feet*
Width: *49'-0"* **Depth:** *45'-0"*

This classy three-bedroom farmhouse has it all. Dormers and Palladian windows welcome visitors to step onto the wraparound porch and come inside for apple pie. To the right of the foyer, a large formal entertainment area is enhanced by double French-door access to the wraparound porch. A hearth-warmed family room also enjoys double French doors to the great outdoors and sits open to the kitchen and sun room. Three family bedrooms and a master suite reside on the second floor. Note the optional bonus room—perfect for an office, bedroom or multimedia room.

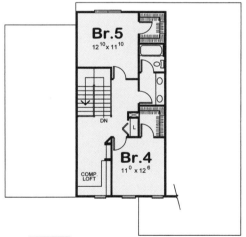

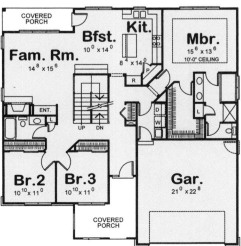

Plan HPT700139

First Floor: *1,724 square feet*
Second Floor: *701 square feet*
Total: *2,425 square feet*
Width: *50'-0"* **Depth:** *51'-8"*

Here's a comfortable cottage with plenty of windows to bring in views and fresh air. An open interior allows flexible space and room for family and friends to gather. A gourmet kitchen provides a food preparation counter and an inviting breakfast area that leads out to the rear covered porch. Triple-window views in the family room take advantage of the gorgeous scenery, while a fireplace and an entertainment center warm up the interior atmosphere. A private vestibule leads to the master suite, which boasts a walk-in closet and a dual vanity. Upstairs, two secondary bedrooms share a computer loft. Please specify basement, crawlspace or slab foundation when ordering.

155

© Stephen Fuller, Inc.

Plan HPT700140

First Floor: *1,786 square feet*
Second Floor: *1,378 square feet*
Total: *3,164 square feet*
Bonus Room: *800 square feet*
Width: *69'-2"* **Depth:** *55'-8"*

Sweet and simple, this Carpenter cottage is a two-story home with a one-story elevation. Classic and Country styles blend to create a rustic facade with a spacious interior. The double-columned, covered entry opens into a two-story foyer. A quiet study or guest suite provides ample wardrobe space and a private hall with a full bath. The kitchen overlooks the breakfast area and employs a service entrance from the two-car garage. A traditional keeping room nearby is warmed by a quaint country fireplace. On the second floor, the master suite provides a pampering bath and two walk-in closets. Bedrooms 2 and 3 also offer walk-in closets and share a full bath. This home is designed with a walkout basement foundation.

© Stephen Fuller, Inc

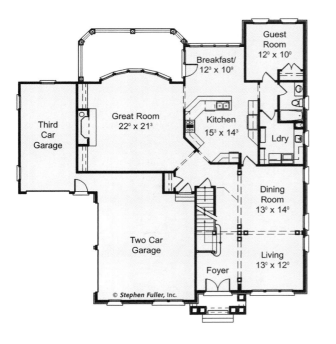

Third Car Garage

Great Room
22⁰ x 21³

Breakfast/
12³ x 10⁹

Guest Room
12⁰ x 10⁰

Kitchen
15³ x 14³

Ldry

Dining Room
13⁰ x 14⁰

Two Car Garage

Living
13⁰ x 12⁰

Foyer

© Stephen Fuller, Inc.

© Stephen Fuller, Inc.

Master Sitting
12³ x 7⁹

Covered Porch

Hers

Master Bedroom
15³ x 17³

Master Bath

His

Bedroom #4
11⁶ x 13⁰

Bedroom #3
13⁰ x 14³

Bedroom #2
13⁹ x 12⁹

Elegance and old-fashioned country charm enhance this home's good looks. The double-columned, covered entranceway makes a stately first impression. Inside, the formal living and dining rooms are open to one another for easy entertaining. The dining room connects to the kitchen, which offers an abundance of counter space and an informal breakfast room. The great room dazzles with natural light allowed by a curved wall of windows overlooking the rear porch and backyard. Upstairs, the master suite provides a sitting area, a private porch and a luxury bath flanked by His and Hers walk-in closets. This home is designed with a walkout basement foundation.

Plan HPT700141

First Floor: *1,820 square feet*
Second Floor: *1,710 square feet*
Total: *3,530 square feet*
Width: *59'-8"* **Depth:** *62'-3"*

© Stephen Fuller, Inc.

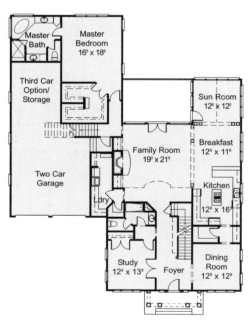

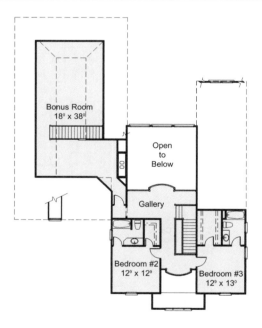

Plan HPT700142

First Floor: *2,682 square feet*
Second Floor: *847 square feet*
Total: *3,529 square feet*
Bonus Room: *770 square feet*
Width: *62'-8"* **Depth:** *81'-8"*

This formal, shingle-style home offers symmetry and elegance, starting with a grand entry porch. Inside, a balcony hall overlooks the family room and foyer. Double doors lead to a private study—the perfect spot for a good read. An island cooktop counter highlights the kitchen, which is set between the dining and breakfast rooms. The spacious two-story great room offers a fireplace and double-door access to the rear porch, also accessed by the sun room. The master suite is secluded on the first floor for privacy and features a whirlpool bath and a double walk-in closet. Two family bedrooms reside upstairs and share a gallery hall that leads to a large bonus room. This home is designed with a walkout basement foundation.

Screen Porch

Storage

Garage

Breakfast
24⁰ x 17⁰

Kitchen
14³ x 16³

Ldry

Two Story
Great Room
22³ x 20⁰

Study
13⁹ x 11⁰

Two Car Garage

Dining Room
13³ x 14⁶

Foyer

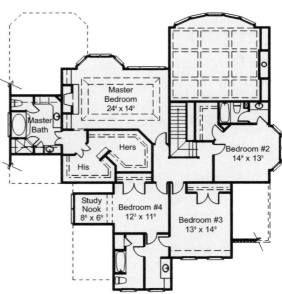

Master Bath

Master Bedroom
24⁰ x 14⁰

Hers

His

Bedroom #2
14⁹ x 13³

Study Nook
8⁸ x 6⁹

Bedroom #4
12³ x 11⁶

Bedroom #3
13⁹ x 14⁹

With an informal European Country flavor, this home speaks volumes about great design. Romantic rooflines sweep over the entry, which leads through double doors to a fabulous foyer. The formal dining room connects with the kitchen via a spacious butler's pantry. Double-hung floor-length windows provide plenty of natural light in the study. A curved wall of windows enhances the two-story great room, which features a fireplace. The island kitchen overlooks the breakfast room, also warmed by a fireplace. A screened porch resides to the rear of the plan and is accessed by the breakfast room. A split three-car garage offers additional storage. Upstairs, the spacious master suite boasts a bay window and features a romantic fireplace. This home is designed with a walkout basement foundation.

Plan HPT700143

First Floor: *1,840 square feet*
Second Floor: *1,888 square feet*
Total: *3,728 square feet*
Width: *61'-6"* **Depth:** *64'-4"*

Plan HPT700144

First Floor: *1,623 square feet*
Second Floor: *418 square feet*
Total: *2,041 square feet*
Width: *70'-8"* **Depth:** *45'-0"*

The wraparound front porch presents a strong welcoming feature with this lovely facade. The living portion is further emphasized by the central gable containing an all-purpose room on the second floor. The front porch leads to an open foyer and coat closet. The great room boasts a massive fireplace flanked by built-in cabinetry. The large dining room shares space with the great room and leads to the kitchen, which opens to a grand dinette bay. A large deck extends across the rear of the plan, accessed from the dining room and dinette via French doors.

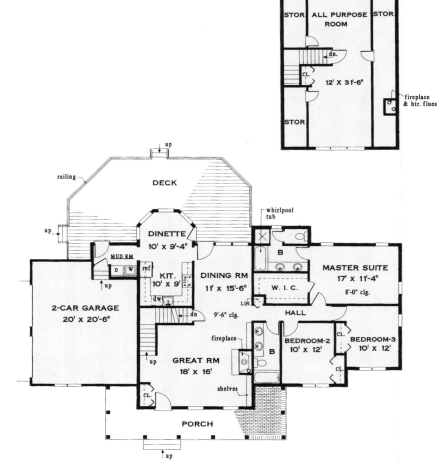

Plan HPT700145

Square Footage: *2,329*
Width: *72'-6"* **Depth:** *73'-4"*

The entrance to this alluring French Country home is graced by stately columns and a vibrant window display. The home's distinctive high-pitched hip roof is decked out with a trio of dormers. Stone sets off the mirrored chimneys in the front elevation. Arches, neoclassical detailing, shutters and window planter boxes add to the home's country adaptation. Open rooms, French doors and specialty ceilings add an air of spaciousness throughout the home. Interior columns set apart the formal dining room. The leisure room boasts a fireplace, built-in cabinetry and dazzling views.

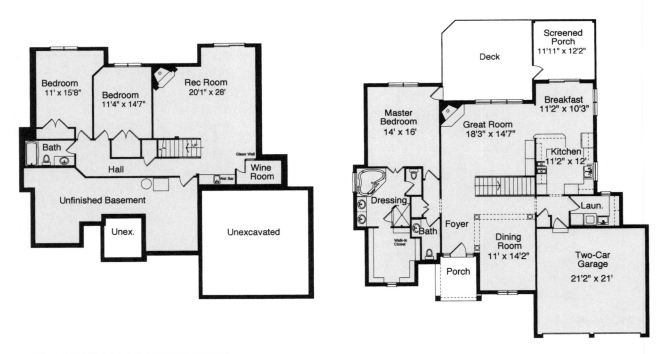

Plan HPT700146

Square Footage: *1,681*
Finished Basement: *1,088 square feet*
Width: *57'-6"* **Depth:** *63'-11"*

A great empty-nester home, this three-bedroom house offers a classic brick exterior and well planned interior. Inside, the foyer introduces a raised ceiling in the great room, deluxe master suite with a spacious walk-in closet, formal and informal dining and a delightful screened porch. The large kitchen features a pantry, cooktop and wall oven. An open rail decorates the stairs to the lower level, which provides a recreation room.

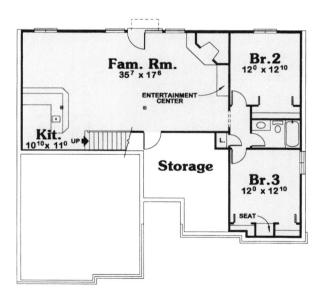

Fam. Rm.
35⁷ x 17⁶

Br.2
12⁰ x 12¹⁰

ENTERTAINMENT CENTER

Kit.
10¹⁰ x 11⁰ UP

Storage

Br.3
12⁰ x 12¹⁰

SEAT

Bfst.
13⁰ x 10⁰

Fam. Rm.
15⁰ x 17⁹

10'-0" CEILING

Kit.
13⁰ x 11⁴ R.

WHIRLPOOL

Mbr.
14⁰ x 14⁴

E.

Gar.
21⁴ x 22⁸

PORCH

Den
10⁰ x 12⁰

W. D.

This European-style exterior offers plenty of curb appeal, with its combination of stone and stucco, engaging window treatments and paneled front door. The family room boasts a fireplace, while the kitchen has a work island and opens into a breakfast nook. The master suite offers a whirlpool tub, two walk-in closets and easy access to a den, which also opens off the front entry. An optional basement provides two bedrooms, a second family room, a bath and a sizable storage area.

Plan HPT700147

Square Footage: *1,472*
Finished Basement: *1,169*
Width: *49'-8"* **Depth:** *45'-0"*

Plan HPT700148

Square Footage: *2,441*
Bonus Room: *366 square feet*
Width: *42'-10"* **Depth:** *92'-11"*

Abrick facade with stucco highlights and quoins creates a simple and elegant exterior for this three-bedroom home. The foyer opens to a trayed dining room. The nearby U-shaped kitchen includes a walk-in pantry and breakfast nook. A corner fireplace, tray ceiling and French-door access to the rear porch enhance the living room. Two family bedrooms share a bath to the right of the design, while the master bedroom sits to the rear. A tray ceiling and luxurious bath make the master bedroom a comfortable retreat. Future expansion is possible with a bonus room on the second level.

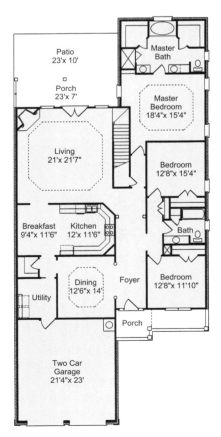

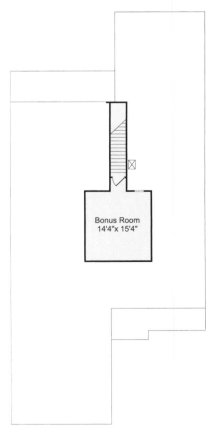

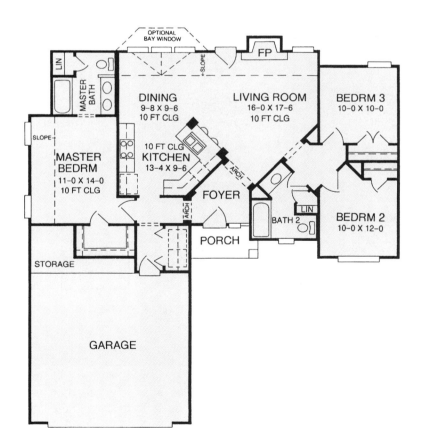

Floor plan labels:

- OPTIONAL BAY WINDOW
- LIN
- MASTER BATH
- FP
- SLOPE
- DINING 9-8 X 9-6 10 FT CLG
- LIVING ROOM 16-0 X 17-6 10 FT CLG
- BEDRM 3 10-0 X 10-0
- MASTER BEDRM 11-0 X 14-0 10 FT CLG
- 10 FT CLG KITCHEN 13-4 X 9-6
- ARCH
- FOYER
- BATH 2
- LIN
- BEDRM 2 10-0 X 12-0
- STORAGE
- PORCH
- GARAGE

Plan HPT700149

Square Footage: *1,282*
Width: *48'-10"* **Depth:** *52'-6"*

Brick detailing and corner quoins lend charm to this traditional exterior. Inside, a graceful arch announces the living room, complete with a fireplace and a French door to the back property. The angled kitchen is conveniently positioned to offer service to the dining room, and provides a snack counter for easy meals. Split sleeping quarters offer a private wing to the sumptuous master suite, which has a twin-lavatory bath. Please specify crawlspace or slab foundation when ordering.

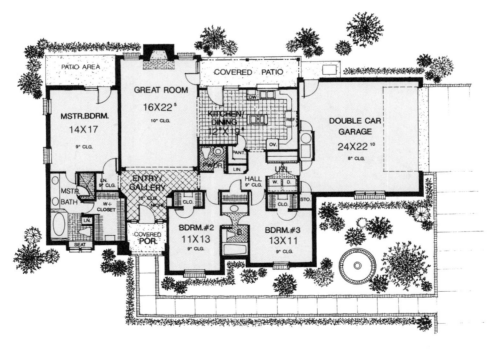

Plan HPT700150

Square Footage: *1,807*
Width: *74'-0"* **Depth:** *44'-0"*

The striking European facade of this home presents a beautiful stone exterior, complete with stone quoins, a shingled rooftop and French-style shutters on the front windows. Step inside the great room where a ten-foot ceiling and fireplace will greet you. A large island in the kitchen provides plenty of much-needed counter space for the cook of the family. An element of privacy is observed, with the master suite separated from the other two bedrooms, which share a full bath. An oversized two-car garage and a covered patio are just some of the added amenities.

Double doors crowned by a fanlight provide an impressive entry to this stately home. Inside, built-in bookshelves and a fireplace occupy one wall of the great room, where double doors lead to a rear porch. The gourmet kitchen includes a walk-in pantry and built-in cabinets. Family and friends can share meals in a snug, well-lit breakfast room or an elegant, formal dining room. A dramatic master suite features a private sitting area with back-porch access. Two second-floor bedrooms share a full bath, while two spacious future bedroom areas border another full bath. This home is designed with a basement foundation.

Plan HPT700151

First Floor: *1,966 square feet*
Second Floor: *696 square feet*
Total: *2,662 square feet*
Bonus Space: *458 square feet*
Width: *56'-6"* **Depth:** *60'-0"*

Plan HPT700152

Square Footage: *2,140*
Width: *62'-0"* **Depth:** *60'-6"*

Imagine the luxurious living you'll enjoy in this beautiful home! The natural beauty of stone combined with sophisticated window detailing represent the good taste you'll find carried throughout the design. Common living areas occupy the center of the plan and include the great room with a fireplace, the sun room and the breakfast area, plus rear and side porches. A second fireplace is located in the front den. The master suite features private access to the rear porch and a wonderfully planned bath. This home is designed with a walkout basement foundation.

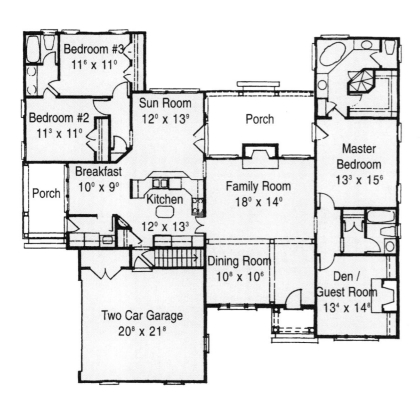

Bedroom #3
11⁶ x 11⁰

Bedroom #2
11³ x 11⁰

Sun Room
12⁰ x 13⁹

Porch

Master Bedroom
13³ x 15⁶

Breakfast
10⁰ x 9⁰

Porch

Kitchen
12⁰ x 13³

Family Room
18⁰ x 14⁰

Dining Room
10⁸ x 10⁶

Den / Guest Room
13⁴ x 14⁸

Two Car Garage
20⁸ x 21⁸

Plan HPT700153

Square Footage: *2,140*
Width: *62'-0"* **Depth:** *60'-8"*

Decorative columns define the formal dining room of this lovely traditional home and announce casual living space that features a fireplace and porch access. Split sleeping quarters allow the master suite a private wing which includes a den or guest room with its own fireplace and full bath. An angled, oversized shower, a compartmented toilet and a corner whirlpool tub highlight the master bath. The gourmet kitchen overlooks the sun room, which opens to the rear porch through French doors. A covered side porch invites morning meals outdoors, while the breakfast room offers a casual dining area inside. This home is designed with a basement foundation.

Plan HPT700154

First Floor: *1,078 square feet*
Second Floor: *313 square feet*
Total: *1,391 square feet*
Width: *43'-0"* **Depth:** *38'-0"*

Stucco brings a pure and simple aura to this home. Porch space is plentiful, making outdoor entertaining and relaxing a delight. Family time is enjoyable in the spacious living and dining rooms. The beauty of this house is emphasized by the natural light beaming in through the large windows. Kitchen space is ample and preparing dinner will be a treat. Storage space is conveniently located around the front porch. The master suite sports a large walk-in closet, spacious bath and private access to the rear porch. The second floor is complete with a bedroom, full bath, balcony and access to the attic. Please specify crawlspace or slab foundation when ordering.

Plan HPT700155

Square Footage: *2,391*
Width: *61'-10"* **Depth:** *64'-11"*

Quoins, keystoned lintels and two picture windows adorn the stucco exterior of this charming four-bedroom home. Inside, the foyer introduces a dining room adorned with graceful columns. The nearby kitchen features a sunny breakfast nook, walk-in pantry and an angled serving bar to the living room. A hearth with built-in shelves enhances the living room, which also includes rear-porch access. Two family bedrooms to the right share a two-sink bath, while on the left a third family bedroom comes with a walk-in closet and a private bath. A tray ceiling accents the master suite, which also enjoys two walk-in closets, two vanities and a separate shower and tub.

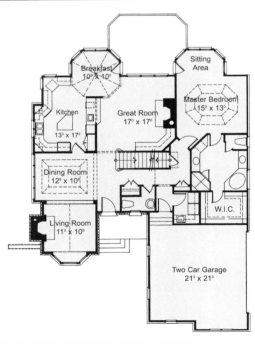

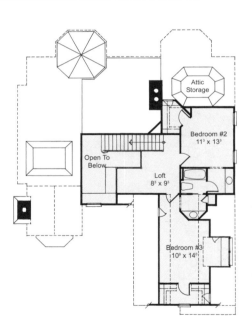

Plan HPT700156

First Floor: *1,724 square feet*
Second Floor: *700 square feet*
Total: *2,424 square feet*
Width: *47'-10"* **Depth:** *63'-6"*

There's nowhere to go but up in this bright and airy three-bedroom home. Nearly every room has a unique ceiling treatment, including the living room, dining room, breakfast nook, master suite and T-shaped secondary bedroom on the second floor. The living room features a grand hearth. Another fireplace is located in the comfortable great room. The dining room is easily accessed by a uniquely designed kitchen which provides extra counter space. The breakfast nook is flooded by natural light and allows access to the backyard. The upstairs loft overlooks main-floor action below. Two family bedrooms are kept on the second level as well as attic storage space. This home is designed with a walkout basement foundation.

Plan HPT700157

Square Footage: *2,174*
Width: *63'-0"* **Depth:** *59'-6"*

With the blending of stucco and stone, this home draws its inspiration from country French tradition. Beginning at the dramatic entrance, the open floor plan flows gracefully from room to room. From the foyer and across the great room, French doors and large side windows give a generous view of the rear porch. The adjoining dining room is subtly defined by columns and a large triple window. The accommodating kitchen, with its generous work island, adjoins the breakfast area and keeping room. The bedroom at the front of the home has direct access to a full bath, which makes it a good choice as guest quarters or a children's den. This home is designed with a basement foundation.

Plan HPT700158

Square Footage: *2,048*
Width: *38'-10"* **Depth:** *75'-0"*

Presenting a narrow frontage, this plan extends back 75 feet and provides spacious rooms for a family. Enter the home through a front corner porch or through a side courtyard that opens to the dining room. A fireplace warms the family room, which accesses the rear yard through French doors. A bright corner breakfast nook highlights the kitchen, which provides a cooktop island and laundry-room access. The master suite features a walk-in closet and separate vanities in the compartmented bath.

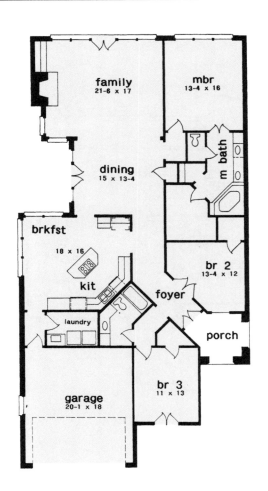

Plan HPT700159

Square Footage: *2,300*
Width: *58'-10"* **Depth:** *83'-0"*

This French Provincial charmer offers a stunning stucco and brick exterior and classic European style. At the heart of the home, the family room provides a fireplace and access to a rear covered porch. The island kitchen serves a breakfast bay that overlooks the backyard. The master suite is tucked away at the back of the plan with a fine bath and walk-in closet. Two family bedrooms—or make one a study—share a full bath and a hall that leads to the family room. An additional suite or guest quarters resides near the service entrance—a perfect arrangement for a live-in relative.

Plan HPT700160

Square Footage: *1,751*
Width: *55'-6"* **Depth:** *59'-6"*

A brick facade and central gable with arched-window accents introduce this stunning Early American home. Double-hung windows are crested by cut-brick jack arches. The foyer opens to a large great room, emphasizing the open and airy floor plan with French doors that lead to a back deck for a warm, inviting feeling. Convenient to both the great room and dining room, the kitchen opens to a bright breakfast bay. The master bath features a garden tub, separate shower and double vanities. This home is designed with a walkout basement foundation.

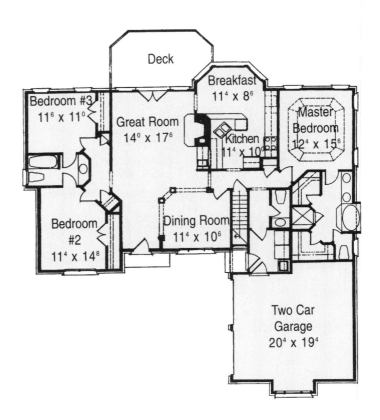

Plan HPT700161

Square Footage: *2,598*
Width: *68'-3"* **Depth:** *78'-3"*

The overall design of this home is reminiscent of a European country cottage. French accents are highlighted inside and out. Stucco and stone create a fairy tale ambiance on the exterior, while amenities enhance the interior. From the arched double-door entry, columns add a stately elegance to the foyer and to the exquisite great room with its warming fireplace. A wall of French doors accesses the rear deck from the dining and great rooms and illuminates interior spaces. The formal dining room connects to the L-shaped kitchen. A bayed breakfast nook opens to a wonderful keeping room with outdoor access and a fireplace. A large utility room separates two family bedrooms and their shared bath from the master suite. This home is designed with a walkout basement foundation.

Plan HPT700162

Square Footage: *2,745*
Width: *69'-6"* **Depth:** *76'-8"*

A gentle European charm flavors the facade of this ultra-modern home. The foyer opens to a formal dining room, which leads to the kitchen through privacy doors. Here, a center cooktop island complements wrapping counter space, a walk-in pantry and a snack counter. Casual living space shares a through-fireplace with the formal living room and provides its own access to the rear porch. Clustered sleeping quarters include a well-appointed master suite, two family bedrooms and an additional bedroom which could double as a study. Please specify basement, crawlspace or slab foundation when ordering.

Plan HPT700163

Square Footage: *2,494*
Width: *65'-4"* **Depth:** *61'-8"*

Stucco and stone, multi-pane windows and a covered porch are all elements of a fine European-flavored home. Inside, the foyer is flanked by formal living and dining rooms, and leads back to more casual areas. Here, a great room with a warming fireplace is framed by windows, with a nearby kitchen and breakfast room finishing off the gathering areas. Two family bedrooms reside to the right and share a full bath that includes two vanities. The master suite is sure to please with a walk-in closet and a sumptuous bath. This home is designed with a walkout basement foundation.

Photo courtesy of Stephen Fuller, Inc.

This home, as shown in the photograph, may differ from the actual blueprints. For more detailed information, please check the floor plans carefully.

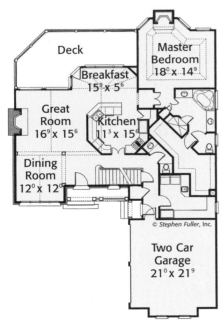

Deck

Breakfast
15⁹ x 5⁶

Master
Bedroom
18⁰ x 14⁹

Great
Room
16⁹ x 15⁶

Kitchen
13³ x 15⁶

Dining
Room
12⁰ x 12⁰

© Stephen Fuller, Inc.

Two Car
Garage
21⁰ x 21⁹

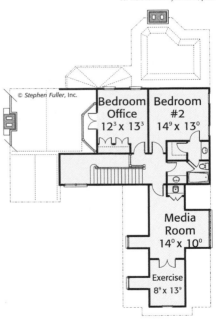

© Stephen Fuller, Inc.

Bedroom
Office
12³ x 13³

Bedroom
#2
14⁹ x 13⁰

Media
Room
14⁰ x 10⁰

Exercise
8⁹ x 13⁹

Plan HPT700164

First Floor: *1,746 square feet*
Second Floor: *651 square feet*
Total: *2,397 square feet*
Exercise/Media: *283 square feet*
Width: *50'-0"* **Depth:** *75'-4"*

Complementary details make this home an enjoyable sight. The stone details, bayed garage window and covered porch create elegant country styling. The grand window in the dining room floods the interior with natural light. The semi-circular kitchen uses space wisely and provides extra counter space. The ribbon of windows in the breakfast nook offers views of the rear deck. French doors open to the master suite, where a private fireplace greets the homeowners. The second level includes an office/bedroom, media room, an exercise room and family bedroom. This home is designed with a walkout basement foundation.

Mountains

top-of-the-world retreats

Plan HPT700165

First Floor: *1,022 square feet*
Second Floor: *551 square feet*
Total: *1,573 square feet*
Width: *39'-0"* **Depth:** *32'-0"*

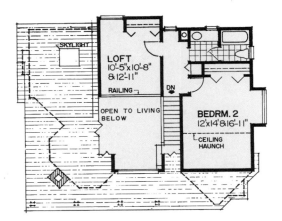

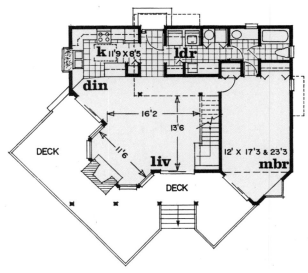

This quaint cottage works equally well in the mountains or by the lake. Its entry is sliding glass, which opens to a vaulted living room with a fireplace tucked into a wide windowed bay. The dining room has sliding glass access to the deck. The skylit kitchen features a greenhouse window over the sink and is just across from a handy laundry room. The master bedroom captures views through sliding glass doors and a triangular feature window. The second floor holds another bedroom, a full bath and a loft area that could be used as a bedroom, if you choose.

br3
10'x11'2

br4
10'7 x 11'2

25'2 x 12
mbr

BALCONY

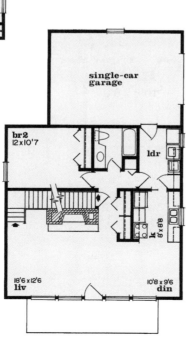

single-car
garage

br2
12x10'7

ldr

k
8'x8'8

18'6 x 12'6
liv

10'8 x 9'6
din

Plan HPT700166

First Floor: *900 square feet*
Second Floor: *780 square feet*
Total: *1,680 square feet*
Width: *30'-0"* **Depth:** *46'-5"*

The master bedroom of this leisure home invites relaxation around the fireplace or on the private balcony. The second fireplace warms the living room and dining room. A galley kitchen adjacent to the dining room features a window sink, and the laundry room, which provides access to the garage, is just across the hall. There's one family bedroom on the first floor, next to a full bath. The second floor contains two more family bedrooms, the master bedroom and a full bath.

Plan HPT700167

Square Footage: *1,244*
Width: *38'-0"* **Depth:** *46'-0"*

With a simple floor plan and a lovely facade—including vertical siding and brick—this casual ranch design is the ideal retirement home. It features an open plan with a living/dining area to the front and bedrooms to the rear. The convenient kitchen connects directly to the dining room and shares its view of the front deck through sliding glass doors. The master suite holds His and Hers closets and a private half-bath. Family bedrooms share a full hall bath. Make one of them into a den or guest room to fit your lifestyle. If you choose, a full basement could be developed later into livable space—or keep it as a storage area.

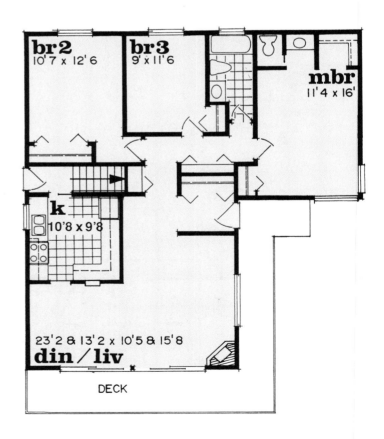

br2
10'7 x 12'6

br3
9' x 11'6

mbr
11'4 x 16'

k
10'8 x 9'8

23'2 & 13'2 x 10'5 & 15'8
din / liv

DECK

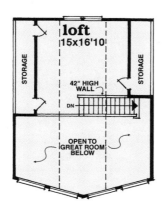

loft
15x16'10

STORAGE

STORAGE

42" HIGH
WALL

DN

OPEN TO
GREAT ROOM
BELOW

Plan HPT700168

First Floor: *1,375 square feet*
Second Floor: *284 square feet*
Total: *1,659 square feet*
Width: *58'-0"* **Depth:** *32'-0"*

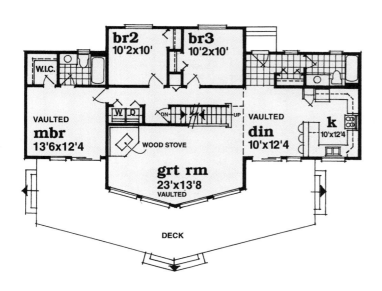

W.I.C.

br2
10'2x10'

br3
10'2x10'

VAULTED
mbr
13'6x12'4

W D

DN

UP

WOOD STOVE

VAULTED
din
10'x12'4

k
10'x12'4

grt rm
23'x13'8
VAULTED

DECK

An expansive window wall across the great room of this home adds a spectacular view and accentuates the high ceiling. The open kitchen shares an eating bar with the dining room and features a convenient "U" shape. Sliding glass doors in the dining room lead to the deck. Two family bedrooms sit to the back of the plan and share the use of a full bath. The master suite provides a walk-in closet and private bath. The loft on the upper level adds living or sleeping space.

Plan HPT700169

Square Footage: *988*
Width: *38'-0"* **Depth:** *26'-0"*

This cozy design serves nicely as a leisure home for vacations or as a full-time retirement residence. Horizontal siding and a solid-stone chimney stack are a reminder of a rustic retreat. A spacious living/dining area has a full wall of glass overlooking a deck with views beyond. A masonry fireplace warms the space in the cold months. A U-shaped kitchen is nearby and has a pass-through counter to the dining room. A large laundry/mud room is across the hall and holds storage space. Sleeping quarters are comprised of a large master suite and smaller family bedroom, both with hall closets.

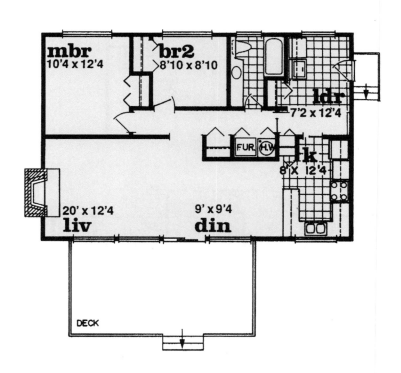

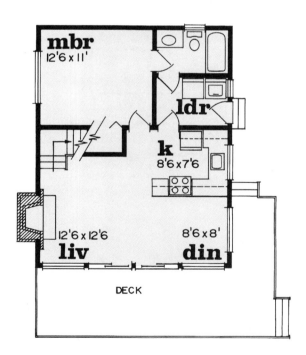

mbr
12'6 x 11'

ldr

k
8'6 x7'6

12'6 x 12'6

8'6 x 8'

liv

din

DECK

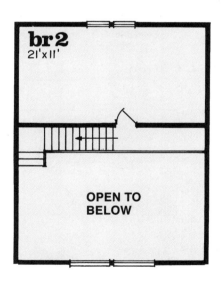

br2
21'x 11'

OPEN TO
BELOW

Rustic details such as a stone fireplace work well for a country cottage such as this. A floor-to-ceiling window wall accents the living and dining rooms and provides an expansive view past a wide deck. Twin sliding glass doors access the deck from the living space. The U-shaped kitchen offers roomy counters and is open to the dining room. Behind it is a laundry room and then a full bath serving the master bedroom. An additional bedroom sits on the second floor and may be used as a studio.

Plan HPT700170
First Floor: *616 square feet*
Second Floor: *300 square feet*
Total: *916 square feet*
Width: *22'-0"* **Depth:** *28'-0"*

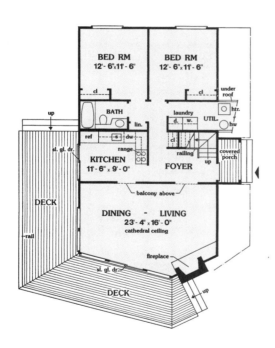

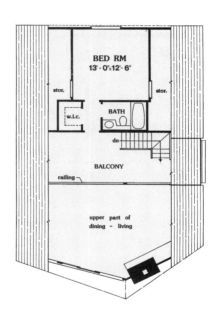

Plan HPT700171

First Floor: *1,016 square feet*
Second Floor: *400 square feet*
Total: *1,416 square feet*
Width: *24'-0"* **Depth:** *44'-4"*

This cleverly modified home combines a dramatic exterior with an exciting interior, which offers a commanding view through a vast expanse of windows. The central foyer leads to the spacious living/dining room on the left, which features a soaring cathedral ceiling and stone fireplace. Just ahead is the kitchen with sliding glass doors opening onto the wraparound deck. Two bedrooms and a bath are located at the rear, while another bedroom and bath reside upstairs. The broad balcony overlooking the living room serves as a lounge or extra guest room. Natural wood siding and shingles, and plank flooring add to the rustic effect.

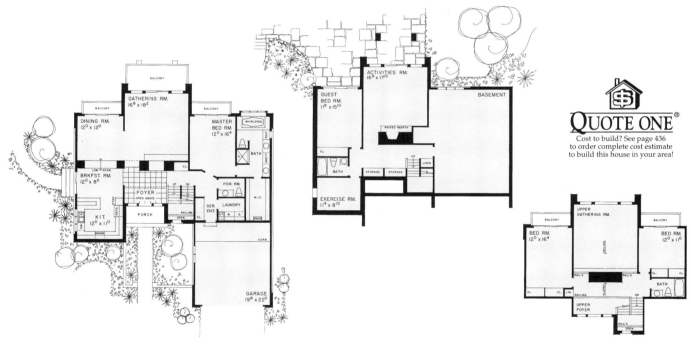

Quote One®

Cost to build? See page 436
to order complete cost estimate
to build this house in your area!

This lavish modern design has it all, including an upper lounge, a family room and a large tiled foyer. A centrally located atrium with a skylight provides focal interest downstairs. A large, efficient kitchen with snack bar service to the breakfast room enjoys its own greenhouse window. The spacious family room offers a warming fireplace and a view of the rear covered terrace. To the front, a living room with a fireplace offers a view of the garden court as well as the atrium. The deluxe master suite features a relaxing whirlpool tub, a dressing area and two walk-in closets.

Plan HPT700172

Main Level: *1,650 square feet*
Upper Level: *628 square feet*
Lower Level: *977 square feet*
Total: *3,255 square feet*
Width: *52'-0"* **Depth:** *60'-0"*

L

Plan HPT700173

Square Footage: *1,574*
Width: *32'-4"* **Depth:** *24'-4"*

This chalet-style design offers wonderful views for vacations and plenty of comfort for year-round living. The main level includes complete living quarters, with one bedroom, a full bath and an open living and dining area. Sliding glass doors lead from the eat-in kitchen to the wraparound deck, and a V-shaped fireplace warms the entire area. The lower level provides two more bedrooms, a full bath with laundry facilities, and a family room with outdoor access. This home is designed with a basement foundation.

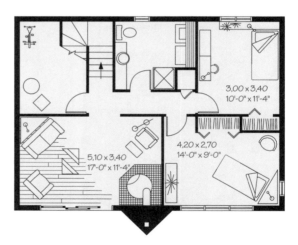

3,00 x 3,40
10'-0" x 11'-4"

4,20 x 2,70
14'-0" x 9'-0"

5,10 x 3,40
17'-0" x 11'-4"

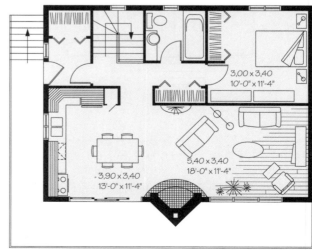

3,00 x 3,40
10'-0" x 11'-4"

5,40 x 3,40
18'-0" x 11'-4"

3,90 x 3,40
13'-0" x 11'-4"

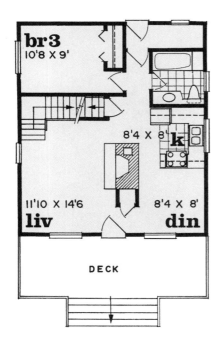

br3
10'8 X 9'

8'4 X 8' k

11'10 X 14'6 8'4 X 8'
liv din

DECK

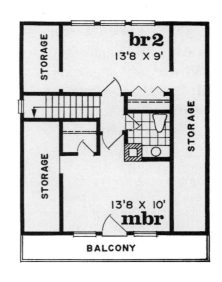

STORAGE br2
13'8 X 9'

STORAGE

STORAGE

13'8 X 10'
mbr

BALCONY

This chalet plan is enhanced by a steep gable roof, scalloped fascia boards and fieldstone chimney detail. The front-facing deck and covered balcony add to outdoor living spaces. The fireplace is the main focus in the living room. The bedroom on the first floor enjoys access to a full hall bath. A storage/mudroom at the back of the plan is perfect for keeping skis and boots. Two additional bedrooms and a full bath occupy the second floor. The master bedroom provides a walk-in closet. Three storage areas are also found on the second floor.

Plan HPT700174

First Floor: *672 square feet*
Second Floor: *401 square feet*
Total: *1,073 square feet*
Width: *24'-0"* **Depth:** *36'-0"*

Plan HPT700175

First Floor: *1,580 square feet*
Second Floor: *812 square feet*
Total: *2,392 square feet*
Sunroom: *130 square feet*
Width: *47'-4"* **Depth:** *69'-0"*

Bold, contemporary lines strike an elegant chord in this two-story plan. The entry foyer leads to a multi-purpose great room with a fireplace and sliding glass doors to a rear deck. The formal dining room is nearby and there is a connecting sun room. A U-shaped kitchen features an attached breakfast room and large walk-in pantry. Two bedrooms on this floor share a full bath. The master suite dominates the second floor. It features a large walk-in closet, double lavatories, a corner tub, and spiral stairs from its private balcony to the sun room below. The upstairs balcony connects it to a study or optional bedroom. Please specify basement or crawlspace foundation when ordering.

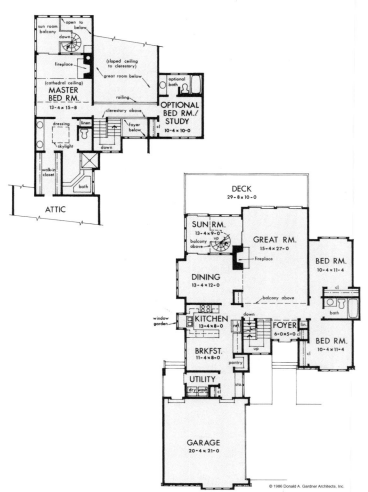

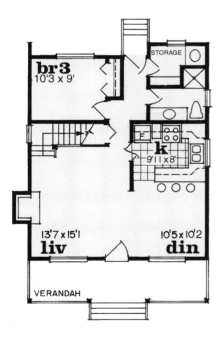

Quote One®

Cost to build? See page 436
to order complete cost estimate
to build this house in your area!

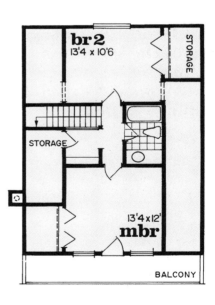

This cozy chalet design begins with a railed veranda opening to a living room with a warm fireplace and a dining room with a snack-bar counter through to the kitchen. The kitchen itself is U-shaped and has a sink with window over. A full bath and large storage area sit just beyond the kitchen. One bedroom with a roomy wall closet is on the first floor. The second floor holds two additional bedrooms—one a master bedroom with a private balcony—and a full bath. Additional storage is found on the second floor as well.

Plan HPT700176

First Floor: *725 square feet*
Second Floor: *561 square feet*
Total: *1,286 square feet*
Width: *25'-0"* **Depth:** *36'-6"*

Plan HPT700177

First Floor: *1,216 square feet*
Second Floor: *478 square feet*
Total: *1,694 square feet*
Bonus Room: *115 square feet*
Width: *38'-0"* **Depth:** *38'-8"*

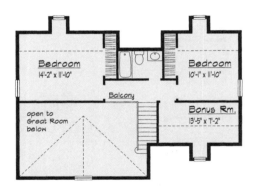

Pillars support a roof topped by an attractive gable—all covering the front porch of this fine three-bedroom home. Inside, the entrance opens directly to the great room, where a cathedral ceiling and a fireplace are enhancements. A gourmet kitchen offers a work island with a sink and serving counter for the nearby dining room. Located on the main level for privacy, the master bedroom is sure to please with two closets—one a walk-in—and a private bath with a separate tub and shower. Upstairs, two family bedrooms share a hall bath and access to a bonus room—perfect for a study or computer room. Please specify basement or crawlspace foundation when ordering.

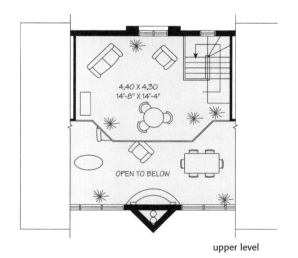

4,40 X 4,30
14'-8" X 14'-4"

OPEN TO BELOW

upper level

Plan HPT700178

Main Level: *790 square feet*
Upper Level: *287 square feet*
Lower Level: *787 square feet*
Total: *1,864 square feet*
Width: *32'-4"* **Depth:** *24'-4"*

3,00 X 3,40
10'-0" X 11'-4"

3,90 X 3,40
13'-0" X 11'-4"

5,40 X 3,40
18'-0" X 11'-4"

main level

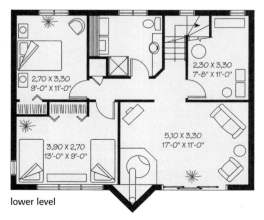

2,70 X 3,30
9'-0" X 11'-0"

2,30 X 3,30
7'-8" X 11'-0"

3,90 X 2,70
13'-0" X 9'-0"

5,10 X 3,30
17'-0" X 11'-0"

lower level

Here's a mountain cabin with plenty of space for entertaining. Three levels include a loft with space for computers, books and games. The main level features an open living area set off with views from tall windows. The kitchen embraces a casual eating space and provides sliding-glass doors that lead to the wraparound deck. Double doors open from the living room to a master bedroom. The lower level provides a sitting room with a fireplace.

195

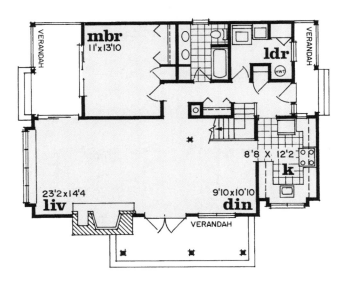

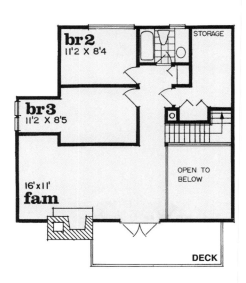

Plan HPT700179

First Floor: *1,094 square feet*
Second Floor: *576 square feet*
Total: *1,670 square feet*
Width: *43'-0"* **Depth:** *35'-4"*

A covered veranda with covered patio above opens through French doors to the living/dining area of this vacation cottage. A masonry fireplace with a wood storage bin warms this area. A modified U-shaped kitchen serves the dining room; a laundry is just across the hall with access to a side veranda. The master bedroom is on the first floor and has the use of a full bath. Sliding glass doors in the master bedroom and the living room lead to still another veranda. The second floor has two family bedrooms, a full bath and a family room with a balcony overlooking the living room and dining room, a fireplace and double doors to a patio. A large storage area on this level adds convenience.

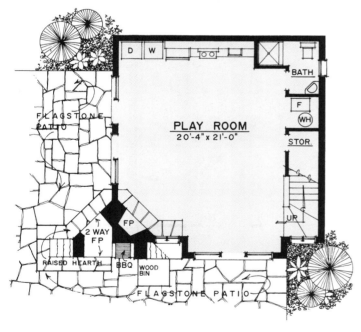

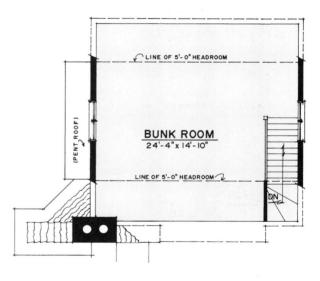

With woodsy charm and cozy livability, this cottage plan offers comfortable living space in a smaller footprint. The exterior is geared for outdoor fun, with two flagstone patios connected by a two-way fireplace and graced by a built-in barbecue. French doors on two sides lead into the large playroom, which features a kitchen area, washer and dryer space and a bath with corner sink and shower. Take the L-shaped stairway to the bunk room upstairs, where there is space for sleeping and relaxing.

Plan HPT700180

First Floor: *665 square feet*
Second Floor: *395 square feet*
Total: *1,060 square feet*
Width: *34'-3"* **Depth:** *32'-5"*

Plan HPT700181

First Floor: *1,530 square feet*
Second Floor: *1,268 square feet*
Total: *2,798 square feet*
Bonus Room: *354 square feet*
Width: *60'-0"* **Depth:** *53'-0"*

BR. 3
12/0 X 10/0 +/-
(9' CLG.)

BR. 4
11/10 X 11/0
(9' CLG.)

BONUS RM.
14/6 X 23/0 +/-
(8' CLG.)

BR. 2
13/0 X 12/0
(9' CLG.)

LIN.

FOYER BELOW

SCISSOR VAULTED
MASTER
13/0 x 16/6 +

Behind this soothing exterior is a floor plan for the space-age family. On the first floor, both the family room and living room include fireplaces. The family room is open to the kitchen and breakfast nook while the living room shares space with the dining area. A full bath, utility room and a den featuring French doors are located near the staircase. On the second floor are four bedrooms, including the master suite which boasts a walk-in closet and private bath with a tub and a separate shower. Three family bedrooms share a full hall bath with a double-bowl sink. A bonus room is available above the three-car garage.

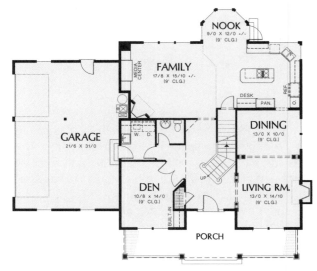

NOOK
9/0 X 12/0 +/-
(9' CLG.)

MEDIA CENTER

FAMILY
17/8 X 15/10 +/-
(9' CLG.)

DESK   PAN.   REF.

GARAGE
21/6 X 31/0

W. D.

DINING
13/0 X 10/0
(9' CLG.)

UP

DEN
10/8 X 14/0
(9' CLG.)

BUILT-IN

LIVING RM.
13/0 X 14/10
(9' CLG.)

PORCH

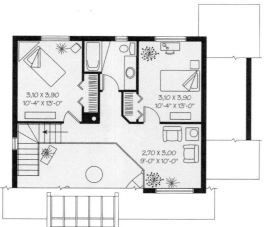

3,10 X 3,90
10'-4" X 13'-0"

3,10 X 3,90
10'-4" X 13'-0"

2,70 X 3,00
9'-0" X 10'-0"

3,30 X 3,90
11'-0" X 13'-0"

8,00 X 4,00
26'-8" X 13'-4"

Plan HPT700182

First Floor: *946 square feet*
Second Floor: *604 square feet*
Total: *1,550 square feet*
Width: *37'-0"* **Depth:** *30'-8"*

This contemporary four-season cottage offers plenty of windows to take in great views. Excellent for gatherings, the living room boasts a cathedral ceiling and a cozy fireplace. The compartmented entry features a coat closet. The U-shaped kitchen includes a built-in pantry which accesses a side porch. Upstairs, two family bedrooms share a hall bath. A balcony hall leads to a sitting area with views of the front property. This home is designed with a basement foundation.

Plan HPT700183

First Floor: *617 square feet*
Second Floor: *972 square feet*
Third Floor: *332 square feet*
Total: *1,921 square feet*
Width: *36'-0"* **Depth:** *30'-0"*

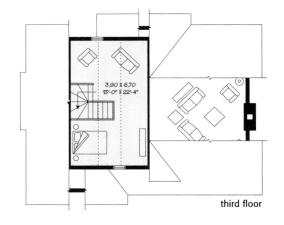

third floor

second floor

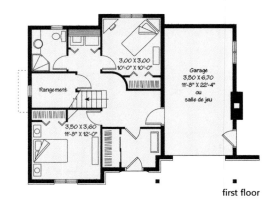

first floor

This unique home boasts shutters, a siding exterior, stone detailing and an attractive front-facing balcony. Two family bedrooms and a full bath reside on the first floor. The second floor is home to the kitchen, dining room and hearth-warmed family room, which all flow into each other smoothly. The second-floor master bedroom enjoys a walk-through closet and private bath. The third floor is open for future expansion—more family bedrooms, a playroom or a rec room.

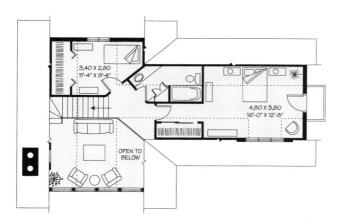

Plan HPT700184

First Floor: *856 square feet*
Second Floor: *636 square feet*
Total: *1,492 square feet*
Width: *44'-0"* **Depth:** *26'-0"*

A standing-seam metal roof, horizontal siding and a massive deck combine to create a mosaic of parallel lines on this rustic two-story home. Sunlight spills into the great room through four beautiful clerestory windows. A generous L-shaped kitchen with a work island adjoins the dining area. A bedroom and powder room are neatly tucked behind the staircase that leads to the second-floor sleeping quarters. Upstairs, a loft allows plenty of space for a computer in kick-off-your-shoes comfort. This home is designed with a basement foundation.

Plan HPT700185

First Floor: *898 square feet*
Second Floor: *358 square feet*
Total: *1,256 square feet*
Width: *34'-0"* **Depth:** *32'-0"*

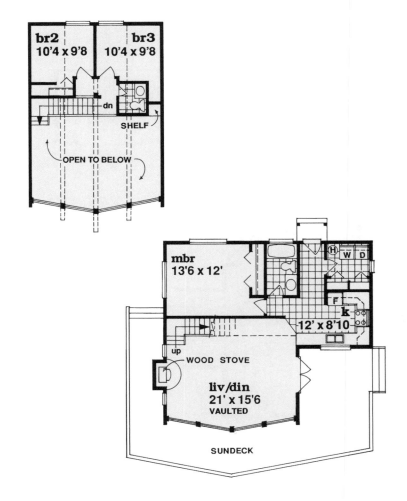

A surrounding sun deck and an expansive window wall capitalize on vacation-home views in this design. The full-height windows flood the living and dining rooms with abundant natural light and bring attention to the high vaulted ceilings. A wood stove in the living area warms cold winter nights. The efficient U-shaped kitchen has ample counter and cupboard space. Behind it is a laundry room and rear entrance. The master bedroom sits on this floor and has a large wall closet and full bath. Two family bedrooms on the second floor share a half-bath.

4,30 X 3,30
14'-4" X 11'-0"

6,00 X 3,90
20'-0" X 13'-0"

3,30 X 3,40
11'-0" X 11'-4"

3,50 X 5,80
11'-8" X 19'-4"

The modern exterior of this home sports a uniquely shaped deck and customized windows. This lovely cottage features a second-floor hall with an overlook to the living room. A spacious secondary bedroom on this floor has a walk-in closet and a private door to the shared bath. On the first floor, a cathedral ceiling highlights the living room, which opens to the dining area and kitchen. A full bath and a storage area complete the plan. This home is designed with a basement foundation.

Plan HPT700186

First Floor: *713 square feet*
Second Floor: *598 square feet*
Total: *1,311 square feet*
Width: *30'-8"* **Depth:** *26'-0"*

Plan HPT700187

First Floor: *905 square feet*
Second Floor: *863 square feet*
Total: *1,768 square feet*
Width: *40'-8"* **Depth:** *46'-0"*

Multiple gables and different window treatments create an interesting exterior on this plan. A covered porch and Victorian accents create a classical elevation. Double doors to the entry open to a spacious great room and an elegant dining room. In the gourmet kitchen, features include an island snack bar and a large pantry—French doors lead to the breakfast area. Cathedral ceilings in the master suite and dressing area add an exquisite touch. A vaulted ceiling in Bedroom 2 accents a window seat and an arched transom window.

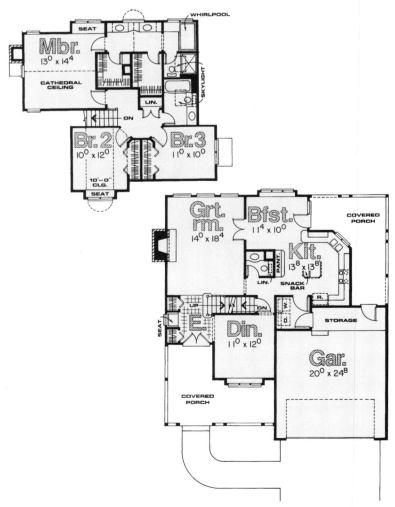

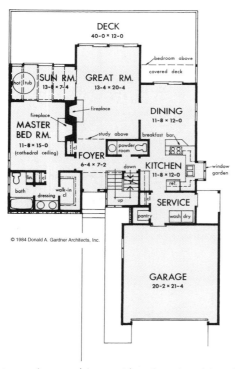

DECK
40-0 × 12-0

bedroom above

covered deck

SUN RM.
13-8 × 7-4

GREAT RM.
13-4 × 20-4

hot tub

fireplace

fireplace

study above

DINING
11-8 × 12-0

MASTER
BED RM.
11-8 × 15-0
(cathedral ceiling)

breakfast bar

FOYER
6-4 × 7-2

powder
room

KITCHEN
11-8 × 12-0

window
garden

cl

down

bath

lin

cl

up

ref.

cl

walk-in
cl

SERVICE

dressing

pantry

wash dry

© 1984 Donald A. Gardner Architects, Inc.

GARAGE
20-2 × 21-4

(sloped ceiling
to clerestory)

great room below

railing

BED RM.
11-8 × 12-10

cl

bath

STUDY/ PLAY
13-4 × 6-6

open to
below

down

cl

BED RM.
11-8 × 11-10

ATTIC

An elegant exterior combines with a functional interior to offer an exciting design for the contemporary minded homeowner. Notice the cheery sun room that captures natural light. The master suite and great room enjoy access to this bright space through sliding glass doors, and each features a fireplace. A U-shaped kitchen has a window garden, a breakfast bar and ample cabinet space. The second floor includes two bedrooms and a study/play area across from the full hall bath. ©1984 Donald A. Gardner Architects, Inc.

Plan HPT700188

First Floor: *1,345 square feet*
Second Floor: *536 square feet*
Total: *1,881 square feet*
Width: *45'-0"* **Depth:** *69'-4"*

Plan HPT700189

Square Footage: *1,377*
Width: *50'-0"* **Depth:** *45'-0"*

Brick and siding lend country charm to the exterior of this three-bedroom home. Inside, a raised-hearth fireplace enhances the spacious living room. The U-shaped kitchen features a large window over the sink and enjoys convenient access to the family room and the dining area. Light will spill in through the bay window in the dining room. The family room has rear-yard access. The laundry room—also great as a mudroom—blocks noise from the single-car garage. Three bedrooms reside to the right of the plan. The master bedroom includes a private bath with a shower and the two secondary bedrooms share a full bath.

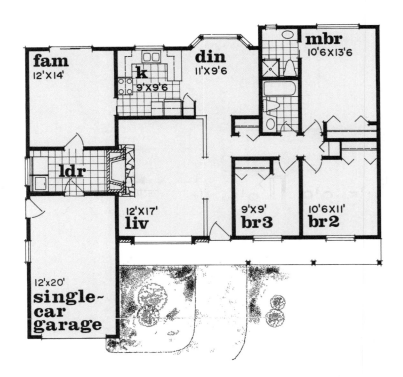

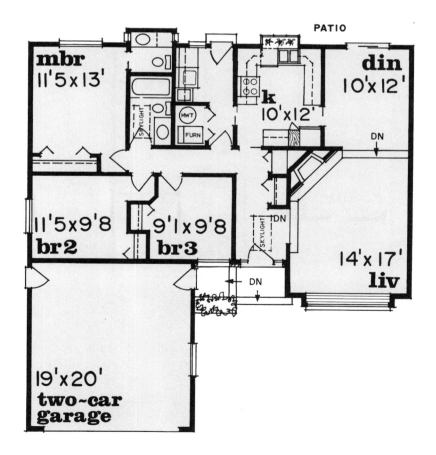

mbr
11'5x13'

br2
11'5x9'8

br3
9'1x9'8

k
10'x12'

PATIO

din
10'x12'

DN

DN

DN

liv
14'x17'

SKYLIGHT

HWT

FURN

SKYLIGHT

**19'x20'
two-car
garage**

Plan HPT700190

Square Footage: *1,289*
Width: *46'-0"* **Depth:** *48'-8"*

This contemporary bungalow offers two different elevations—included in the plans—with different rooflines. One of the options allows for a vaulted ceiling in the living room. The foyer of the plan is skylit and leads down a few steps on the right to the sunken living room with corner fireplace. A box-bay window allows for room-enhancing natural light. The dining room is nearby and appointed with sliding glass doors to the rear patio. A U-shaped kitchen features a window over the sink and has access to a nearby laundry room. Bedrooms include a master suite with half-bath and two family bedrooms sharing a full, skylit bath. A two-car garage sits in front of the bedrooms to shield them from street noise.

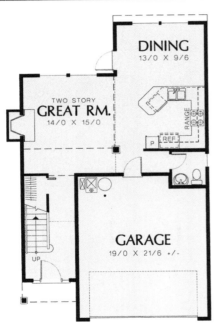

DINING
13/0 X 9/6

TWO STORY
GREAT RM.
14/0 X 15/0

RANGE

REF.

GARAGE
19/0 X 21/6 +/-

UP

MASTER
13/0 X 11/0

GREAT RM
BELOW

DN

LINEN

LINEN

D

FOYER
BELOW

BR. 3
9/4 X 11/0

BR. 2
9/4 X 10/0

Plan HPT700191

First Floor: *704 square feet*
Second Floor: *782 square feet*
Total: *1,486 square feet*
Width: *28'-0"* **Depth:** *47'-0"*

A simple design with a smaller floor plan, this home has just the right appeal—especially for empty-nesters or small families. The garage shields living spaces on the first floor: a two-story great room, modified U-shaped kitchen and a dining area. A half-bath is found in the service hallway. Bedrooms on the second floor include two family bedrooms with large closets and a master suite with a separate bath. Each of these baths contains its own linen closet—the one for the hall bath is a walk-in. Note the laundry alcove on the second floor for convenience.

NOOK
9/0 X 10/0

7/0 X 11/4 +/-

GREAT RM.
15/0 X 15/0

REF. P.

GARAGE
19/0 X 21/6 +/-

UP

MASTER
14/0 X 11/2

LIN. LINEN

DN.

D. W.

BR. 2
9/4 X 11/6

BR. 3
9/4 X 11/0 +/-

FOYER
BELOW

Traditional and Craftsman elements shape the exterior of this lovely family home. The two-story foyer leads down the hall to a great room with a warming fireplace. The U-shaped kitchen includes a window sink and is open to the breakfast nook. A powder room is located near the garage. Upstairs, the master suite provides a private bath and walk-in closet. The two family bedrooms share a full hall bath, across from the second-floor laundry room. Linen closets are available in the hall and inside the full hall bath.

Plan HPT700192

First Floor: *636 square feet*
Second Floor: *830 square feet*
Total: *1,466 square feet*
Width: *28'-0"* **Depth:** *43'-6"*

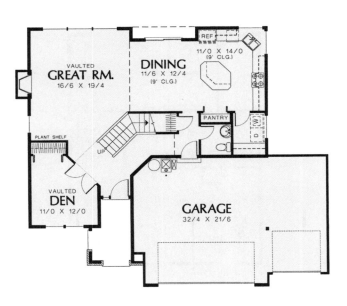

Plan HPT700193

First Floor: *1,097 square feet*
Second Floor: *807 square feet*
Total: *1,904 square feet*
Width: *40'-0"* **Depth:** *45'-0"*

The combination of rafter tails and stone-and-siding gabled rooflines gives this home plenty of curb appeal. The Craftsman styling on this bungalow is highly attractive. Inside, a vaulted den is entered through double doors, just to the left of the foyer. A spacious, vaulted great room features a fireplace and is located near the dining room. The kitchen offers an octagonal island, a corner sink with a window, and a pantry. Up the angled staircase are the sleeping quarters. Here two secondary bedrooms share a hall bath, while the master suite is enhanced with a private bath and a walk-in closet. The three-car garage easily shelters the family fleet.

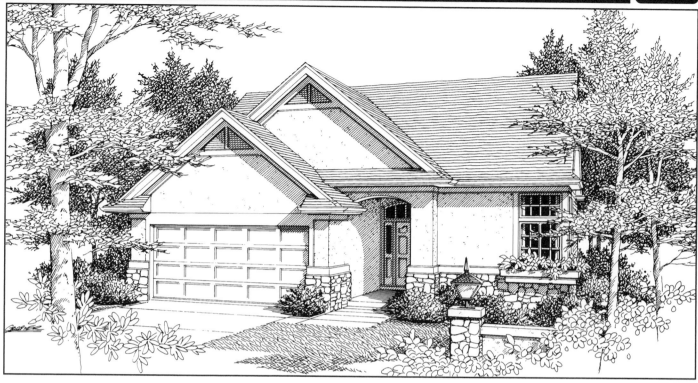

Cozy in a style reminiscent of Craftsman homes, this three-bedroom plan has livablity on two levels. The main level has a vaulted great room with corner fireplace, a vaulted dining room and a vaulted modified-U-shaped kitchen. A half bath sits in the hall to the master suite. A vaulted ceiling also graces the master bedroom. The master bath has double sinks and a walk-in closet. Two family bedrooms are on the lower level and share a full bath. Doors on the lower level lead out to a covered patio. The master bedroom and the great room also have doors to a deck in the back. Please specify basement or crawlspace foundation when ordering.

Plan HPT700194

Square Footage: *1,120 square feet*
Finished Basement: *620 square feet*
Width: *40'-0"* **Depth:** *47'-0"*

Plan HPT700195

First Floor: *917 square feet*
Second Floor: *742 square feet*
Total: *1,659 square feet*
Width: *38'-0"* **Depth:** *36'-0"*

Arch-top windows offer charming accents to this distinctive contemporary exterior. The entry leads to the living room, which has a fireplace and a cathedral ceiling. A gourmet kitchen serves the dining room, which opens to the outdoors. The upper-level mezzanine offers a reading area plus space for lounging. An angled whirlpool tub and a double vanity enhance the master suite. This home is designed with a basement foundation.

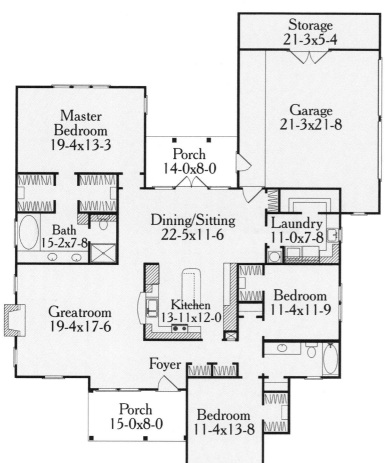

Plan HPT700196

Square Footage: *2,053*
Width: *57'-8"* **Depth:** *71'-10"*

Shutters, multi-pane glass windows and a cross-hatched railing on the front porch make this a beautiful country cottage. To the left of the foyer is a roomy great room and a warming fireplace, framed by windows. To the right of the foyer, two family bedrooms feature walk-in closets and share a fully appointed bath. The efficient kitchen centers around a long island workstation and opens to the large dining/sitting room. The rear porch adds living space to view the outdoors. French doors, a fireplace and columns complete this three-bedroom design. Please specify basement, crawlspace or slab foundation when ordering.

Plan HPT700197

First Floor: *872 square feet*
Second Floor: *734 square feet*
Total: *1,606 square feet*
Width: *40'-0"* **Depth:** *29'-6"*

Cozy and quaint, this home provides an open and spacious floor plan. The oversized living room includes a fireplace and is adjacent to the kitchen. Down the hall is a family bedroom, which can also serve as a guest room, and a full hall bath. Upstairs, the master bedroom contains two wall closets and a master bath with a compartmented toilet and dual vanities. Across the way is a second family bedroom with a wall closet and a full private bath.

Bedroom
14'-2" X 11'-10"

Bedroom
13'-5" X 11'-10"

Balcony

open to
Great Room
below

Bonus Rm.
13'-5" X 7'-2"

Plan HPT700198

First Floor: *1,216 square feet*
Second Floor: *478 square feet*
Total: *1,694 square feet*
Bonus Room: *115 square feet*
Width: *38'-0"* **Depth:** *63'-3"*

Deck
14'-4" x 22'-4"

Garage
20'-0" x 20'-0"

Storage
14'-0" x 4'-0"

Kitchen
10'-0" x 14'-5"

Utility

Dining Rm.
10'-0" x 14'-5"

Pantry

Great Room
20'-0" x 16'-3"
(cathedral clg.)

Master
Bedroom
13'-5" x 16'-3"

Porch
22'-8" x 6'-8"

This charming cottage fits effortlessly in either the wooded countryside or a manicured suburb. A multitude of well-placed windows fills the interior with fresh air and sunlight. The great room, with its warming fireplace, is open to the formal dining room where sliding glass doors open to the expansive backyard deck. The lavish master suite on the first floor offers privacy and a luxurious bath. Two additional bedrooms share a full bath on the second floor.

Plan HPT700199

First Floor: *772 square feet*
Second Floor: *411 square feet*
Total: *1,183 square feet*
Width: *32'-0"* **Depth:** *28'-7"*

Perfect for a lakeside, vacation or starter home, this two-story design with Victorian details is sure to be a favorite. A large covered porch is available for watching sunsets, while inside, the spacious living room sits conveniently close to the kitchen and dining area. A bedroom and a full hall bath finish off the first floor. Upstairs, a second bedroom, the laundry area and a full bath round out the plan. Note how the first-floor bedroom features its own bumped-out window balcony.

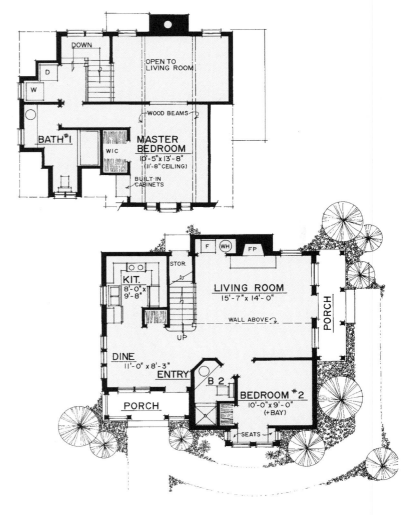

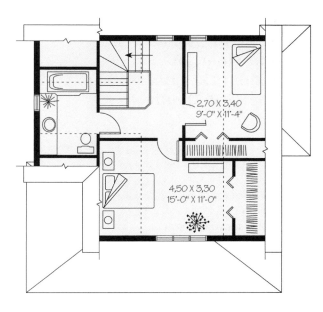

This lovely country cottage features a cozy wraparound covered porch, extending outdoor living for seasonal occasions. Double doors open into a spacious living area that extends to the dining room and kitchen. A casual snack bar adds counter space for the kids. A door near the kitchen accesses the backyard. A mudroom and powder/utility room are located on the left side of the house, completing the first floor. Upstairs, two family bedrooms share a full hall bath. This home is designed with a basement foundation.

Plan HPT700200

First Floor: *630 square feet*
Second Floor: *546 square feet*
Total: *1,176 square feet*
Width: *26'-8"* **Depth:** *24'-0"*

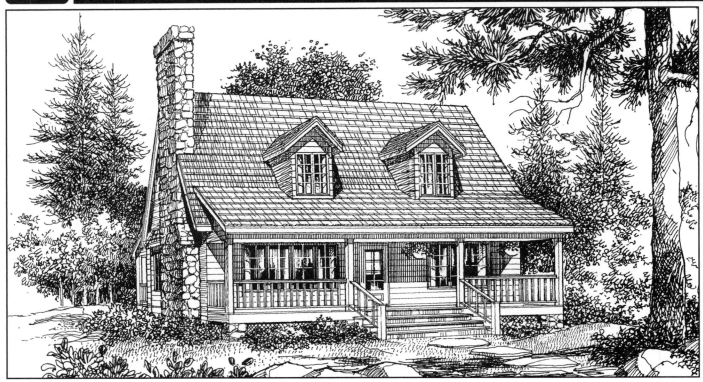

Plan HPT700201

First Floor: *1,039 square feet*
Second Floor: *583 square feet*
Total: *1,622 square feet*
Width: *37'-9"* **Depth:** *44'-8"*

Charming and compact, this delightful two-story cabin is perfect for the small family or empty-nester. Designed with casual living in mind, the two-story great room is completely open to the dining area and the spacious island kitchen. The master suite is on the first floor for privacy and convenience. It features a roomy bath and a walk-in closet. Upstairs, two comfortable bedrooms—one includes a dormer window, the other features a balcony overlooking the great room—share a full hall bath.

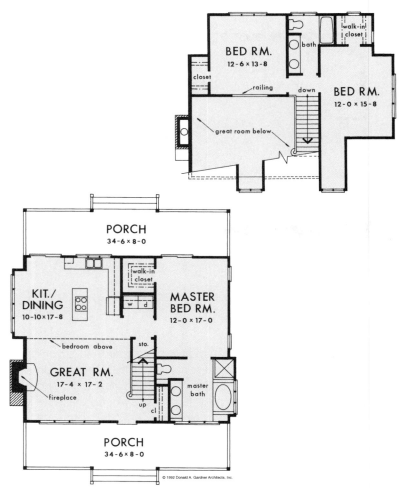

© 1992 Donald A. Gardner Architects, Inc.

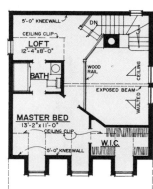

Plan HPT700202

First Floor: *576 square feet*
Second Floor: *489 square feet*
Total: *1,065 square feet*
Width: *24'-0"* **Depth:** *31'-0"*

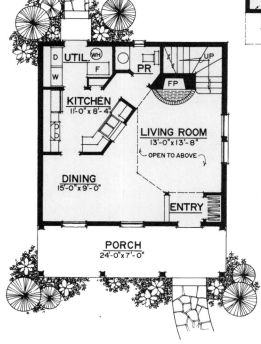

D
UTIL.
WH
PR
UP
W
F
FP
KITCHEN
11'-0" x 8'-4"
LIVING ROOM
13'-0"x 13'-8"
OPEN TO ABOVE
DINING
15'-0"x 9'-0"
ENTRY
PORCH
24'-0"x 7'-0"

The steep rooflines on this home offer a sophisticated look that draws attention. Three dormers bring in plenty of natural light. A vestibule entry offers a coat closet and leads to the two-story living room, which provides a fireplace. The dining room is quite spacious and contains convenient access to the kitchen where a pantry room and plenty of counter space make cooking a treat in this home. The stairs to the second floor wrap around the fireplace and take the homeowners to the master bedroom and loft area.

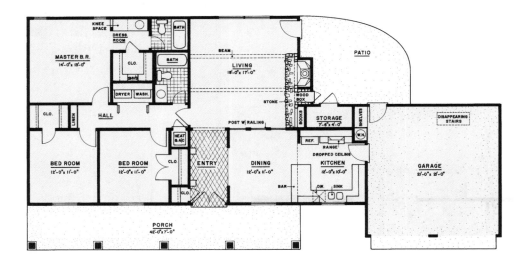

Plan HPT700203

Square Footage: *1,395*
Width: *73'-0"* **Depth:** *37'-0"*

This charming ranch-style home has much to offer in livability. The entry leads to the vaulted living room where the stone fireplace is easy to enjoy and provides a warm welcome on chilly evenings. There's an ingenious pass-through wood box so owners can replenish the fuel supply without venturing outside. The formal dining room adjoins the efficient kitchen with its convenient garage access. The pampering master suite boasts a dressing room and a full bath while two additional family bedrooms share a second full bath. Please specify crawlspace or slab foundation when ordering.

Plan HPT700204

Square Footage: *1,191*
Width: *44'-6"* **Depth:** *59'-0"*

A covered front porch gives this home country charm and makes family and guests feel welcome. Graced by a sloped ceiling and warmed by a stone fireplace, the living room provides the perfect gathering spot. The well-equipped kitchen easily serves the dining room, and adjoins a utility room that opens to the patio. The master suite offers an adjoining bath with a separate dressing area and double vanities. Two family bedrooms share a full bath. The two-car garage includes a large storage area. Please specify crawlspace or slab foundation when ordering.

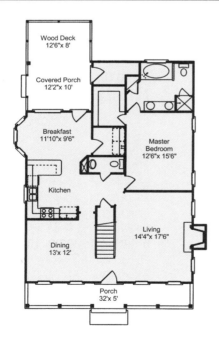

Wood Deck
12'6"x 8'

Covered Porch
12'2"x 10'

Breakfast
11'10"x 9'6"

Master
Bedroom
12'6"x 15'6"

Kitchen

Dining
13'x 12'

Living
14'4"x 17'6"

Porch
32'x 5'

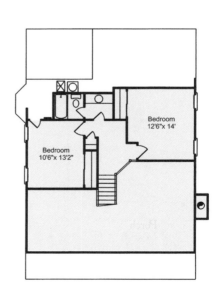

Bedroom
12'6"x 14'

Bedroom
10'6"x 13'2"

Plan HPT700205

First Floor: *1,247 square feet*
Second Floor: *521 square feet*
Total: *1,768 square feet*
Width: *36'-6"* **Depth:** *57'-0"*

This Creole cottage has only 1,768 square feet of living space, but has the feel of a much larger house. Natural light streaming through the full-length windows that span the entire front wall combines with the seventeen-foot sloped ceiling in the front rooms to create a sense of spaciousness. The feeling of airiness is carried into the kitchen, which opens to a breakfast room featuring a bay window. The master bedroom features a walk-in closet. The master bath includes an oversized tub and separate shower. Two bedrooms and a balcony that opens to the living area occupy the second floor. Please specify crawlspace or slab foundation when ordering.

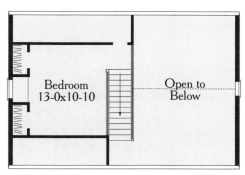

Bedroom
13-0x10-10

Open to
Below

Plan HPT700206

First Floor: *720 square feet*
Second Floor: *203 square feet*
Total: *923 square feet*
Width: *32'-0"* **Depth:** *38'-6"*

This compact design offers a host of extras beginning with its charming exterior. Wide country-style porches grace both the front and back of this cozy home. The focus of the interior centers on the open living area with a vaulted ceiling. Split into a great room and dining room, this area includes a large warming fireplace and lots of windows for outdoor viewing and increased natural lighting. The fully equipped kitchen is located near the rear porch for convenient outdoor dining. The master bedroom finishes the first floor. An extra bedroom upstairs includes two closets. Storage space is located in the eaves. Please specify basement, slab or crawlspace foundation when ordering.

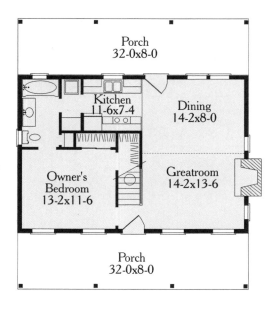

Porch
32-0x8-0

Kitchen
11-6x7-4

Dining
14-2x8-0

Owner's
Bedroom
13-2x11-6

Greatroom
14-2x13-6

Porch
32-0x8-0

Plan HPT700207

Square Footage: *2,796*
Width: *70'-9"* **Depth:** *66'-6"*

This home warmly welcomes both family and visitors with its charming covered front porch and multipane windows. Inside, the formal dining room opens directly off the foyer and has access to the porch. At the back of the plan, a large country kitchen includes an island counter and opens to a bay-windowed breakfast area. Just off the kitchen is a comfortable great room enhanced by a fireplace, a beam ceiling and access to a second covered porch. The luxurious master suite has many tempting amenities, such as a pampering bath, a huge walk-in closet and access to the rear covered porch. This home is designed with a walkout basement foundation.

Plan HPT700208

First Floor: *1,355 square feet*
Second Floor: *490 square feet*
Total: *1,845 square feet*
Bonus Room: *300 square feet*
Width: *46'-0"* **Depth:** *51'-8"*

A pair of rocking chairs will add a charming touch to this traditional porch. Inside, a fireplace dresses up the great room, which opens to the rear deck. Also accessible to the rear deck is the breakfast room, which is a handy extension of the well-appointed kitchen. Directly off the breakfast room you will find a laundry that leads off to the master bedroom, which itself has access to the deck. The master bath includes a separate shower, dual-basin vanity, compartmented toilet and walk-in closet. Upstairs, two secondary bedrooms share a bath, and there's room for a future study or office. This home is designed with a basement foundation.

Plan HPT700209

Square Footage: *1,573*
Width: *40'-0"* **Depth:** *56'-4"*

Charm the neighborhood with the unique exterior on this three-bedroom cottage—the fireplace is set between two windows. Inside, a vaulted great room boasts a centerpiece fireplace, decorative columns and an open layout. The dining room can enjoy the fireplace display while receiving convenient service from the pass-through bar of the nearby galley kitchen. A tray ceiling adorns the master suite and the luxurious bathroom features a radius window by the oval tub. Two family bedrooms share a full hall bath. Please specify basement or crawlspace foundation when ordering.

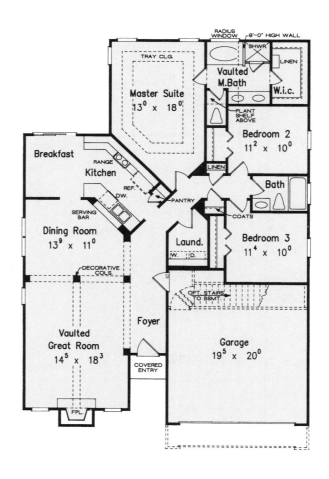

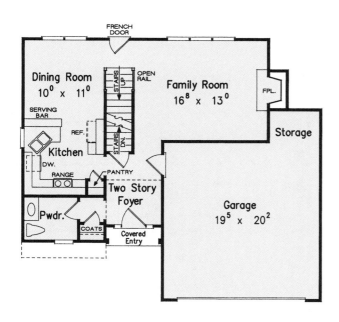

This plan starts with a two-story foyer that opens to a family room with a fireplace and windows overlooking the rear yard. Just off the foyer, a vestibule provides a coat closet and a convenient powder room. The dining room leads to the gourmet kitchen, which includes a pantry and a serving bar. Upstairs, sleeping quarters include two family bedrooms sharing a full bath, and a master suite with a tray ceiling, a vaulted bath and a walk-in closet. Please specify basement or crawlspace foundation when ordering.

Plan HPT700210

First Floor: *637 square feet*
Second Floor: *730 square feet*
Total: *1,367 square feet*
Width: *37'-6"* **Depth:** *34'-0"*

Plan HPT700211

Square Footage: *1,559*
Width: *54'-4"* **Depth:** *52'-0"*

Both formal and informal rooms are found in this one-story country home—even though it contains a smaller square footage. The foyer opens to a formal dining room to the right and a great room with a cathedral ceiling straight ahead. The breakfast room and kitchen lie just to the right of the great room. Family bedrooms are on the left side of the plan. They share a full hall bath. The master suite is tucked in behind the two-car garage and has access to the rear deck, as does the great room.

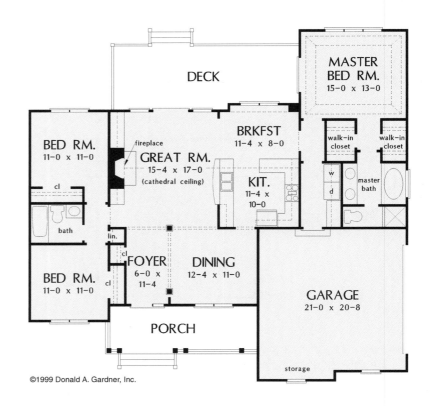

DECK

BED RM.
11-0 x 11-0
cl

fireplace
GREAT RM.
15-4 x 17-0
(cathedral ceiling)

bath

lin.

cl
FOYER
6-0 x
11-4
cl

BED RM.
11-0 x 11-0

BRKFST
11-4 x 8-0

KIT.
11-4 x
10-0

DINING
12-4 x 11-0

PORCH

MASTER
BED RM.
15-0 x 13-0

walk-in
closet

walk-in
closet

w
d

master
bath

GARAGE
21-0 x 20-8

storage

Plan HPT700212

First Floor: *1,222 square feet*
Second Floor: *521 square feet*
Total: *1,743 square feet*
Width: *35'-4"* **Depth:** *68'-8"*

This eye-catching cottage offers a livable and satisfying floor plan. Past the foyer, the great room provides a fireplace and a cathedral ceiling, and opens to the dining room. The U-shaped kitchen leads to a breakfast room that's accessible to the deck. The short hall holds the laundry area and directs traffic to family bedrooms and a full hall bath. The second floor provides a secluded area for the master bedroom and its private bath with a tub and a separate shower.

© 1997 Donald A Gardner Architects, Inc.

229

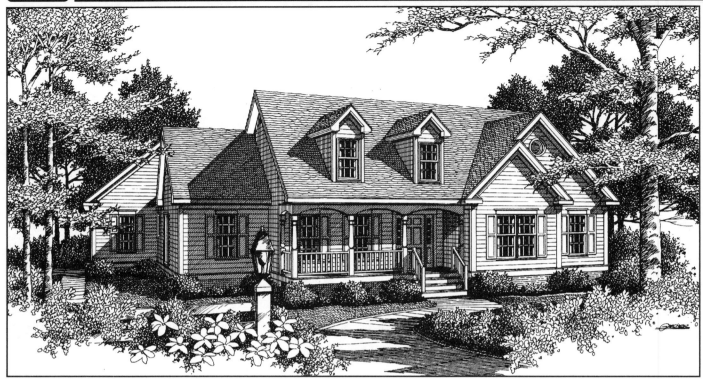

Plan HPT700213

Square Footage: *2,012*
Width: *65'-0"* **Depth:** *64'-0"*

Double gables add a noticeable touch to this charming three-bedroom home. Inside, the master suite offers a private bath with two vanities and a walk-in closet. Two family bedrooms are accessible to a full bath with private sinks. The dining room is just off the foyer, and the living room features French doors that open to the sun deck. The kitchen includes a breakfast area and leads to the powder room and the laundry area. A double garage is located to the rear of the home.

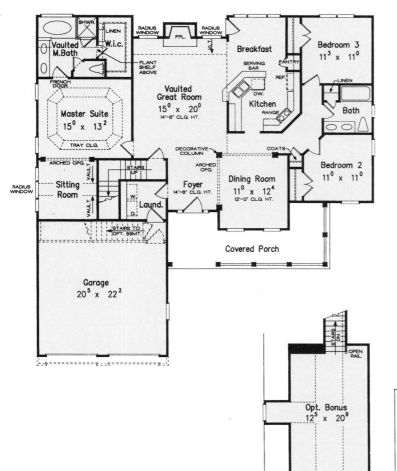

Master Suite 15⁰ x 13²

Vaulted M.Bath

W.i.c.

SHWR

LINEN

RADIUS WINDOW

FPL.

RADIUS WINDOW

Breakfast

Bedroom 3 11³ x 11⁰

LINEN

SERVING BAR

PANTRY

REF.

DW.

Kitchen

RANGE

Bath

Vaulted Great Room 15⁰ x 20⁰
14'-6" CLG. HT.

PLANT SHELF ABOVE

FRENCH DOOR

TRAY CLG.

DECORATIVE COLUMN

COATS

ARCHED OPG.

Sitting Room

STAIRS UP

Laund.

Foyer 14'-6" CLG. HT.

ARCHED OPG.

Dining Room 11⁰ x 12⁴
12'-0" CLG. HT.

Bedroom 2 11⁰ x 11⁰

VAULT

VAULT

W. D.

RADIUS WINDOW

STAIRS TO OPT. BSMT.

Garage 20⁵ x 22²

Covered Porch

STAIRS DN.

OPEN RAIL

Opt. Bonus 12⁵ x 20⁹

Plan HPT700214

Square Footage: *1,692*
Bonus Room: *358 square feet*
Width: *54'-0"* **Depth:** *56'-6"*

This cozy country cottage is enhanced with a front-facing planter box above the garage and a charming covered porch. The foyer leads to a vaulted great room, complete with a fireplace and radius windows. Decorative columns complement the entrance to the dining room, as does a decorative arch. On the left side of the plan resides the master suite, which is resplendent with amenities including a vaulted sitting room, tray ceiling, French doors to the vaulted full bath and an arched opening to the sitting room. On the right side, two additional bedrooms share a full bath. Please specify basement or crawlspace foundation when ordering.

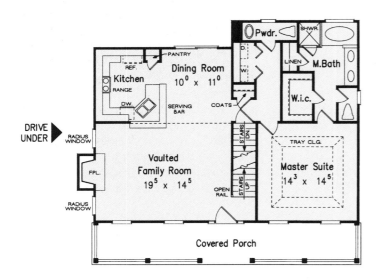

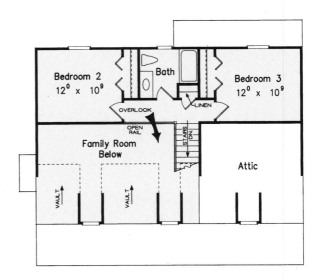

Plan HPT700215

First Floor: *1,061 square feet*
Second Floor: *430 square feet*
Total: *1,491 square feet*
Width: *40'-4"* **Depth:** *36'-0"*

This country cottage boasts a wide covered porch that offers room to sit and enjoy the sunrise. Inside, the vaulted family room provides a warming fireplace. The kitchen features a snack bar and a pantry and opens to the dining area. A tray ceiling in the master bedroom adds depth, and the master bath includes a tub, separate shower, linen closet and walk-in closet. The powder room sits near the laundry room. Bedrooms 2 and 3 are on the second floor and share a full hall bath and a linen closet.

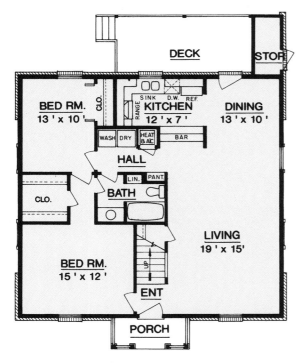

The brick facade of this house lends a rustic air to the general appearance, and an overhang protects the entryway from rain or snow. The front door opens to a spacious living room that flows to the dining room, which allows access to the rear deck. Storage space is available directly off of the deck, and ample attic space provides further storage possibilities. The U-shaped kitchen faces the dining room and sports an eating bar that overlooks the living room. A skylight in the attic at the rear of the house allows natural light to fill the kitchen below. An unfinished second floor offers the possibility of two additional bedrooms and a full bath. Please specify crawlspace or slab foundation when ordering.

Plan HPT700216

Square Footage: *1,088*
Unfinished Second Floor: *580 square feet*
Width: 34'-0" **Depth:** 44'-0"

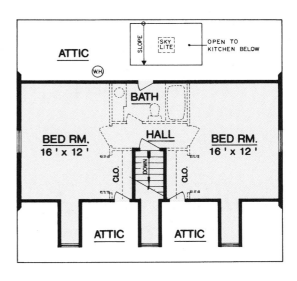

233

Plan HPT700217

Square Footage: *2,078*
Width: *75'-0"* **Depth:** *47'-10"*

Colonial style meets farmhouse style in this home, furnishing old-fashioned charisma with a flourish. From the entry, double doors open to the country dining room and a large island kitchen. Nearby, the spacious great room takes center stage and is warmed by a fireplace flanked by large windows. Tucked behind the three-car garage, the master suite features a vaulted ceiling in the bedroom. The master bath contains a relaxing tub, double-bowl vanity, separate shower and a compartmented toilet. Beyond the bath is a huge walk-in closet with two built-in chests. Three family bedrooms—one doubles as a study or home office—a full bath and a utility room complete the plan.

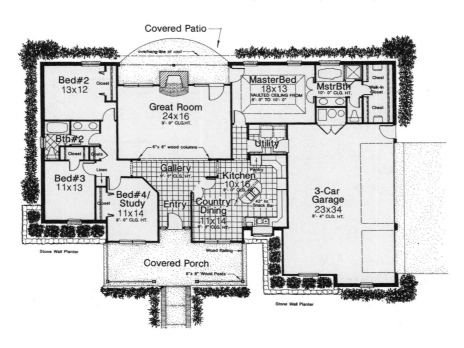

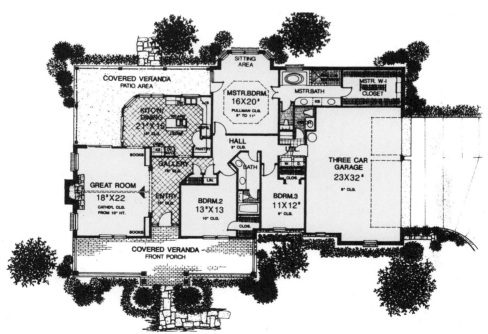

Plan HPT700218

Square Footage: *2,172*
Width: *79'-0"* **Depth:** *47'-0"*

The simplicity of the ranch lifestyle is indicated in every detail of this charming country design. Front and rear verandas along with earthy materials combine to give the exterior of this home a true land-lover's look. A central fireplace warms the cathedral-enhanced space of the formal great room. The casual kitchen area features an island workstation overlooking the rear veranda. The master suite is a sumptuous retreat with a sitting area, private bath and walk-in closet. Two additional bedrooms share a full hall bath.

Plan HPT700219

Square Footage: *2,360*
Width: *75'-2"* **Depth:** *68'-0"*

Columns, transoms and a clerestory lend this house a stylish country charm. Inside, a built-in media center, fireplace and columns add to the wonderful livability of this home. The modified galley kitchen features a serving bar and an island workstation. Escape to the relaxing master suite featuring a private sitting room and a luxurious bath set between His and Hers walk-in closets. Three bedrooms share a bath on the other side of the plan, ensuring privacy. Note the handy storage area in the two-car, side-entry garage. Please specify basement, crawlspace or slab foundation when ordering.

Retreat
15-3x8-6

Bath
12-0x11-9

Owner's
Bedroom
15-3x15-8

Laundry
12-0x7-6

Porch
28-4x11-0

Bedroom
11-9x13-6

Greatroom
14-6x17-5

Dining
11-0x17-5

Garage
23-6x21-6

Bedroom
11-6x13-6

Bedroom
11-8x13-6

Foyer

Kitchen
12-6x13-9

Storage
13-4x5-8

Porch
32-0x8-0

Basement Stair
Location

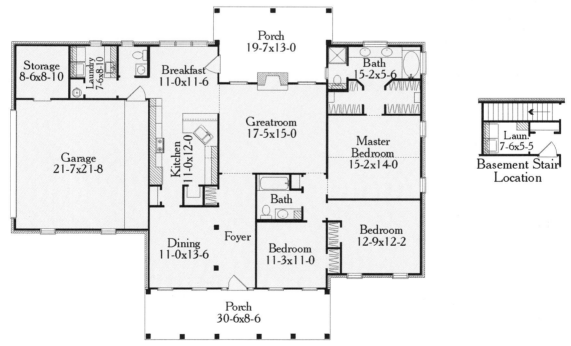

Porch
19-7x13-0

Storage
8-6x8-10

Laundry
7-6x8-10

Breakfast
11-0x11-6

Bath
15-2x5-6

Garage
21-7x21-8

Kitchen
11-0x12-0

Greatroom
17-5x15-0

Master
Bedroom
15-2x14-0

Bath

Dining
11-0x13-6

Foyer

Bedroom
11-3x11-0

Bedroom
12-9x12-2

Porch
30-6x8-6

Laun.
7-6x5-5

Basement Stair
Location

Plan HPT700220

Square Footage: *1,894*
Width: *68'-0"* **Depth:** *56'-6"*

Multiple windows offer insight into this beautiful home and accent this brilliant design. Entering from the garage, a laundry room is on the left, while to the right await a powder room and breakfast room. The kitchen provides plenty of counter space and opens to the dining room. The great room includes a fireplace framed by windows. A lavish master suite is home to two walk-in closets, dual sinks, a separate shower and a garden tub. Please specify basement, crawlspace or slab foundation when ordering.

Plan HPT700221

Square Footage: *1,828*
Bonus Room: *352 square feet*
Width: *53'-8"* **Depth:** *55'-8"*

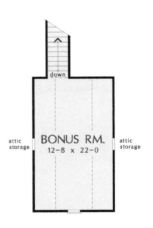

A simple footprint and easy roofline make this mid-size home affordable, and families will appreciate its split-bedroom design and stylish exterior. Interior columns and a tray ceiling accent the formal dining room, while a vaulted ceiling enhances the great room, kitchen and breakfast area. A rear clerestory dormer window further embellishes the open great room, which features a cozy fireplace and built-in bookshelves. The adjacent back porch increases living space. The master suite is secluded from the two family bedrooms for privacy. A tray ceiling, back-porch access, a walk-in closet and a whirlpool tub enrich the master suite's luxury.

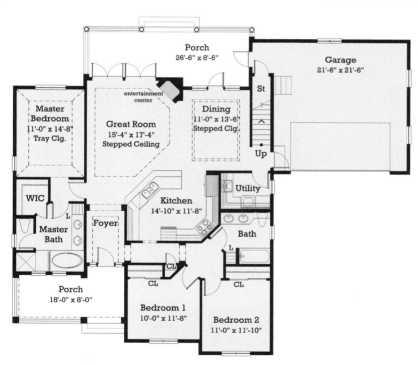

B uild this home in your local neighborhood or on a secluded mountaintop. Two sets of French doors brighten the great room and lead out to the rear covered porch. The dining room—also with porch access—and kitchen are connected to the great room. The utility room is just around the hall near the garage entrance. The master bedroom features a tray ceiling and a private bath with a tub, separate shower, walk-in closet and dual vanities. Two family bedrooms are located toward the front of the home, with wall closets and a full hall bath.

Plan HPT700222
Square Footage: *1,616*
Bonus Room: *362 square feet*
Width: *64'-0"* **Depth:** *54'-6"*

Deck
36'-0" x 12'-0"

Kitchen
18'-0" x 14'-5"

Utility

Pantry

Great Room
18'-0" x 16'-4"
(cathedral clg.)

Master
Bedroom
13'-5" x 16'-3"

Porch
36'-0" x 8'-0"

Bedroom
12'-2" x 11'-10"

Bedroom
10'-0" x 11'-10"

Balcony

open to
Great Room
below

Bonus Rm.
13'-5" x 7'-2"

Plan HPT700223

First Floor: *1,152 square feet*
Second Floor: *452 square feet*
Total: *1,604 square feet*
Bonus Room: *115 square feet*
Width: *36'-0"* **Depth:** *40'-0"*

Three dormers, two chimneys and a covered front porch combine to make this home attractive in any neighborhood. Inside, a great room greets both family and friends with a cathedral ceiling and a warming fireplace. An L-shaped kitchen features a cooktop island. The nearby dining area offers rear-porch access. Upstairs, two secondary bedrooms share a hall bath and access a bonus room—perfect for a study or computer room. Please specify basement or crawlspace foundation when ordering.

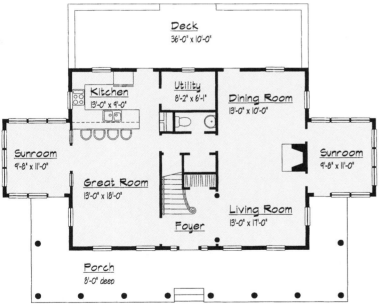

Note the clean lines and attractive front porch of this symmetrical design. Inside, the two-story foyer is flanked by a formal living room and a more casual great room. Two sun rooms echo each other at opposite ends of the home. The U-shaped kitchen offers a snack bar into the great room and has access to the rear deck. If entertaining is your forte, the formal dining room flows into the formal living room, perfect for after-dinner conversation. Upstairs, a lavish master bedroom features a walk-in closet, private fireplace and sumptuous private bath. Two large secondary bedrooms and a hall bath complete this level. Please specify basement or crawlspace foundation when ordering.

Plan HPT700224

First Floor: *1,008 square feet*
Second Floor: *917 square feet*
Total: *1,925 square feet*
Sun Rooms: *240 square feet*
Width: *56'-0"* **Depth:** *36'-0"*

Plan HPT700225

Square Footage: *1,792*
Bonus Space: *494 square feet*
Width: *63'-3"* **Depth:** *52'-0"*

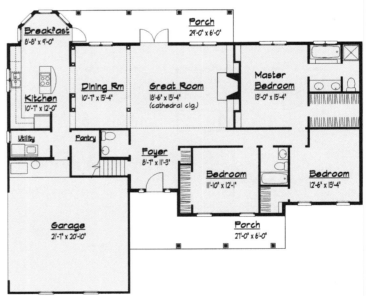

Three dormers and pedimented columns lend a country feeling to this home. The covered porch won't be complete until there is a swinging bench in place. This home is efficiently laid out to any family's liking. The foyer leads into the great room where a warming hearth is waiting. The dining room is separated from both the kitchen and the great room by columns. The L-shaped kitchen features an island and a bayed breakfast nook. The master suite is to the right of the plan with a private bath, and two more family bedrooms are located at the front of the plan.

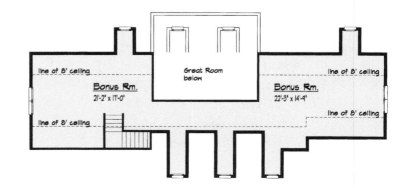

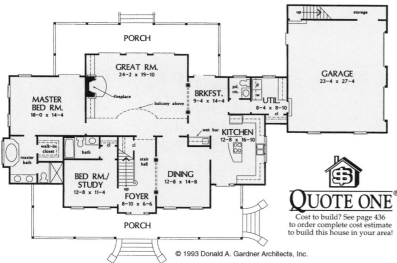

PORCH

GREAT RM.
24-2 x 19-10

MASTER
BED RM.
18-0 x 14-4

fireplace

balcony above

BRKFST.
9-4 x 14-4

pd.
rm.

d
w

UTIL.
8-4 x 8-10

cl

GARAGE
23-4 x 27-4

up

storage

wet bar

KITCHEN
12-8 x 16-10

walk-in
closet

bath

cl

master
bath

a

cl

stair
hall

BED RM./
STUDY
12-8 x 11-4

FOYER
8-10 x 6-6

up

DINING
12-8 x 14-8

PORCH

Quote One®
Cost to build? See page 436
to order complete cost estimate
to build this house in your area!

© 1993 Donald A. Gardner Architects, Inc.

arched windows above
clerestory windows

(cathedral ceiling)

great room
below

railing

bath

attic storage

BED RM.
12-8 x 11-3

down

BED RM.
12-8 x 11-3

attic storage

cl

cl

cl

cl

foyer
below

clerestory with palladian window

down

BONUS RM.
27-4 x 14-0

Plan HPT700226

First Floor: *2,064 square feet*
Second Floor: *594 square feet*
Total: *2,658 square feet*
Bonus Room: *483 square feet*
Width: *92'-0"* **Depth:** *57'-8"*

You'll find country living at its best when mean-dering through this four-bedroom farmhouse with its wraparound porch. A front Palladian dormer window and rear clerestory windows in the great room add exciting visual elements to the exterior while providing natural light to the interior. The large great room boasts a fireplace, bookshelves and a raised cathedral ceiling, allow-ing a curved balcony overlook above. The great room, master bedroom and breakfast room are accessible to the rear porch for greater circulation and flexibility. Special features such as the large cooktop island in the kitchen, the wet bar, the bedroom/study, the generous bonus room over the garage and ample storage space set this plan apart.

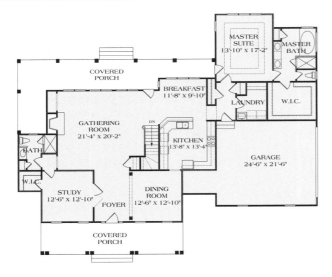

Plan HPT700227

First Floor: *2,131 square feet*
Second Floor: *1,030 square feet*
Total: *3,161 square feet*
Width: *73'-11"* **Depth:** *61'-7"*

This country home displays a quaint rural character outside and a savvy sophistication inside. Double columns support the covered porch of this large four-bedroom design. A study or optional fifth bedroom with a bath is to the left of the foyer. The kitchen opens to the breakfast area and the gathering room—which features a fireplace. The master bedroom boasts a tray ceiling and a private bath with a walk-in closet. A loft reached by a stairway from the large, open gathering room provides an added activity center or convenient home office. Two family bedrooms and a full hall bath are located on the second floor.

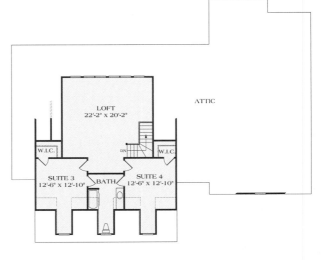

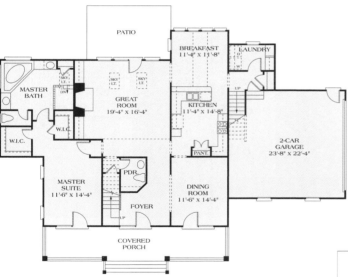

Skylights, an abundance of windows and five gable-roofed dormers fill this three-bedroom country design with natural light. The central living area is a skylit comfort zone with a fireplace and built-in bookshelves. Nearby, a wall of glass brightens the breakfast area, which shares its bounty of natural light with the kitchen. The first-floor master suite features a corner tub and His and Hers bath on the second floor and overlooks the great room.

Plan HPT700228

First Floor: *1,669 square feet*
Second Floor: *706 square feet*
Total: *2,375 square feet*
Bonus Room: *342 square feet*
Width: 70'-8" **Depth:** 48'-0"

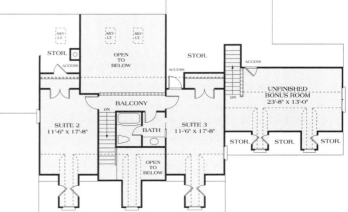

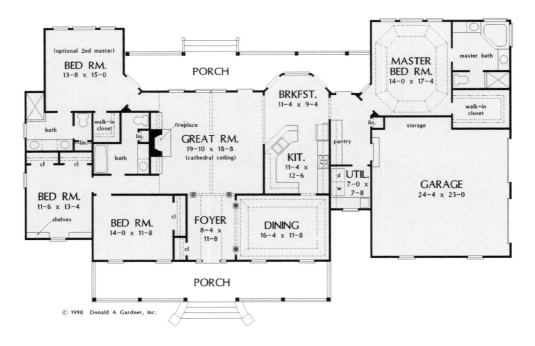

© 1998 Donald A Gardner, Inc.

Plan HPT700229

Square Footage: *2,487*
Width: *86'-2"* **Depth:** *51'-8"*

A trio of dormers and a front porch adorn the facade of this sprawling four-bedroom country home. Illuminated by the center dormer, the vaulted foyer gives way to the dining room with a tray ceiling and the spacious great room with a cathedral ceiling, a fireplace and built-in shelves. A split-bedroom layout provides privacy for homeowners in a generous master suite with a tray ceiling and private bath.

© 1998 Donald A Gardner, Inc.

Teeming with luxury and style, this gracious country estate features spacious rooms, volume ceilings and four porches for extended outdoor living. Fireplaces in the living and family rooms grant warmth and character to these spacious gathering areas, while columns add definition to the open living and dining rooms. Built-in bookshelves in the living room are both attractive and functional, as is the built-in desk adjacent to the open U-shaped staircase. The master suite is a haven with a tray ceiling, sitting alcove, dual walk-in closets and a luxurious bath. The upstairs balcony overlooks both the foyer and the living room while serving as an open, central hallway for the home's three family bedrooms and bonus room.

Plan HPT700230

First Floor: *2,676 square feet*
Second Floor: *1,023 square feet*
Total: *3,699 square feet*
Bonus Room: *487 square feet*
Width: *87'-8"* **Depth:** *63'-0"*

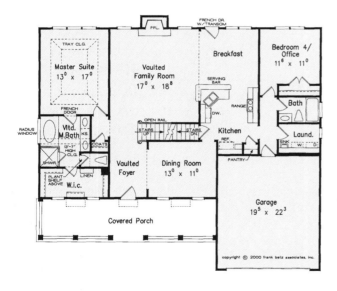

Plan HPT700231

First Floor: *1,668 square feet*
Second Floor: *638 square feet*
Total: *2,306 square feet*
Bonus Room: *298 square feet*
Width: *54'-0"* **Depth:** *50'-4"*

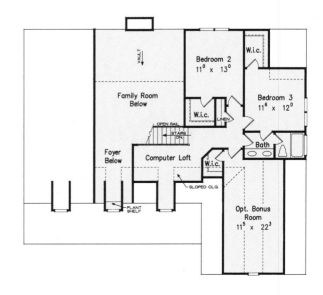

This home's covered front porch says welcome! Shuttered windows, dormers and a cupola offer a farmhouse look. A vaulted foyer introduces the formal dining room to the right and the vaulted family room with a fireplace directly ahead. The kitchen offers a serving bar and a walk-in pantry. The master suite displays luxury with a tray ceiling and sumptuous bath. A bedroom to the rear is perfect for either a guest suite or home office. Two family bedrooms, a computer loft and an optional bonus room expand the second floor. Please specify basement or crawlspace foundation when ordering.

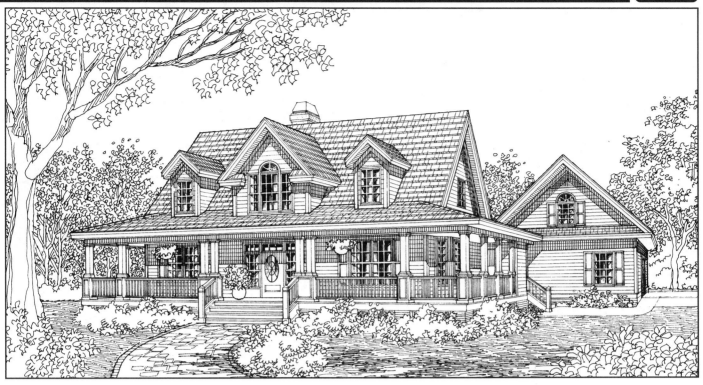

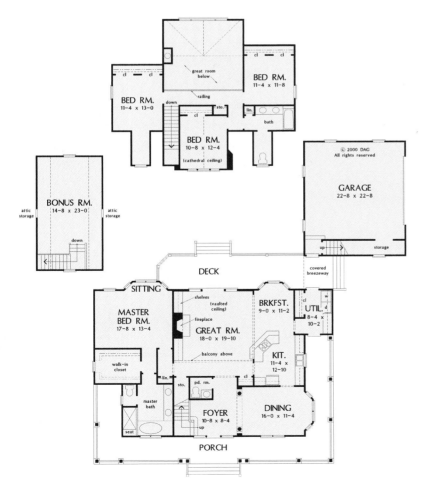

Plan HPT700232

First Floor: *1,706 square feet*
Second Floor: *776 square feet*
Total: *2,482 square feet*
Bonus Room: *414 square feet*
Width: *54'-8"* **Depth:** *43'-0"*

The cozy charm of this country farmhouse—complete with a wraparound porch—belies the spaciousness that lies within. A large great room lies directly beyond the foyer and boasts a fireplace, shelves, a vaulted ceiling and a door to the rear deck. A bayed breakfast room, located just off the kitchen, looks to a covered breezeway that leads from the house to the garage. The first-floor master bedroom is enhanced with a sitting area, a walk-in closet and a full bath with a garden tub and dual sinks. The second floor includes three additional bedrooms, one with a cathedral ceiling.

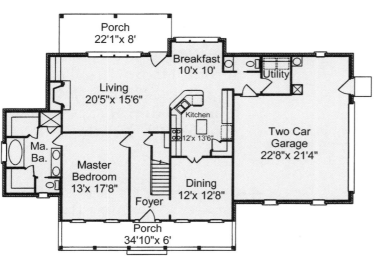

Porch
22'1"x 8'

Breakfast
10'x 10'

Utility

Living
20'5"x 15'6"

Kitchen
12'x 13'6"

Two Car
Garage
22'8"x 21'4"

Ma.
Ba.

Master
Bedroom
13'x 17'8"

Dining
12'x 12'8"

Foyer

Porch
34'10"x 6'

Plan HPT700233

First Floor: *1,557 square feet*
Second Floor: *774 square feet*
Total: *2,331 square feet*
Bonus Room: *264 square feet*
Width: *68'-10"* **Depth:** *48'-7"*

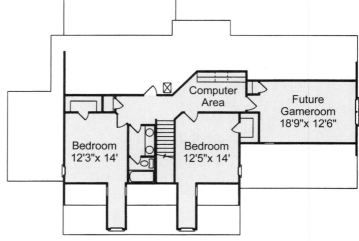

Computer
Area

Future
Gameroom
18'9"x 12'6"

Bedroom
12'3"x 14'

Bedroom
12'5"x 14'

Pillars, pedimented dormers and a covered porch make this home a Southern treat. Rows of windows along the exterior of this facade shine light into the master bedroom and dining room. The master bedroom offers a private bath with dual vanities and two walk-in closets. Double doors lead from the dining room to the kitchen for planned events. Plenty of counter space is available in the kitchen. A ribbon of windows lend themselves well to the kitchen and breakfast nook area. The spacious living room has a warming hearth and access to the backyard. Upstairs, two family bedrooms and a future game room complete the plan.

Photo by Chris A. Little of Atlanta, courtesy of Chatham Home Planning, Inc.

This home, as shown in the photograph, may differ from the actual blueprints. For more detailed information, please check the floor plans carefully.

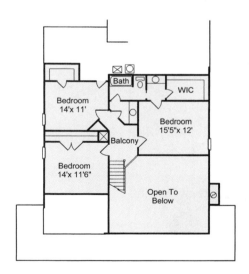

Plan HPT700234

First Floor: *1,516 square feet*
Second Floor: *840 square feet*
Total: *2,356 square feet*
Width: *46'-10"* **Depth:** *73'-5"*

Looking for a home with a country attitude and modern amenities? Welcome home! A wide, columned porch graced by tall shuttered windows will greet guests with the feeling of comfort. The formal living room is enhanced by a central fireplace, while the dining room is situated just off the U-shaped kitchen. Sunshine pours in from the breakfast area, flooding the kitchen with light. The master bedroom features a walk-in closet and double doors to the dual-vanity bathroom. Upstairs, three family bedrooms—two enjoy walk-in closets—share a compartmented bath. The rear-loading two-car garage doesn't detract from the symmetry of the home.

Plan HPT700235

Square Footage: *2,919*
Width: *70'-10"* **Depth:** *66'-6"*

This plan was made for entertaining. Its entry and center hall are lined with columns that help define, but not limit, the great room, dining room and bedroom wing. A beam ceiling, a fireplace and covered rear-porch access highlight the great room. This room also opens to a sun room and the bay-windowed breakfast room. A large gourmet kitchen makes a great work center. Bedrooms include two family suites with a shared bath and private vanity areas and the master suite with a tray ceiling in the bedroom. The master bath offers His and Hers walk-in closets, a garden whirlpool tub, separate shower, compartmented toilet and make-up vanity. This home is designed with a walkout basement foundation.

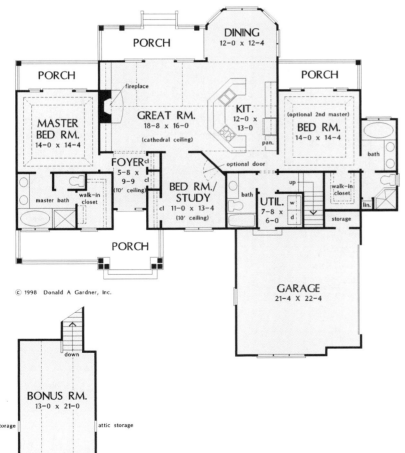

© 1998 Donald A Gardner, Inc.

PORCH

DINING
12-0 x 12-4

PORCH

fireplace

PORCH

MASTER BED RM.
14-0 x 14-4

GREAT RM.
18-8 x 16-0
(cathedral ceiling)

KIT.
12-0 x 13-0

(optional 2nd master)

BED RM.
14-0 x 14-4

bath

pan.

FOYER
5-8 x 9-9
(10' ceiling)

cl

optional door

cl

BED RM./ STUDY
11-0 x 13-4
(10' ceiling)

cl

bath

UTIL.
7-8 x 6-0

w d

up

walk-in closet

storage

lin.

master bath

walk-in closet

PORCH

GARAGE
21-4 x 22-4

down

BONUS RM.
13-0 x 21-0

attic storage   attic storage

Plan HPT700236

Square Footage: *1,792*
Bonus Room: *338 square feet*
Width: *66'-4"* **Depth:** *62'-4"*

Stucco, stone and shingles combined with Craftsman windows, rafter tails and a pillared porch give this home plenty of curb appeal. The great room features a fireplace, built-ins, access to the rear porch and a cathedral ceiling. The unique kitchen offers tons of counter and cabinet space and easily accesses the bayed dining area. Two full bedroom suites could serve as separate master suites, or one as a fine guest suite. A bedroom/study is available for an in-home office or unexpected guests. Note the large bonus room over the two-car garage.

Plan HPT700237

Square Footage: *1,822*
Width: *58'-0"* **Depth:** *66'-8"*

Country charm at its best and a design that suits your every need combine to create a very livable floor plan. French doors off the foyer open to a study/office with a walk-in closet. Across the hall is the living room with a fireplace and built-ins. The dining area is defined by columns and is easily served by the kitchen—which includes a breakfast nook. The master suite includes a walk-in closet and a private bath. The utility area is near the two-car garage. A full hall bath is available to the two family bedroom; one of the bedrooms includes a walk-in closet.

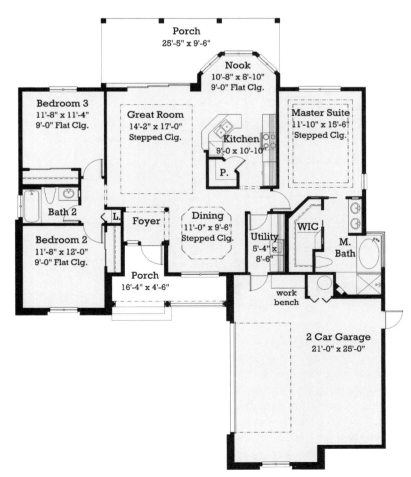

Plan HPT700238

Square Footage: *1,487*
Width: *52'-6"* **Depth:** *66'-0"*

Simple yet captivating, this brick home is full of charming country flavor. Beyond the inviting porch and the foyer resides a design that's perfect for a family getaway. The open great room is adjacent to the kitchen, which features a snack bar, walk-in pantry and bayed breakfast nook. To the far right of the plan is the master bedroom with a large walk-in closet, tub, separate shower and two sinks. Two additional bedrooms to the left of the great room are separated by a full hall bath. The two-car garage includes a work bench and enters the home through the utility room.

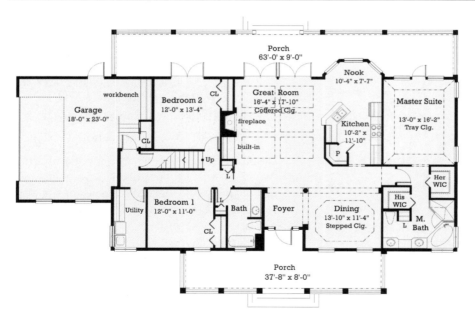

Porch
63'-0" x 9'-0"

Nook
10'-4" x 7'-7"

workbench

Garage
18'-0" x 23'-0"

Bedroom 2
12'-0" x 13'-4"

CL

Great Room
16'-4" x 17'-10"
Coffered Clg.

fireplace

built-in

Kitchen
10'-2" x
11'-10"

P

Master Suite
13'-0" x 16'-2"
Tray Clg.

CL

Up

L

Her
WIC

His
WIC

Utility

Bedroom 1
12'-0" x 11'-0"

L

Bath

Foyer

Dining
13'-10" x 11'-4"
Stepped Clg.

M.
Bath

L

CL

Porch
37'-8" x 8'-0"

Bonus Room
16'-6" x 11'-0"

Bath

Dn

Plan HPT700239

Square Footage: *1,989*
Bonus Room: *291 square feet*
Width: *80'-6"* **Depth:** *50'-0"*

Beneath this attractive exterior is a comfortable and unique design. The tray ceiling in the dining room adds depth, and a decorative column helps define the space. The master bedroom includes a tray ceiling and features the ultimate master bath with His and Her closets. In the kitchen, the pantry provides extra storage space, and the snack bar is open to the nook. The great room contains a fireplace and two sets of French doors that open to the rear porch. Please specify basement or crawlspace foundation when ordering.

Plan HPT700240

Square Footage: *2,555*
Width: *70'-6"* **Depth:** *76'-6"*

A striking pediment hovers above a columned porch and a glass-paneled entry, introducing a well-planned interior. The foyer leads to a study and to the formal dining room. The great room offers a fireplace and a wall of French doors to the backyard. The island kitchen includes a nook and plenty of counter space. Two family bedrooms reside near the laundry and offer individual access to a full bath with dual vanities. The master bedroom provides His and Her closets and a lavish bath with a tub and a separate shower. A workbench is featured in the garage.

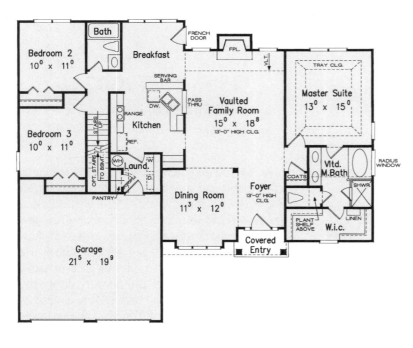

This comfortable cottage is well suited to an alpine environment yet, with a flexible interior and superior architecture, will build anywhere. Open living and dining space is anchored by a decorative column and a fireplace surrounded by views. A well-planned kitchen features a food-preparation island and a serving bar. A triple window in the breakfast area brightens the kitchen, while a French door allows access to the rear property. To the right of the plan, the master suite boasts a vaulted bath, a plant shelf and a walk-in closet. Two secondary bedrooms share a full bath. Please specify basement or crawlspace foundation when ordering.

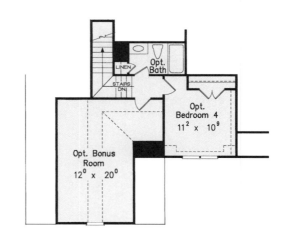

Plan HPT700241

Square Footage: *1,583*
Optional Second Floor: *532 square feet*
Width: 54'-0" **Depth:** 47'-6"

Plan HPT700242

Square Footage: *2,090*
Width: *61'-0"* **Depth:** *70'-6"*

This traditional home features board-and-batten and cedar shingles in an attractively proportioned exterior. Finishing touches include a covered entrance and porch with column detailing and an arched transom, flower boxes and shuttered windows. The foyer opens to both the dining room and the great room beyond with French doors leading to the porch. To the right of the foyer is the combination bedroom/study. A short hallway leads to a full bath and a secondary bedroom with ample closet space. The spacious master bedroom offers walk-in closets on both sides of the entrance to the master bath. This home is designed with a walkout basement foundation.

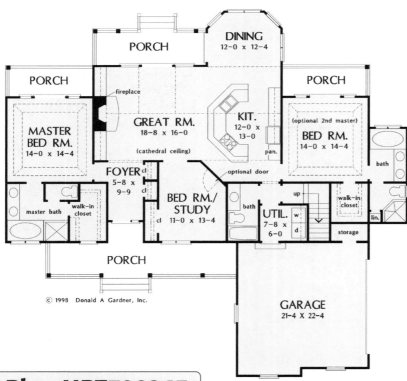

PORCH

DINING
12-0 x 12-4

PORCH

PORCH

fireplace

GREAT RM.
18-8 x 16-0

(cathedral ceiling)

KIT.
12-0 x 13-0

pan.

(optional 2nd master)
BED RM.
14-0 x 14-4

bath

MASTER BED RM.
14-0 x 14-4

FOYER
5-8 x 9-9

cl
cl

optional door

master bath

walk-in closet

BED RM./STUDY
11-0 x 13-4

cl

bath

UTIL.
7-8 x 6-0

w
d

up

walk-in closet

lin.

storage

PORCH

© 1998 Donald A Gardner, Inc.

GARAGE
21-4 X 22-4

Plan HPT700243

Square Footage: *1,792*
Bonus Room: *338 square feet*
Width: *66'-4"* **Depth:** *62'-4"*

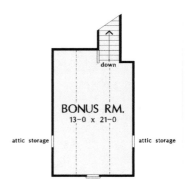

down

BONUS RM.
13-0 x 21-0

attic storage

attic storage

Cedar shakes, siding and stone blend with the Craftsman details of a custom design in this stunning home. An open common area separates two suites, including an optional second master suite that would be great for guests or a roommate. Note the fireplace and direct porch access in the great room. Watch the glow of the fire from the kitchen's five-sided island. Enjoy the light-filled dining area for formal and informal dining situations. Added flexibility is found in the bedroom/study and bonus room.

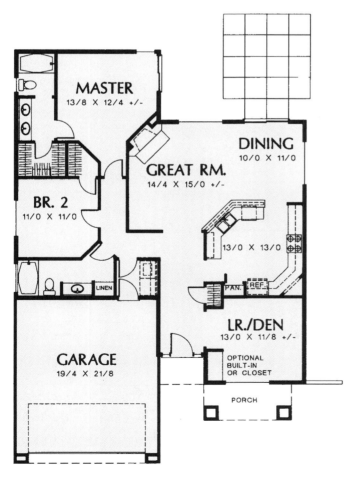

MASTER
13/8 X 12/4 +/-

GREAT RM.
14/4 X 15/0 +/-

DINING
10/0 X 11/0

BR. 2
11/0 X 11/0

13/0 X 13/0

LINEN

PAN. REF.

LR./DEN
13/0 X 11/8 +/-

GARAGE
19/4 X 21/8

OPTIONAL
BUILT-IN
OR CLOSET

PORCH

Plan HPT700244

Square Footage: *1,420*
Width: *40'-0"* **Depth:** *58'-0"*

L

This efficient floor plan displays a charming exterior elevation that's just right for any neighborhood. Inside, a living room or den opens to the right of the entry and offers an optional built-in or closet. In the kitchen, an abundance of counter space and an accommodating layout make meal preparations simple. A great room and dining room connect to this area and will conform to everyday living. The master suite has a private bath, ample closet space and rear-yard access. A secondary bedroom and a full hall bath complete this plan.

Siding, stone and a trio of front-facing gables add character to the facade of this captivating cottage with a courtyard garage. A second-floor balcony looks over the two-story foyer and the great room with its cathedral ceiling. An open and undefined central hall on the first floor is bordered on either end by built-in art niches. Bay windows extend both the breakfast area and master bedroom. The master suite features dual walk-in closets and a private bath with His and Her vanities, a separate tub and shower, and a compartmented toilet. Divided by the upstairs balcony are two family bedrooms. Accessed from the first floor, a bonus room offers options for future expansion.

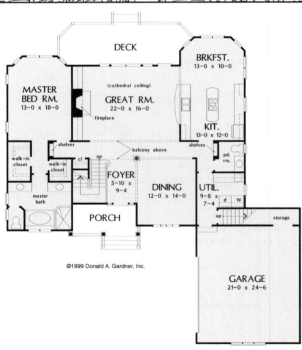

©1999 Donald A. Gardner, Inc.

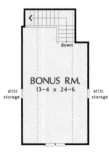

Plan HPT700245

First Floor: *1,734 square feet*
Second Floor: *547 square feet*
Total: *2,281 square feet*
Bonus Room: *381 square feet*
Width: *60'-8"* **Depth:** *65'-6"*

Plan HPT700246

Square Footage: *1,700*
Bonus Room: *294 square feet*
Width: *50'-0"* **Depth:** *63'-8"*

Stone, stucco and cedar shakes create an interesting exterior for this attractive three-bedroom bungalow. A cathedral ceiling with a rear clerestory dormer embellishes the generous great room, creating additional space and appeal. The dining room and efficiently designed kitchen are open to one another and to the great room for casual, relaxed living. The master suite features an elegant tray ceiling and a private bath with a compartmented toilet and a walk-in closet. Two secondary bedrooms enjoy a spacious hall bath with dual lavatories and a linen closet. A bonus room over the garage allows for ample storage and future expansion.

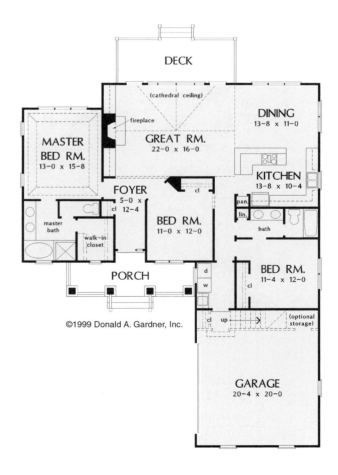

©1999 Donald A. Gardner, Inc.

Looking a bit like a mountain resort, this fine Craftsman home is sure to be the envy of your neighborhood. Entering through the elegant front door, one finds an open staircase to the right and a spacious great room directly ahead. Here, a fireplace and a wall of windows give a cozy welcome. A lavish master suite begins with a sitting room—complete with a fireplace—and continues to a private porch, large walk-in closet and sumptuous bedroom area. The gourmet kitchen adjoins a sunny dining room and leads to a screened porch. ©1998 Donald A. Gardner, Inc.

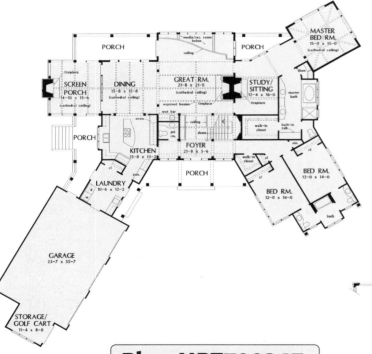

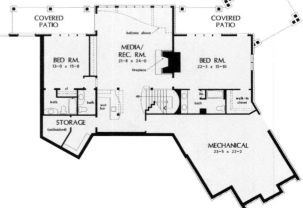

Plan HPT700247

Main Level: *3,040 square feet*
Lower Level: *1,736 square feet*
Total: *4,776 square feet*
Width: *106'-5"* **Depth:** *104'-2"*

Plan HPT700248

Main Level: *2,065 square feet*
Lower Level: *1,216 square feet*
Total: *3,281 square feet*
Width: 82'-2" **Depth:** 43'-6"

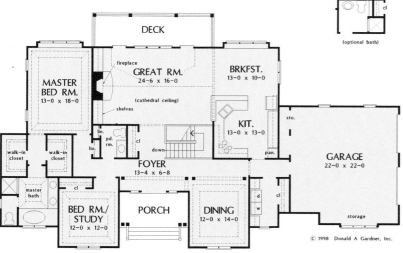

Stone, siding and multiple gables combine beautifully on the exterior of this hillside home. Taking advantage of rear views, the home's most oft-used rooms are oriented at the back with plenty of windows. Augmented by a cathedral ceiling, the great room features a fireplace, built-in shelves and access to the rear deck. Twin walk-in closets and a private bath infuse the master suite with luxury. The nearby powder room offers an optional full-bath arrangement, allowing the study to double as a bedroom. Downstairs, a large media/recreation room with a wet bar and fireplace separates two more bedrooms, each with a full bath and walk-in closet.

Plan HPT700249

Main Level: *1,734 square feet*
Upper Level: *546 square feet*
Lower Level: *788 square feet*
Total: *3,068 square feet*
Bonus Room: *381 square feet*
Width: *60'-8"* **Depth:** *68'-0"*

Multiple gables, cedar shakes, stucco and stone provide plenty of enchantment for the exterior of this hillside home. Craftsman character abounds inside as well as out, evidenced by the home's functional floor plan. Built-ins flank the great room's fireplace for convenience, and a rear deck extends living space outdoors. The exceptionally well-designed kitchen features an island cooktop and an adjacent breakfast bay. The master suite, also with a bay window, enjoys twin walk-in closets and a delightful bath with dual vanities. Two upstairs bedrooms are divided by an impressive balcony that overlooks the foyer and great room. A fourth bedroom and generous recreation room are located on the lower level, while a spacious bonus room provides more room for expansion above the garage.

©1999 Donald A. Gardner, Inc.

MASTER BED RM. 14-0 x 16-0

BRKFST. 13-0 x 12-8 (vaulted ceiling)

DECK

DECK

KITCHEN 13-4 x 16-0

GREAT RM. 21-0 x 16-0 (cathedral ceiling)

fireplace

SCREEN PORCH 11-10 x 15-8 (cathedral ceiling)

lin.

seat

master bath

walk-in closet

pan.

sto.

lin.

bath

DINING 13-0 x 12-4

FOYER 14-10 x 4-2

down

lin.

cl

cl

walk-in closet

w d

UTIL. 9-8 x 8-0

storage

PORCH

BED RM./ STUDY 11-0 x 13-0

GARAGE 21-8 x 25-8

A Craftsman combination of cedar shake shingles and wood siding lends warmth and style to this four-bedroom home. A stunning cathedral ceiling spans the open great room and spacious island kitchen for exceptional volume. A deep tray ceiling heightens the formal dining room, while the breakfast room is enhanced by a vaulted ceiling. Two rear decks and a screened porch augment the home's ample living space. The master bedroom is topped by a tray ceiling and features two walk-in closets and a generous private bath. A second bedroom is located on the main floor and two more can be found in the finished basement.

Plan HPT700250

Main Level: *2,122 square feet*
Lower Level: *1,290 square feet*
Total: *3,412 square feet*
Width: *83'-0"* **Depth:** *74'-4"*

PATIO

storage

BED RM. 13-4 x 16-0

cl

BED RM. 12-4 x 12-4

REC. RM. 20-0 x 16-0

walk-in closet

bath

lin.

up

sto.

storage

267

DINING
12-0 x 15-0

PORCH

PORCH

MASTER
BED RM.
14-0 x 18-0

fireplace

GREAT RM.
22-0 x 18-8
(cathedral ceiling)

KITCHEN
12-0 x 15-0

walk-in
closet

walk-in
closet

BRKFST.
9-8 x 10-0

railing

down

UTIL.
5-8 x
6-8
d | w

pantry

storage

pd.
rm.

cl FOYER
6-8 x
10-0

master
bath

seat

PORCH

GARAGE
21-8 x 23-4

©1999 Donald A. Gardner, Inc.

storage

Arched windows and arches adorn the covered front porch and complement the gable peaks on the facade of this stylish Craftsman home, complete with a stone-and-siding exterior. Designed for sloping lots, this home positions its common living areas and the master suite on the main floor, while a generous recreation room and two family bedrooms reside on the lower level. A cathedral ceiling expands the foyer and great room, while the dining room and master bedroom and bath enjoy elegant tray ceilings. The island kitchen opens to the great room, dining room and breakfast area and features a nearby walk-in pantry. The master suite boasts dual walk-in closets and a luxurious bath.

Plan HPT700251

Main Level: *1,725 square feet*
Lower Level: *1,090 square feet*
Total: *2,815 square feet*
Width: *59'-0"* **Depth:** *59'-4"*

PATIO

BED RM.
11-6 x 13-4

wet bar

fireplace

BED RM.
13-6 x 11-0

cl

cl

REC. RM.
19-8 x 18-8

cl

lin.

bath

up

bath

sto.

A prominent center gable with an arched window accents the facade of this custom Craftsman home, which features an exterior of cedar shakes, siding and stone. An open floor plan with generously proportioned rooms contributes to the home's spacious and relaxed atmosphere. The vaulted great room boasts a rear wall of windows, a fireplace bordered by built-in cabinets, and convenient access to the kitchen. A second-floor loft overlooks the great room for added drama. The master suite is completely secluded and enjoys a cathedral ceiling, back-porch access, a walk-in closet and a luxurious bath.
©1999 Donald A. Gardner, Inc.

Plan HPT700252

First Floor: *2,477 square feet*
Second Floor: *742 square feet*
Total: *3,219 square feet*
Bonus Room: *419 square feet*
Width: *100'-0"* **Depth:** *66'-2"*

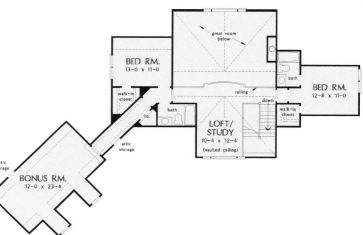

Plan HPT700253

Square Footage: *2,306*
Finished Basement: *1,724 square feet*
Width: *98'-0"* **Depth:** *48'-0"*

Stone and vertical siding enrich this country facade. Beyond the foyer, the spacious great room is shaped by a sloped ceiling—it offers a fireplace and built-in shelves, while overlooking the rear deck. The dining room also features a sloped ceiling and is conveniently placed between the U-shaped island kitchen and the rear screened porch. A laundry room, pantry and half-bath are thoughtfully placed next to the garage, which offers extra storage. A master bedroom with a private bath and a walk-in closet resides on the opposite side of the home. Nearby, two additional family bedrooms share a full bath between them. The basement level includes a playroom, recreation room and unfinished storage area.

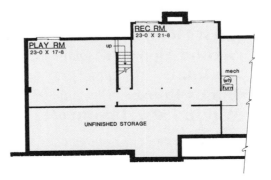

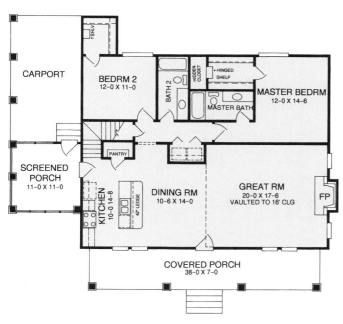

This rustic Craftsman-style cottage provides an open interior with good outdoor flow. The front covered porch invites casual gatherings, while inside, the dining area is set for both everyday and planned occasions. Meal preparations are a breeze with a cooktop/snack-bar island in the kitchen. A centered fireplace in the great room shares its warmth with the dining room. A rear hall leads to the master bedroom and a secondary bedroom, while upstairs, a loft has space for computers.

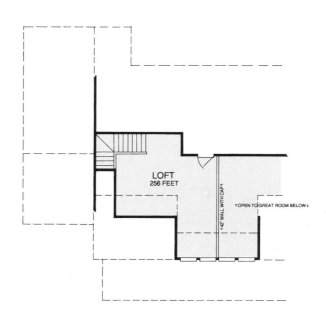

Plan HPT700254

Square Footage: *1,404*
Bonus Room: *256 square feet*
Width: *54'-7"* **Depth:** *46'-6"*

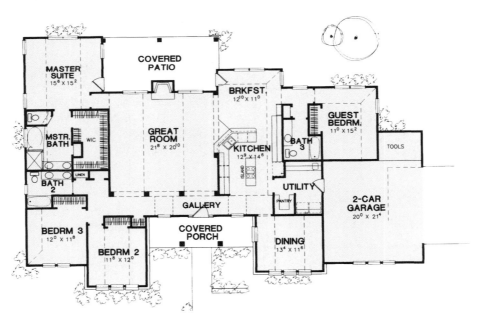

Plan HPT700255

Square Footage: *2,541*
Width: *81'-0"* **Depth:** *54'-0"*

This alluring Craftsman home includes decorative stone detailing, noble pillars and enchanting windows. The covered porch leads into the gallery, and just through the pillars is the great room, where the focal point falls on the fireplace. The kitchen features an island and a snack bar with a breakfast nook nearby. Easy access to the covered rear patio is made through the nook. A guest bedroom is located away from the family sleeping quarters for privacy. Two family bedrooms and a master suite comprise the left side of the plan. Please specify basement, slab or crawlspace foundation when ordering.

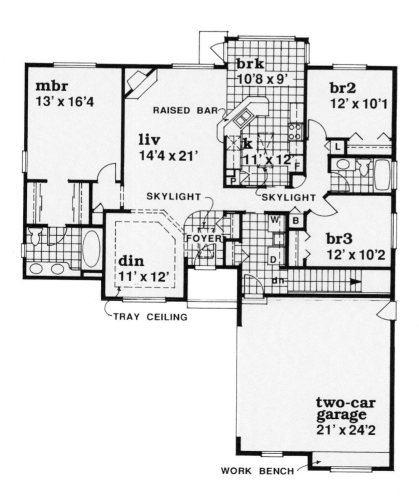

mbr
13' x 16'4

RAISED BAR

liv
14'4 x 21'

SKYLIGHT

din
11' x 12'

FOYER

TRAY CEILING

brk
10'8 x 9'

k
11' x 12'

SKYLIGHT

br2
12' x 10'1

L

W   B

D

br3
12' x 10'2

dn

two-car
garage
21' x 24'2

WORK BENCH

Plan HPT700256

Square Footage: *1,734*
Width: *52'-0"* **Depth:** *62'-0"*

Fish-scale siding, shutters and window boxes provide a charming exterior for this quaint three-bedroom ranch house. The skylit foyer opens to the formal dining room—an elegant atmosphere for entertaining. Adjoining the dining room, the living room boasts a cozy corner fireplace. The gourmet kitchen features a skylit raised eating bar for quick meals and opens to the breakfast area. The master suite offers a dual wardrobe, a dressing area and a bath with a double vanity. Two additional bedrooms cluster around a three-piece bath that features a soaking tub.

273

© Design Traditions

Plan HPT700257

Square Footage: *2,648*
Width: *66'-6"* **Depth:** *62'-0"*

With brick and siding, a hipped roofline, a covered porch accented by columns, and two fireplaces, this three-bedroom home is a perfect example of Old World class. Inside, the foyer is flanked by a formal dining room and a cozy study. Directly ahead is the family room, complete with a fireplace, built-ins and French doors to the rear deck. Nearby, the elegant kitchen is full of amenities, including a snack bar, a pantry and the adjacent bayed breakfast area. Sleeping quarters consist of two family bedrooms that share a bath, and a deluxe master suite. This home is designed with a walkout basement foundation.

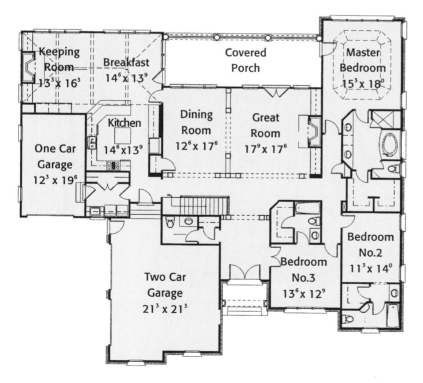

Keeping Room 13³ x 16³

Breakfast 14⁶ x 13⁹

Covered Porch

Master Bedroom 15³ x 18⁰

Dining Room 12⁶ x 17⁶

Great Room 17⁹ x 17⁶

Kitchen 14⁶ x 13⁹

One Car Garage 12³ x 19⁶

Two Car Garage 21³ x 21³

Bedroom No.3 13⁶ x 12⁹

Bedroom No.2 11³ x 14⁰

Plan HPT700258

Square Footage: *2,973*
Width: *75'-0"* **Depth:** *70'-0"*

This home has a rather unique floor plan—and for those who like to entertain in style, it works well. Enter through double doors and find a bedroom or study immediately to the right. Walk through columns straight ahead to find a large, open area, defined by more columns, that holds the formal dining room and the great room (a fireplace and built-in bookshelves are amenities here). Views here are stunning, past the covered porch and on to the backyard. The kitchen separates this area from the breakfast nook and keeping room—perfect for more casual pursuits. Each bedroom has a private bath and a walk-in closet. The master suite provides porch access and a lovely tray ceiling. Notice the two separate garages— one a two-car garage and the other a one-car garage. This home is designed with a walkout basement foundation.

Plan HPT700259

Square Footage: *1,920*
Width: *38'-10"* **Depth:** *74'-4"*

The entry courtyard creates an impressive introduction to this lovely European-style home. Double doors lead to the foyer, which opens through decorative columns to the formal dining room. A view of the enchanting rear garden and fountain enhances the heart of the home and invites guests to linger. Casual living space includes a breakfast nook with a view of the rear courtyard, and a family room with a fireplace and access to a private porch. A secluded master bedroom offers a whirlpool tub.

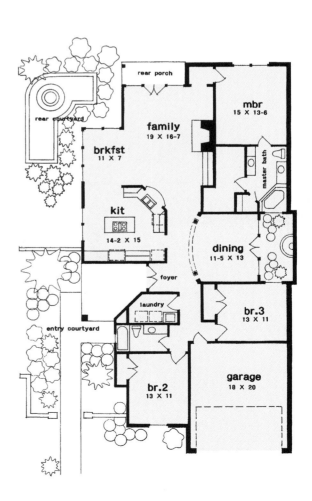

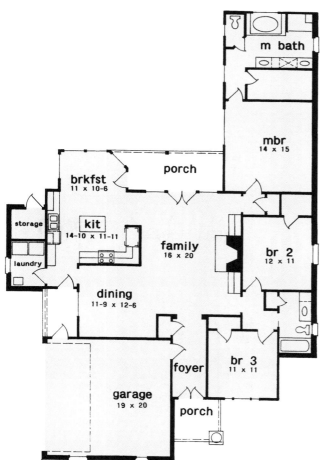

Plan HPT700260

Square Footage: *1,804*
Width: *49'-10"* **Depth:** *74'-9"*

Heavy European influences bring warmth and charm to this lovely cottage home. The family room—with an elaborate fireplace and built-ins—along with the dining room, is the heart of this home. Entertaining will be a snap with the convenience and efficiency of the well-equipped and easily accessible kitchen. An alternate to the formal dining room, the sunny breakfast area allows for more casual dining. A rear porch is accessed via the breakfast area and the family room. An exquisite master suite and two bedrooms with a shared bath complete the living spaces.

Plan HPT700261

Square Footage: *2,396*
Width: *72'-0"* **Depth:** *62'-0"*

Long and low, but sporting a high roofline, this one-story plan offers the best in family livability. The recessed entry opens to an entry hall that leads to a spacious living area with a fireplace. An angled eating area is close by and connects to the galley-style kitchen. The formal dining area also connects to the kitchen, yet retains access to the entry hall for convenience. Family bedrooms reside to the left of the plan and share a full bath. The master suite boasts private patio access and a fine bath. Note the large storage area in the garage. Please specify basement, crawlspace or slab foundation when ordering.

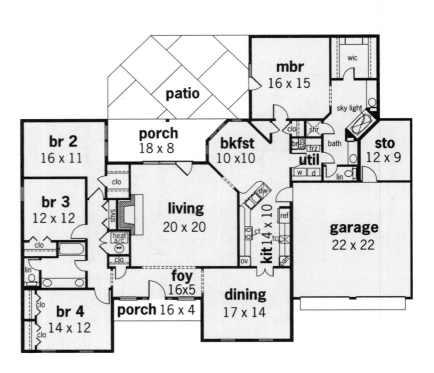

Plan HPT700262

Square Footage: *1,848*
Width: *58'-0"* **Depth:** *59'-6"*

With glorious amenities all on one level, this cozy Victorian home includes two porches and formal and informal living spaces. Beyond the gingerbread-adorned front porch is a vaulted foyer that's open to the formal living and dining rooms. At the heart of the home, casual living space provides a built-in entertainment center. Two family bedrooms to the left of the plan share a bath that's also accessed from the porch. On the opposite side of the plan, the master suite provides a spacious bath and access to the rear porch through lovely French doors.

279

Plan HPT700263

Square Footage: *2,502*
Width: *70'-0"* **Depth:** *72'-0"*

Cottage quaintness and Victorian accents lend a timeless style to this family design. The covered front entry porch welcomes you inside to a foyer open to a combined living room/ dining area, defined by columns. Two sets of double doors open onto the expansive rear porch. The kitchen, open to the dining room, features an island workstation and a casual breakfast nook. Two family bedrooms share a hall bath with the quiet office/study. The master suite provides private access to the rear porch, His and Hers walk-in closets and a spacious bath. Please specify basement or crawlspace foundation when ordering.

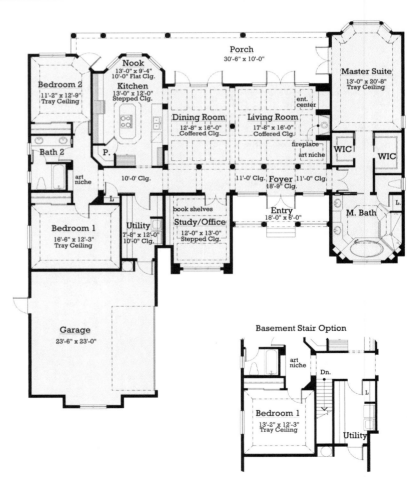

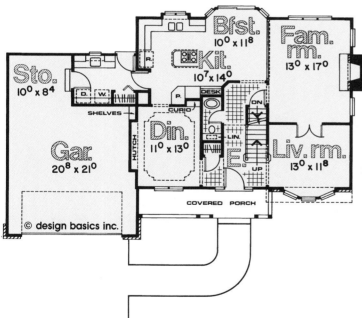

© design basics inc.

Sto.
10⁰ x 8⁴

Gar.
20⁸ x 21⁰

SHELVES

D. W.

HUTCH

Bfst.
10⁰ x 11⁸

Kit.
10⁷ x 14⁰

Fam. rm.
13⁰ x 17⁰

DESK

CURIO

Din.
11⁰ x 13⁰

LIN.

DN

UP

Liv. rm.
13⁰ x 11⁸

COVERED PORCH

Plan HPT700264

First Floor: *1,093 square feet*
Second Floor: *1,038 square feet*
Total: *2,131 square feet*
Width: *55'-4"* **Depth:** *37'-8"*

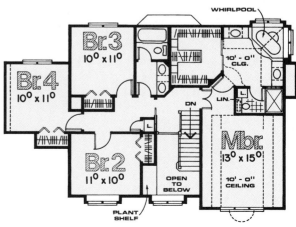

Br.3
10⁰ x 11⁰

Br.4
10⁰ x 11⁰

WHIRLPOOL

10'-0" CLG.

LIN.

DN

Mbr.
13⁰ x 15⁰

10'-0" CEILING

Br.2
11⁰ x 10⁰

OPEN TO BELOW

PLANT SHELF

Bay windows, French doors and a fireplace are just some of the amenities offered in this delightful family plan. A covered front porch offers a warm welcome, while the two-story foyer provides a grand entry to a comfortable interior. The formal dining room has a built-in hutch and a curio cabinet and enjoys a patterned tray ceiling. A bay window highlights the formal living room, and double French doors lead to the spacious family area, which includes a fireplace. Upstairs, the sumptuous master suite features a walk-in closet, a whirlpool tub and ten-foot ceilings.

Plan HPT700265

Square Footage: *2,590*
Width: *73'-6"* **Depth:** *64'-10"*

With a solid exterior of rough cedar and stone, this new French country design will stand the test of time. A wood-paneled study on the front features a large bay window. The heart of the house is found in a large, open great room with a built-in entertainment center. The spacious master bedroom features a corner reading area and access to an adjacent covered patio. A three-car garage and three additional bedrooms complete this generous family home.

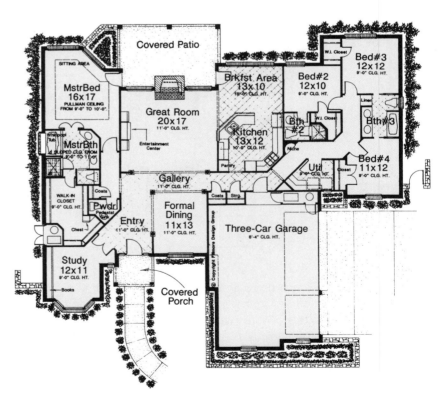

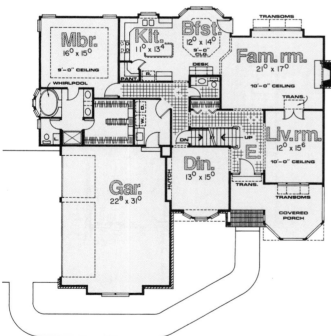

G ables with vergeboard details lend a Victorian charm to this two-story home. The formal dining room to the left of the foyer offers a beautiful bay window, a built-in hutch and access to the island kitchen. The living room, to the right of the foyer, adjoins the family room where a fireplace creates a warm atmosphere. The breakfast area enjoys a sunny bay window and a tray ceiling. The second floor holds three family bedrooms while the master suite finds privacy on the first floor. The three-car garage is accessed through the utility room near the kitchen.

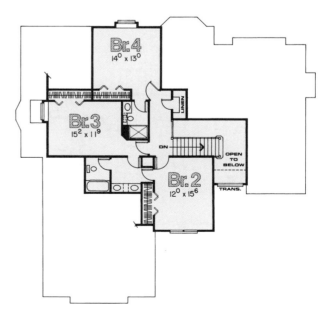

Plan HPT700266

First Floor: *1,953 square feet*
Second Floor: *936 square feet*
Total: *2,889 square feet*
Width: *59'-4"* **Depth:** *61'-4"*

Plan HPT700267

First Floor: *1,010 square feet*
Second Floor: *794 square feet*
Total: *1,804 square feet*
Width: *47'-0"* **Depth:** *51'-6"*

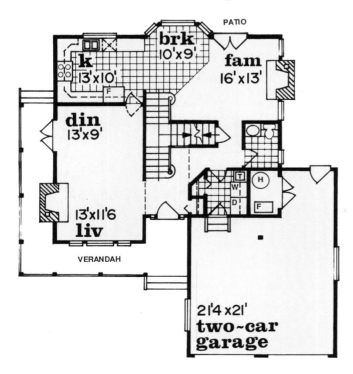

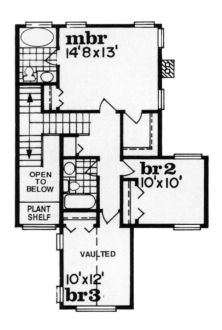

This three-bedroom home possesses a contemporary country charm. The covered veranda provides access from the formal dining room through lovely French doors. The U-shaped kitchen serves the dining room through a privacy door and opens to the breakfast area—a stunning space brightened by a bay window. A dual-access staircase leads from the kitchen and foyer to the second-floor bedrooms. The master suite boasts a walk-in closet and a three-piece ensuite with a whirlpool tub.

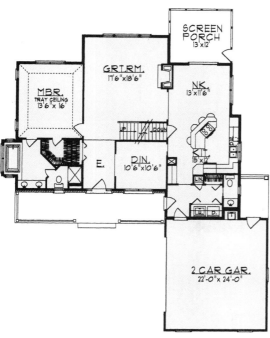

Plan HPT700268

First Floor: *1,563 square feet*
Second Floor: *592 square feet*
Total: *2,155 square feet*
Width: *57'-0"* **Depth:** *70'-0"*

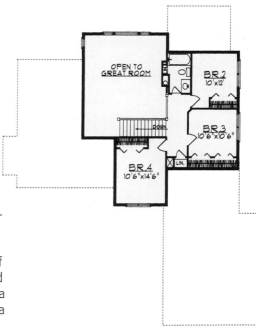

This updated Colonial Revival home has a definite Cape Cod influence while offering a covered front porch as well as a screened porch in the rear. The staircase separates the formal dining room from the two-story great room that boasts a fireplace and a wall of windows. The angled kitchen adjoins the nook that opens to the screened porch. The master suite provides a tray ceiling, a walk-in closet and a lavish bath. Upstairs, three additional bedrooms share a full bath and a gallery overlook to the great room.

Plan HPT700269

First Floor: *1,687 square feet*
Second Floor: *745 square feet*
Total: *2,432 square feet*
Width: *56'-0"* **Depth:** *66'-0"*

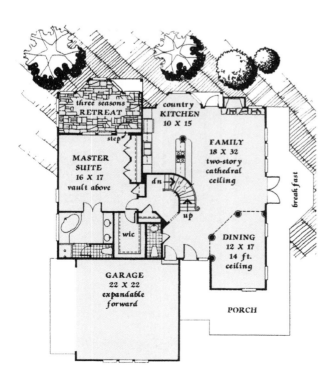

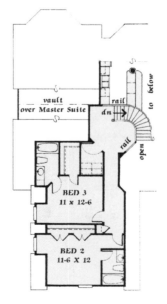

Unique gambrel roof styling and a delicate pinnacle make this home easy to enjoy. Circular windows allow light to roll in. The two-story cathedral ceiling highlights the absolute elegance of the family room. The wraparound porch accesses the family room from the right. Attached to the master suite is a three-seasons retreat. The large country kitchen makes a great cooking atmosphere. Gently winding stairs lead to the second floor where Bedrooms 2 and 3 overlook the foyer and the dining room.

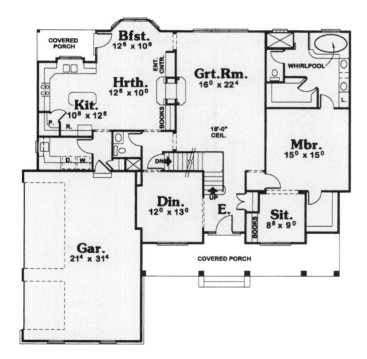

Plan HPT700270

First Floor: *1,955 square feet*
Second Floor: *660 square feet*
Total: *2,615 square feet*
Width: *60'-0"* **Depth:** *60'-4"*

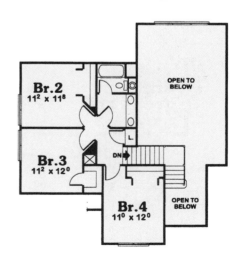

M ultiple gables, shuttered windows and a covered front porch define the exterior of this farmhouse. The great room shares a through-fireplace with the hearth room, which offers a built-in entertainment center and bookshelves. A nearby breakfast bay opens to a small covered porch. The island kitchen boasts a walk-in pantry and easy access to the formal dining room. The master suite provides a sitting room with built-in bookshelves, a large walk-in closet and an opulent bath with a whirlpool tub and double vanities. Please specify basement or block foundation when ordering.

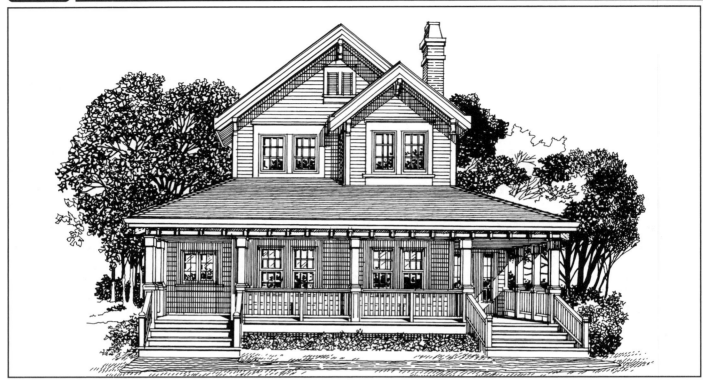

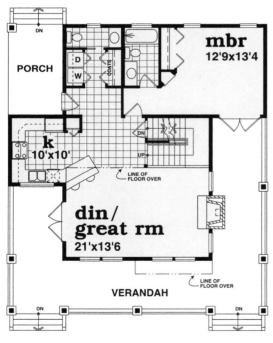

PORCH

D
W

mbr
12'9x13'4

k
10'x10'

DN
UP

LINE OF
FLOOR OVER

din/
great rm
21'x13'6

LINE OF
FLOOR OVER

VERANDAH

DN

QUOTE ONE®

Cost to build? See page 436
to order complete cost estimate
to build this house in your area!

br3
10'4x10'2

br2
10'4x11'2

DN

RAILING

OPEN TO
GREAT ROOM
BELOW

PLANT LEDGE

Plan HPT700271

First Floor: *995 square feet*
Second Floor: *484 square feet*
Total: *1,479 square feet*
Width: *38'-0"* **Depth:** *44'-0"*

What an appealing plan! Its rustic character is defined by cedar lattice, covered columned porches, exposed rafters and multi-pane, double-hung windows. The great room/dining room combination is reached through double doors off the veranda and features a fireplace towering two stories to the lofty ceiling. A U-shaped kitchen contains an angled snack counter that serves this area and loads of space for a breakfast table—or use the handy side porch for alfresco dining. To the rear resides the master bedroom with a full bath and double doors to the veranda. An additional half-bath sits just beyond the laundry room. Upstairs, two family bedrooms and a full bath finish the plan.

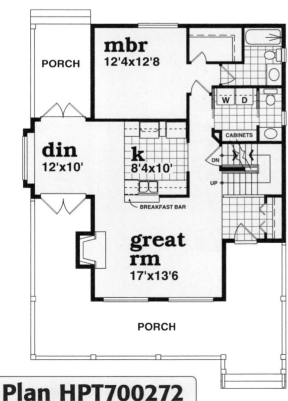

PORCH

mbr
12'4x12'8

W D

CABINETS

din
12'10'

k
8'4x10'

DN

UP

BREAKFAST BAR

great rm
17'x13'6

PORCH

br2
12'4x12'8

br3
10'x10'
OR OPTIONAL LOFT

DN

3'6 RAILING

OPEN TO BELOW

QUOTE ONE®

Cost to build? See page 436
to order complete cost estimate
to build this house in your area!

Plan HPT700272

First Floor: *1,012 square feet*
Second Floor: *556 square feet*
Total: *1,568 square feet*
Width: *34'-0"* **Depth:** *48'-0"*

Country comes home to this plan with details such as a metal roof, horizontal siding, multi-pane double-hung windows, and front and rear porches. The recessed front entry leads to the great room, flanked by a breakfast bar and formal dining room with access to both the front and rear porches. The great room is warmed by a fireplace and features a two-story ceiling. The master suite has a private bath and walk-in closet.

Plan HPT700273

First Floor: *1,493 square feet*
Second Floor: *723 square feet*
Total: *2,216 square feet*
Width: *70'-0"* **Depth:** *55'-8"*

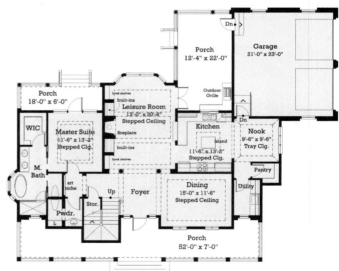

Bask in the glow of the moon from a private deck in either of two upstairs bedrooms in this lovely home. A spacious loft with computer space overlooks the leisure room, which provides access to the rear porch. This casual living space promotes an inviting atmosphere, with a cozy fireplace, a sitting bay and French doors to the outside. The sumptuous master suite features a walk-in closet, dual-sink vanity, a bay-window whirlpool tub and an oversized shower. A stepped ceiling sets off the bedroom and complements the natural light coming from a dual-sidelight French door that leads out to the rear porch. Please specify basement or crawlspace foundation when ordering.

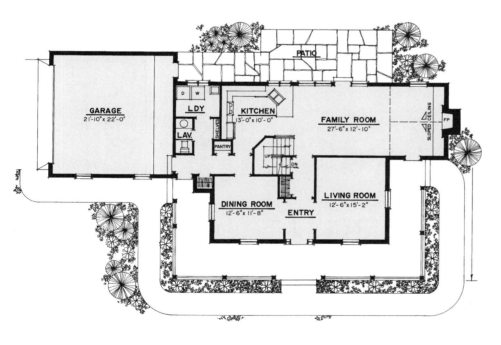

Plan HPT700274

First Floor: *1,229 square feet*
Second Floor: *939 square feet*
Total: *2,168 square feet*
Width: 74'-4" **Depth:** 41'-4"

This symmetrical facade features windows trimmed with rustic wooden shutters. Sidelights flank the paneled front door and fish-scale shingles surround the pedimented gable's mullioned fanlight. The dining room and living room stand on either side of the entrance. The large country kitchen provides plenty of counter space and opens to the family room, which includes a vaulted ceiling, a hearth fireplace and access to the rear patio. A powder room and laundry room complete the first floor. Upstairs, the master bedroom enjoys an opulent compartmented bath that offers a whirlpool tub, dual vanities and a separate shower.

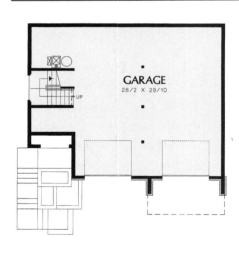

GARAGE
28/2 X 29/10

OPT. FR. DRS

DINING
10/6 X 12/0+

15/0 X 9/0

NOOK
13/10 X 8/4

2 STORY
LIVING
13/0 X 14/0

FAMILY
13/10 X 20/8

DECK

BR. 3
11/0 X 10/8

BR. 2
11/0 X 10/0

LOFT

DN

FOYER
BELOW

LIVING
BELOW

VAULTED
MASTER
15/2 X 12/0

Plan HPT700275

Main Level: *1,106 square feet*
Upper Level: *872 square feet*
Total: *1,978 square feet*
Width: *38'-0"* **Depth:** *35'-0"*

Though this home gives the impression of the Northwest, it will be the winner of any neighborhood. Craftsman style is evident both on the outside and the inside of this three-bedroom home. From the foyer, the two-story living room is just a couple of steps up and features a through-fireplace. The U-shaped kitchen has a cooktop work island, an adjacent nook and easy access to the formal dining room. A spacious family room shares the fireplace with the living room, is enhanced by built-ins and also offers a quiet deck for stargazing. The upstairs consists of two family bedrooms sharing a full bath and a vaulted master suite complete with a walk-in closet and sumptuous bath. Please specify basement or slab foundation when ordering.

Plan HPT700427

First Floor: *784 square feet*
Second Floor: *672 square feet*
Total: *1,456 square feet*
Width: *24'-0"* **Depth:** *34'-0"*

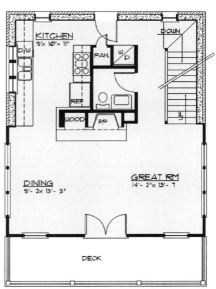

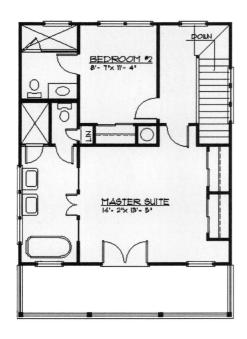

Here's a rustic retreat with a heart of gold: a upper-level master suite with plenty of outdoor views. French doors open this lovely homeowner's retreat to a private deck, while tall windows allow fresh breezes within. A spacious bath includes a garden tub, a dual vanity, an oversized shower and a compartmented toilet. The gallery hall leads to a secondary bedroom suite and to a side staircase which leads down to the living space. The main level is carefully positioned to take full advantage of mountain views. Triple windows frame the open space shared by the great room and dining room, while French doors lead to a deck.

Plan HPT700276

First Floor: *1,269 square feet*
Second Floor: *880 square feet*
Total: *2,149 square feet*
Width: *34'-4"* **Depth:** *54'-4"*

This two-story home offers a grand view through a wall of windows in both the first- and second-floor bedrooms. On the first floor, the bedroom/study includes a walk-in closet and a nearby full bath. The formal dining room is defined by columns, while the great room is open to the kitchen. The second floor holds two bedrooms—one is a master bedroom with a walk-in closet and a private bath, and the second is a family bedroom, also with a private bath.

© 1997 Donald A Gardner Architects, Inc.

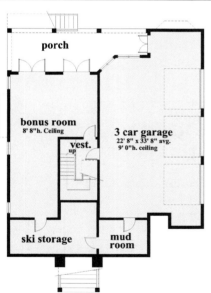

porch

bonus room
8' 8"h. Ceiling

vest.
up

3 car garage
22' 8" x 33' 8" avg.
9' 0"h. ceiling

ski storage

mud room

dn.

porch

window seat

built-in cabinetry

great room
19' 6" x 19' 0"
2-story ceiling
fireplace

nook
11' 0" x 8' 0"
9' 4" clg.

bedroom 3
11' 8" x 12' 4"
9' 4". clg.

kitchen

linen

ut.

up

up

study
11' 0" x 13' 6"
14' 0"h. clg.

foyer

dining
11' 0" x 13' 6"
14' 0"h. clg.

bedroom 2
11' 8" x 10' 6"
9' 4". clg.

entry porch
32' 0" x 8' 6"
14' 0"h. ceiling
dn.

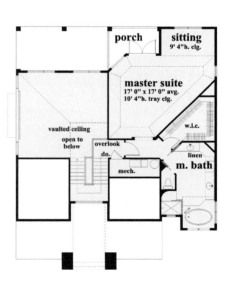

porch

sitting
9' 4"h. clg.

master suite
17' 0" x 17' 0" avg.
10' 4"h. tray clg.

vaulted ceiling

open to below

overlook

dn.

mech.

w.i.c.

linen

m. bath

Plan HPT700277

First Floor: *1,671 square feet*
Second Floor: *846 square feet*
Total: *2,517 square feet*
Lower–Level Entry: *140 square feet*
Width: *44'-0"* **Depth:** *55'-0"*

An array of elegant details creates a welcoming entry to this new-century home, with massive stone pillars, a matchstick pediment and a stunning turret. The main-level foyer leads up to the spacious living area and down to the lower-level bonus room, which boasts a covered porch, ski storage, mudroom and three-car garage. On the main level, a vaulted ceiling highlights the great room, and a fireplace warms the open interior. French doors bring in a feeling of nature and provide access to the rear covered porch. Secondary sleeping quarters reside to the right of the plan, connected by a gallery hall that offers a full bath.

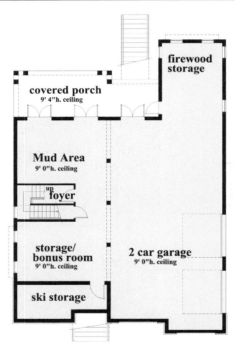

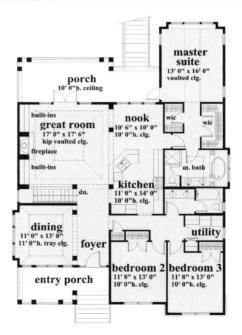

Plan HPT700278

Square Footage: *2,137*
Width: *44'-0"* **Depth:** *63'-0"*

The horizontal lines and straightforward details of this rustic plan borrow freely from the Arts and Crafts style, with a dash of traditional warmth. At the heart of the home, the kitchen and nook bring people together for easy meals and conversation. Clustered sleeping quarters ramble across the right wing and achieve privacy and convenience for the homeowners. The master suite is all decked out with a wall of glass, two walk-in closets and generous dressing space. On the lower level, a mud area leads in from a covered porch, and the two-car garage leaves plenty of room for bicycles.

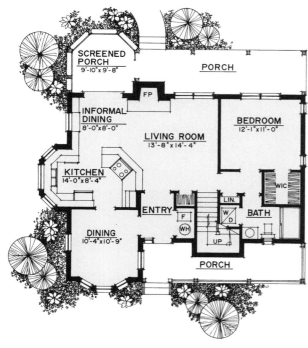

SCREENED PORCH
9'-10"x 9'-8"

PORCH

INFORMAL DINING
8'-0"x8'-0"

FP

LIVING ROOM
13'-8"x14'-4"

BEDROOM
12'-1"x11'-0"

KITCHEN
14'-0"x8'-4"

WIC

ENTRY

LIN.

F

W D

BATH

WH

DINING
10'-4"x10'-9"

UP

PORCH

Plan HPT700279

First Floor: 949 square feet
Second Floor: 633 square feet
Total: 1,582 square feet
Width: 40'-3" **Depth:** 40'-6"

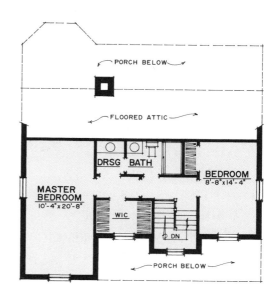

PORCH BELOW

FLOORED ATTIC

DRSG BATH

BEDROOM
8'-8"x14'-4"

MASTER BEDROOM
10'-4"x20'-8"

WIC

DN

PORCH BELOW

Front and rear porches and bay windows lend this three-bedroom home Victorian flavor. Inside, the entry leads to the living room and the formal dining room, which boasts a bay window. The kitchen adjoins the informal dining area as well as the formal dining room and overlooks the living room. On the right of the first floor is a bedroom with a walk-in closet and full bath. Upstairs, a family bedroom and the master bedroom share a full bath.

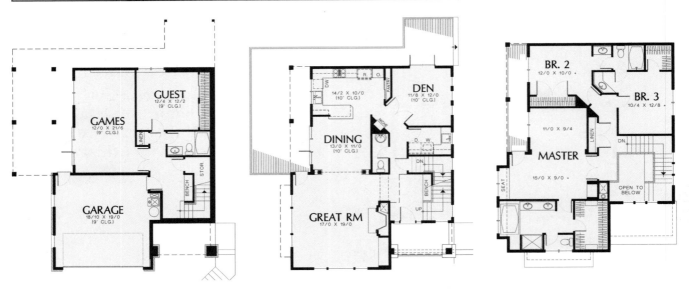

Plan HPT700280

First Floor: *1,158 square feet*
Second Floor: *1,038 square feet*
Total: *2,196 square feet*
Finished Basement: *760 square feet*
Width: *34'-6"* **Depth:** *42'-0"*

Craftsman detailing adorns the exterior of this fine hillside home. Its cozy nature includes horizontal and shingle siding and a covered porch at the entry with a wide-based column. The great room is warmed by a hearth surrounded by built-ins. Columns define the dining room, which separates the great room and the U-shaped kitchen. A wide deck at the side of the home is accessed through the dining room or the great room. A cozy den sits at the back of this level and has double doors to the rear portion of the deck. Three bedrooms on the upper level include two family bedrooms with a shared full bath, and a master bedroom with a sitting area, private bath and walk-in closet.

HOLZHALIER INC.

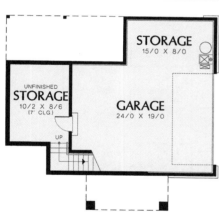

STORAGE
15/0 X 8/0

UNFINISHED
STORAGE
10/2 X 8/6
(7' CLG.)

GARAGE
24/0 X 19/0

UP

9/0 X 14/0

LIVING
15/0 X 17/8 +/-
(10' CLG.)

DINING
13/4 X 15/4 +/-
(10' CLG.)

UP

DN

BUILT-IN

STORAGE

D | W

MASTER
15/0 X 13/0

BR. 3
10/2 X 11/10

LINEN

DN

BR. 2.
10/0 X 11/4

Plan HPT700281

First Floor: *813 square feet*
Second Floor: *726 square feet*
Total: *1,539 square feet*
Width: *36'-0"* **Depth:** *34'-0"*

Wood siding, both vertical and horizontal, works to bring a Craftsman flavor to the exterior of this home. Its wonderful plan has two large storage areas at the garage level. The first floor includes a living room and dining room that are open to one another and to the L-shaped island kitchen. A corner fireplace in the living room and deck access in the dining room are special accents. A half-bath at the entry sits in front of the laundry and a storage closet. The second floor is devoted to bedrooms: the master suite with a private bath and two family bedrooms sharing a full bath.

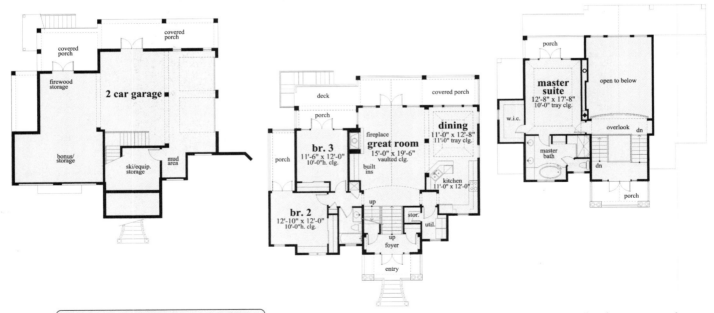

Plan HPT700282

First Floor: *1,383 square feet*
Second Floor: *595 square feet*
Total: *1,978 square feet*
Width: *48'-0"* **Depth:** *48'-8"*

The stone facade and woodwork detail give this home a Craftsman appeal. The foyer opens to a staircase up to the vaulted great room, which features a fireplace flanked by built-ins and French-door access to the rear covered porch. The open dining room with a tray ceiling offers convenience to the spacious kitchen. Two family bedrooms share a bath and enjoy private porches. An overlook to the great room below is a perfect introduction to the master suite. The second level spreads out master-suite luxury with a spacious walk-in closet, private porch and a glorious master bath with a garden tub, dual vanities and compartmented toilet.

Waves

cottages and seaside houses

Plan HPT700283

Square Footage: *1,792*
Width: *32'-0"* **Depth:** *82'-0"*

A blend of Southern comfort and Gulf Coast style sets this home apart. Inside, decorative arches and columns mark the grand entrance to the living and dining areas, while the gourmet kitchen provides a pass-through to the dining room. On cold nights, a fireplace warms the great room, and on warm evenings, French doors to the covered porch let in cool breezes. At the rear of the plan, the master suite privately accesses a sun deck, and French doors open to the covered porch. Two walk-in closets, a garden tub and a bayed sitting area add to the comfort of this suite.

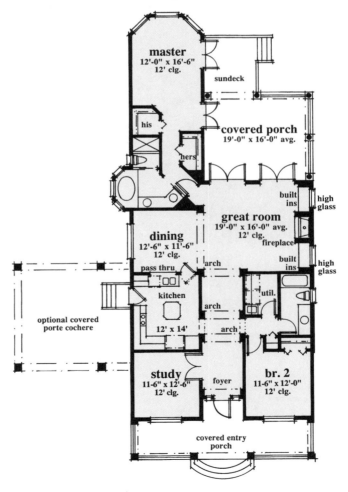

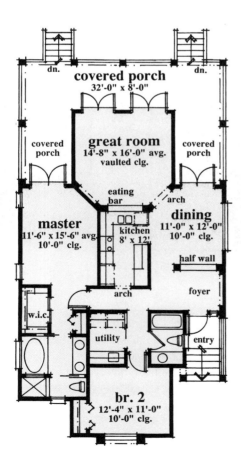

covered porch
32'-0" x 8'-0"

dn.

dn.

covered porch

great room
14'-8" x 16'-0" avg.
vaulted clg.

covered porch

eating
bar

arch

master
11'-6" x 15'-6" avg.
10'-0" clg.

kitchen
8' x 12'

dining
11'-0" x 12'-0"
10'-0" clg.

half wall

foyer

w.i.c.

arch

utility

entry

br. 2
12'-4" x 11'-0"
10'-0" clg.

Plan HPT700284

Square Footage: *1,288*
Width: *32'-4"* **Depth:** *60'-0"*

Welcome home to casual, unstuffy living with this comfortable Tidewater design. Asymmetrical lines celebrate the turn of the new century and blend a current Gulf Coast style with vintage panache brought forward from its regional past. The heart of this home is the great room, where a put-your-feet-up atmosphere prevails, and the dusky hues of sunset can mingle with the sounds of ocean breakers. French doors open the master suite to a private area of the covered porch, where sunlight and sea breezes mingle with a spirit of *bon vivant*.

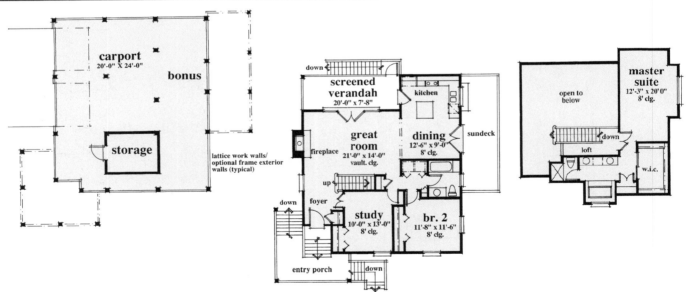

Plan HPT700285

First Floor: *1,136 square feet*
Second Floor: *636 square feet*
Total: *1,772 square feet*
Width: *41'-9"* **Depth:** *45'-0"*

This two-story home's pleasing exterior is complemented by its warm character and decorative "widow's walk." The covered entry—with its dramatic transom window—leads to a spacious great room highlighted by a warming fireplace. To the right, the dining room and kitchen combine to provide a delightful place for mealtimes, with access to a side sun deck through double doors. Two bedrooms and a full bath complete the first floor. The luxurious master suite on the second floor features an oversized walk-in closet and a separate dressing area. The pampering master bath enjoys a relaxing whirlpool tub, double-bowl vanity and compartmented toilet. Please specify slab or pier foundation when ordering.

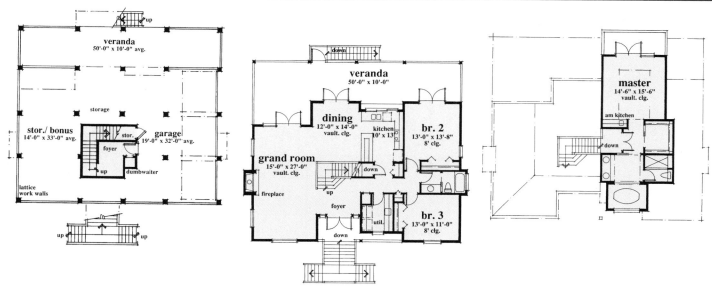

Plan HPT700286

First Floor: *1,586 square feet*
Second Floor: *601 square feet*
Total: *2,187 square feet*
Width: *50'-0"* **Depth:** *44'-0"*

Lattice walls, pickets and horizontal siding complement a relaxed Key West design that's perfect for waterfront properties. The grand room with a fireplace, the dining room and Bedroom 2 open through French doors to the veranda. The master suite occupies the entire second floor and features access to a private balcony through double doors. This pampering suite also includes a spacious walk-in closet and a full bath with a whirlpool tub. Enclosed storage/bonus space and a garage are on the lower level. This home is designed with a pier foundation.

Quote One®

Cost to build? See page 436
to order complete cost estimate
to build this house in your area!

Plan HPT700287

Square Footage: *2,190*
Width: *58'-0"* **Depth:** *54'-0"*

A dramatic set of stairs leads to the entry of this home. The foyer opens to an expansive grand room with a fireplace and built-in bookshelves. For formal meals, a front-facing dining room offers plenty of space and a bumped-out bay. The kitchen serves this area easily as well as the breakfast nook. A study and three bedrooms make up the rest of the floor plan. Two secondary bedrooms share a full bath.

Plan HPT700288

First Floor: *1,798 square feet*
Second Floor: *900 square feet*
Total: *2,698 square feet*
Width: *54'-0"* **Depth:** *57'-0"*

First floor plan labels:
master suite 14' 0" x 15' 0" 11' 4"h. ceiling
veranda
w.i.c.
w.i.c.
great room 22' 0" x 13' 0" 2-story ceiling
built-in cabinetry
2-sided fireplace
dining 13' 6" x 13' 6" 10' 0"h. clg.
up
study 12' 0" x 13' 0" 10' 0"h. clg.
foyer
kitchen 12' 0" x 13' 0" 10' 0"h. clg.
ut.
dn.
dn.
entry porch

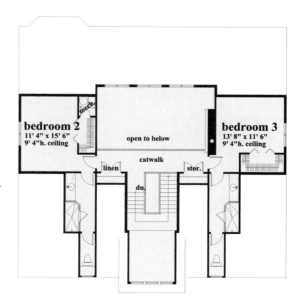

Second floor plan labels:
bedroom 2 11' 4" x 15' 6" 9' 4" ceiling
mech.
open to below
bedroom 3 13' 8" x 11' 6" 9' 4" ceiling
linen
catwalk
stor.
dn.

Symmetry is the key to the appeal of this adorable coastal cottage. A two-story ceiling allows for a dramatic upper-level catwalk in the great room. Built-ins are partnered with a two-sided fireplace that is shared with the formal dining room. French doors in the great room open to the veranda. In the master bedroom, a tray ceiling and bay window add to the sense of spaciousness, while French doors open to the veranda. Each of the upper-level family suites has a walk-in closet and a roomy bath with an oversized shower.

Plan HPT700289

Square Footage: *2,555*
Width: *70'-2"* **Depth:** *53'-0"*

VERANDA
38'-6" x 12'-0"
10' CLG.

BALCONY
18'-8" x 9'-0"
16' CLG.

MASTER PORCH
13'-0" x 12'-0"
10' CLG.

NOOK
9'-0" x 8'-0"
10' CLG.

GUEST 2
11'-2" x 13'-4"
10' CLG.

DINING
10'-0" x 13'-6"
12' CLG.

GREAT ROOM
17'-8" x 21'-0"
16' CLG.

MASTER
12'-6" x 15'-6"
TRAY

KIT.
10'-8" x 14'-8"

12' CLG.

16' CLG.

W.I.C.

W.I.C.

GUEST 3
12'-8" x 11'-0"
10' CLG.

UTIL.

ENTRY

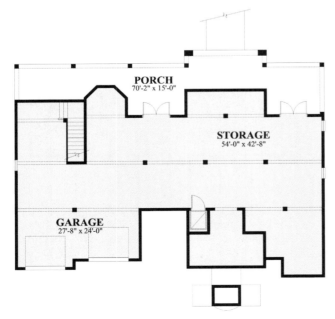

PORCH
70'-2" x 15'-0"

STORAGE
54'-0" x 42'-8"

GARAGE
27'-8" x 24'-0"

This design enjoys a mixture of shingle and siding, twin dormers and beautiful window detailing. High ceilings adorn most of the rooms in this plan, including the sixteen-foot entry hallway. The great room leads to a balcony and is flanked on the left by a spacious dining room. The island kitchen looks to a bayed breakfast nook, which opens to a rear veranda. The sleeping quarters are split, with the master suite on the right side and the family bedrooms on the left. The master suite boasts a tray ceiling, His and Hers walk-in closets, a garden tub, twin vanities, and porch.

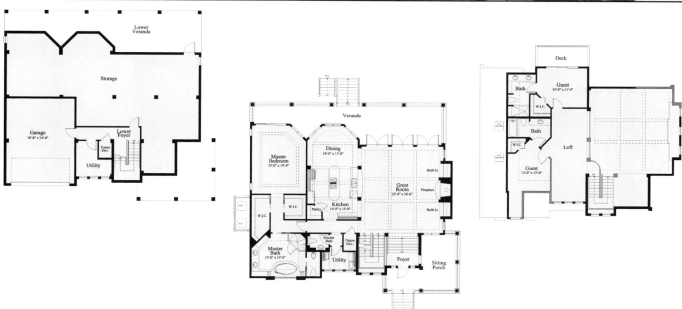

Plan HPT700290

First Floor: *2,096 square feet*
Second Floor: *892 square feet*
Total: *2,988 square feet*
Width: *58'-0"* **Depth:** *54'-0"*

The variety in the rooflines of this striking waterfront home will make it the envy of the neighborhood. The two-story great room, with its fireplace and built-ins, is a short flight down from the foyer. The three sets of French doors give access to the covered lanai. The huge and well-equipped kitchen will easily serve the gourmet who loves to entertain. The step ceiling and bay window of the dining room will add style to every meal. The master suite completes the first level. Two bedrooms and two full baths, along with an expansive loft, constitute the second level. Bedroom 3 has an attached sun deck.

Plan HPT700291

First Floor: *1,266 square feet*
Second Floor: *1,324 square feet*
Total: *2,590 square feet*
Width: *34'-0"* **Depth:** *63'-2"*

This Floridian-style home boasts an impressive balcony that is sure to catch the eye. A large veranda borders two sides of the home. The entry leads into a long foyer, which runs from the entrance to the rear of the design. The coffered great room enjoys a fireplace, built-in cabinetry and French doors to the veranda; the dining room also has this same ability. The island kitchen leads into a bayed nook, perfect for Sunday morning breakfast. The second floor is home to two family bedrooms, both with access to the deck, a study and a luxurious master suite. A vaulted sitting area, full bath and deck access are just some of the highlights of the master suite.

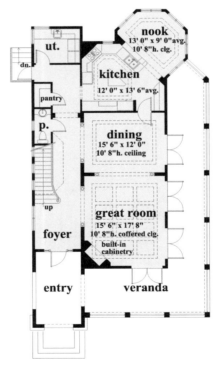

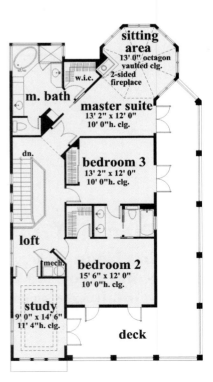

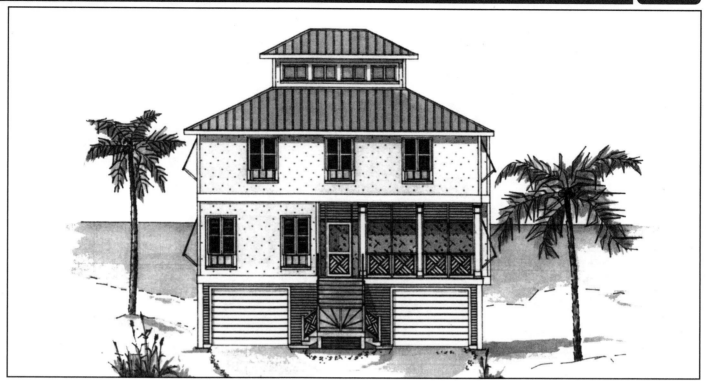

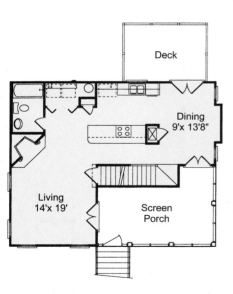

Deck

Dining
9'x 13'8"

Living
14'x 19'

Screen
Porch

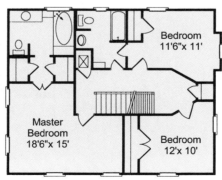

Master
Bedroom
18'6"x 15'

Bedroom
11'6"x 11'

Bedroom
12'x 10'

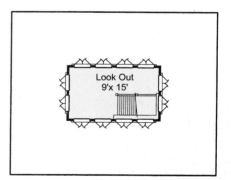

Look Out
9'x 15'

Plan HPT700292

First Floor: *731 square feet*
Second Floor: *935 square feet*
Total: *1,666 square feet*
Lookout: *138 square feet*
Width: *34'-0"* **Depth:** *38'-0"*

Perfect for a seaside abode, this pier-foundation home has an abundance of amenities to offer, not the least being the loft lookout. Here, with a 360-degree view, one can watch the storms come in over the water or gaze with wonder on the colors of the sea. Inside the home just off the screened porch, the living room is complete with a corner gas fireplace. The spacious kitchen features a cooktop island, an adjacent breakfast nook and easy access to the dining room. From this room, a set of French doors leads out to a small deck—perfect for dining *alfresco*. Upstairs, the sleeping zone consists of two family bedrooms sharing a full hall bath, and a deluxe master suite.

Plan HPT700293

First Floor: *1,073 square feet*
Second Floor: *470 square feet*
Total: *1,543 square feet*
Width: *30'-0"* **Depth:** *71'-6"*

Holding the narrowest of footprints, this adorable little plan is big on interior space—perfect for beachfront areas. The family room has three big windows and opens to the tiled U-shaped kitchen and breakfast nook, with access to the rear deck. The master bedroom, which includes a walk-in closet, and another bedroom share a full bath on this floor. Two more bedrooms and another bath are upstairs. Bedroom 4 features a study area in the dormer.

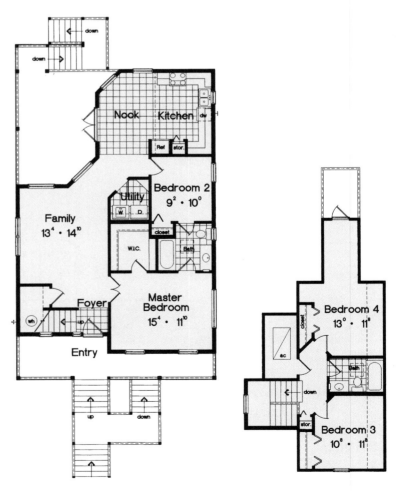

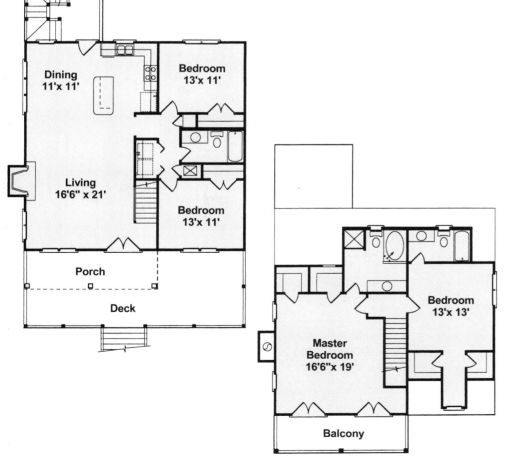

Dining
11'x 11'

Bedroom
13'x 11'

Living
16'6" x 21'

Bedroom
13'x 11'

Porch

Deck

Master
Bedroom
16'6"x 19'

Bedroom
13'x 13'

Balcony

Plan HPT700294

First Floor: *1,056 square feet*
Second Floor: *807 square feet*
Total: *1,863 square feet*
Width: *33'-0"* **Depth:** *54'-0"*

Run up a flight of stairs to an attractive four-bedroom home! With a traditional flavor, this fine pier design is sure to please. The living room features a fireplace and easy access to the L-shaped kitchen. Here, a work island makes meal preparation a breeze. Two family bedrooms share a full bath and access to the laundry facilities. Upstairs, a third bedroom offers a private bath. Please specify crawlspace or pier foundation when ordering.

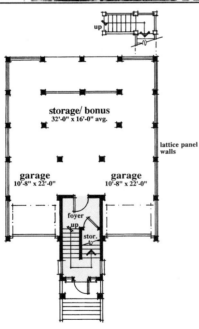

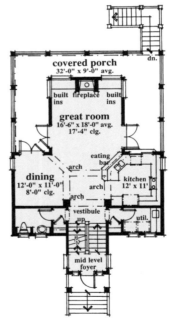

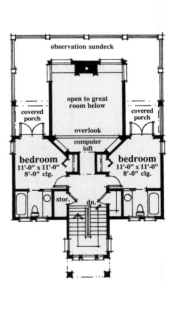

Plan HPT700295

First Floor: *942 square feet*
Second Floor: *571 square feet*
Total: *1,513 square feet*
Width: *32'-0"* **Depth:** *53'-0"*

The modest detailing of Greek Revival style gave rise to this grand home. A mid-level foyer eases the trip from ground level to the raised living area, while an arched vestibule announces the great room. The formal dining room offers French-door access to the covered porch. Built-ins, a fireplace and two ways to access the porch make the great room truly great. A well-appointed kitchen serves a casual eating bar as well as the dining room. Upstairs, each of two private suites has a windowed tub, a vanity and wardrobe space. A pair of French doors opens each of the bedrooms to an observation sun deck through covered porches. This home is designed with a pier foundation.

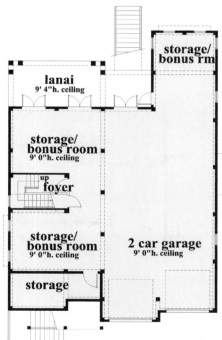

lanai
9' 4"h. ceiling

**storage/
bonus rm**

**storage/
bonus room**
9' 0"h. ceiling

up

foyer

**storage/
bonus room**
9' 0"h. ceiling

2 car garage
9' 0"h. ceiling

storage

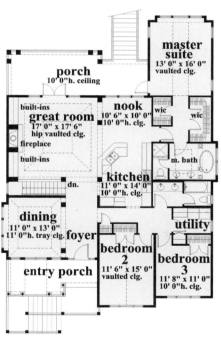

porch
10' 0"h. ceiling

**master
suite**
13' 0" x 16' 0"
vaulted clg.

built-ins

great room
17' 0" x 17' 6"
hip vaulted clg.

nook
10' 6" x 10' 0"
10' 0"h. clg.

wic

wic

fireplace

built-ins

m. bath

kitchen
11' 0" x 14' 0"
10' 0"h. clg.

dn.

dining
11' 0" x 13' 0"
11' 0"h. tray clg.

foyer

utility

**bedroom
2**
11' 6" x 15' 0"
vaulted clg.

**bedroom
3**
11' 8" x 11' 0"
10' 0"h. clg.

entry porch

Plan HPT700296

Square Footage: *2,136*
Width: *44'-0"* **Depth:** *63'-0"*

This raised Tidewater design is well suited for many building situations, with comfortable outdoor areas that encourage year-round living. A hip vaulted ceiling highlights the great room, made comfy by a centered fireplace, extensive built-ins and French doors that let in fresh air and sunlight. The formal dining room opens from the entry hall and features a triple-window view of the side property. Family members will gather in the morning nook or at the snack counter in the kitchen. The master suite features a sitting area with a wide window and a door to a private area of the rear porch. Each of two secondary bedrooms has a triple window.

With its wide windows and wraparound porch, this traditional design is ideal for a site with splendid views. Families will also enjoy special features designed with teenagers in mind. On the lower level, they will find their own bedroom and bathroom, access to a private patio and their own living area on the main floor—stairs are located in front of their rooms. Direct access to a shower from the backyard make this home perfect for outdoor pursuits. There are gorgeous views from the "parent" living room on the main floor and the master bedroom on the lower level.

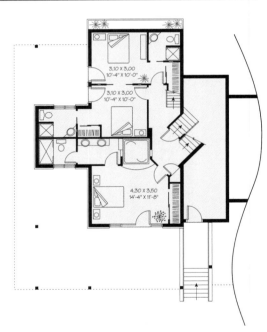

Plan HPT700297

Main Level: *1,099 square feet*
Lower Level: *822 square feet*
Total: *1,921 square feet*
Width: *60'-0"* **Depth:** *39'-0"*

Photo by Chris A. Little of Atlanta, courtesy of Chatham Home Planning, Inc.

This home, as shown in the photograph, may differ from the actual blueprints. For more detailed information, please check the floor plans carefully.

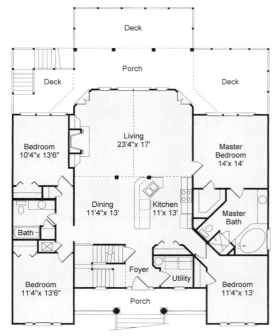

Plan HPT700298

Square Footage: *1,936*
Bonus Room: *448 square feet*
Width: *49'-0"* **Depth:** *62'-0"*

An enormous bay window fitted with French doors and wonderful views is the highlight of this four-bedroom waterfront home. A living room with a warming fireplace sits inside the bay, at the center of the home. The kitchen easily serves both the living room and dining area via a serving bar. Three family bedrooms share a full bath, while the master suite includes a walk-in closet and a bath with a soaking tub and separate shower.

Plan HPT700299

First Floor: *873 square feet*
Second Floor: *1,037 square feet*
Total: *1,910 square feet*
Width: *27'-6"* **Depth:** *64'-0"*

This efficient saltbox design includes three bedrooms and two full baths, plus a handy powder room on the first floor. A large great room at the front of the home features a fireplace. The rear of the home is left open, with space for the kitchen with a snack bar, the breakfast area with a fireplace, and the dining room with outdoor access. If you wish, use the breakfast area as an all-purpose dining room and turn the dining room into a library or sitting room. Upstairs, the vaulted master suite accesses its own private sun deck and a full bath, while two additional second-floor bedrooms share a full bath.

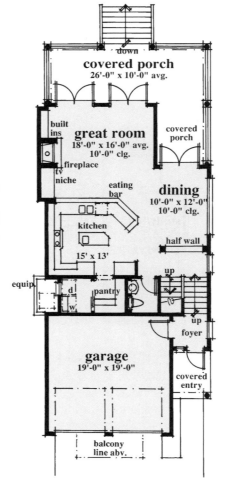

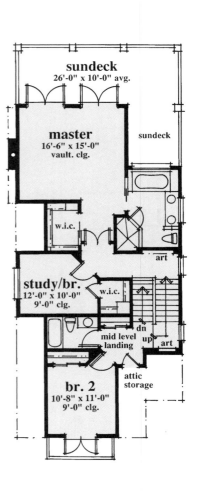

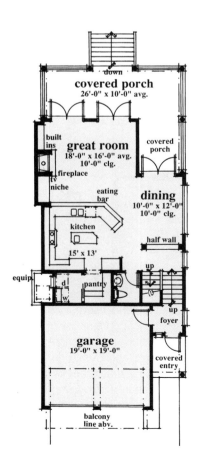

covered porch
26'-0" x 10'-0" avg.

down

built ins

great room
18'-0" x 16'-0" avg.
10'-0" clg.

covered porch

fireplace

tv niche

eating bar

dining
10'-0" x 12'-0"
10'-0" clg.

kitchen

15' x 13'

half wall

up

equip

pantry

up

foyer

garage
19'-0" x 19'-0"

covered entry

balcony line abv.

sundeck
26'-0" x 10'-0" avg.

master
16'-6" x 15'-0"
vault. clg.

sundeck

w.i.c.

art

study/br.
12'-0" x 10'-0"
9'-0" clg.

w.i.c.

dn.

landing

up

art

br. 2
9'-8" x 11'-0"
9'-0" clg.

br. 3
9'-8" x 11'-0"
9'-0" clg.

Plan HPT700300

First Floor: *878 square feet*
Second Floor: *1,245 square feet*
Total: *2,123 square feet*
Width: *27'-6"* **Depth:** *64'-0"*

Key West Conch style blends Old World charm with New World comfort in this picturesque design. A glass-paneled entry lends a warm welcome and complements a captivating front balcony. Reminiscent of the Caribbean "shotgun" houses, the narrow floor plan works well. Two sets of French doors open the great room to wide views and extend the living areas to the back covered porch. A gourmet kitchen is prepared for any occasion with a prep sink, plenty of counter space, an ample pantry and an eating bar. The mid-level landing leads to two additional bedrooms, a full bath and a windowed art niche. Double French doors open the upper-level master suite to a sun deck.

Plan HPT700301

First Floor: *1,290 square feet*
Second Floor: *548 square feet*
Total: *1,838 square feet*
Width: *38'-0"* **Depth:** *51'-0"*

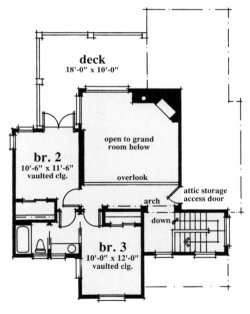

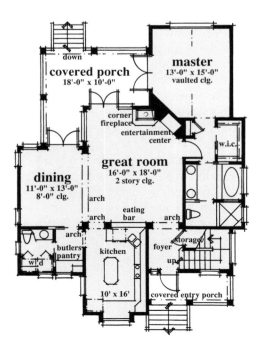

A romantic air flirts with the clean, simple lines of this seaside getaway, set off by stunning shingle accents and a sunburst transom. Horizontal siding complements an insulated metal roof to call up a sense of 19th-Century style. Inside, an unrestrained floor plan harbors cozy interior spaces and offers great outdoor views through wide windows and French doors. At the heart of the home, the two-story great room features a corner fireplace, an angled entertainment center and an eating bar shared with the gourmet kitchen. Columns and sweeping archways define the formal dining room, while French doors open to the veranda, inviting dreamy ocean breezes inside. Please specify basement or crawlspace foundation when ordering.

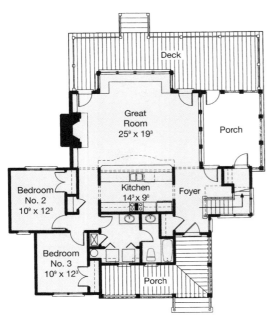

Plan HPT700302

First Floor: *1,341 square feet*
Second Floor: *598 square feet*
Total: *1,939 square feet*
Width: *50'-3"* **Depth:** *46'-3"*

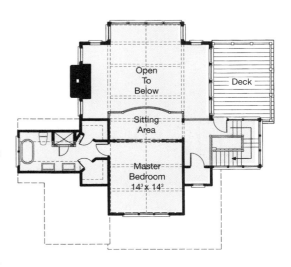

H orizontal siding, plentiful windows and a wraparound porch grace this comfortable home. The great room is aptly named, with a fireplace, built-in seating and access to the rear deck. Meal preparation is a breeze with a galley kitchen designed for efficiency. A screened porch is available for sipping lemonade on warm summer afternoons. The second floor offers a private getaway with a master suite that supplies panoramic views from its adjoining sitting area. A master bath with His and Hers walk-in closets and a private deck complete the second floor.

©1998 Donald A. Gardner, Inc.

Plan HPT700303

First Floor: *965 square feet*
Second Floor: *739 square feet*
Total: *1,704 square feet*
Width: *41'-4"* **Depth:** *30'-10"*

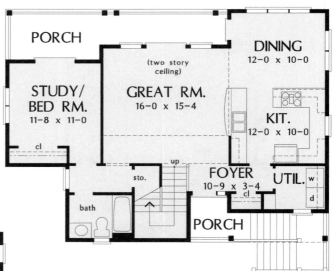

PORCH

STUDY/
BED RM.
11-8 x 11-0

cl

GREAT RM.
16-0 x 15-4

(two story ceiling)

DINING
12-0 x 10-0

KIT.
12-0 x 10-0

up

sto.

FOYER
10-9 x 3-4

UTIL.

w
d

cl

bath

PORCH

BED RM.
11-8 x 13-0

cl

lin.

great room
below

railing

down

bath

foyer
below

**MASTER
BED RM.**
12-0 x 15-0

(cathedral ceiling)

walk-in
closet

master
bath

With its elevated pier foundation, this home is well suited to coastal locations. Principal rooms are oriented toward the rear of the home for premium waterfront views. On the first floor, a two-story ceiling adds drama and space to the great room, which is open to the dining room and kitchen for a large gathering area. The great room, dining room and study/bedroom all open to the rear porch. Upstairs, a balcony overlooking the great room and foyer joins the master suite and a secondary bedroom and bath. ©1998 Donald A. Gardner, Inc.

This lovely seaside vacation home is perfect for seasonal family getaways or for the family that lives coastal year round. The spacious front deck is great for private sunbathing or outdoor barbecues, providing breathtaking ocean views. The two-story living room is warmed by a fireplace on breezy beach nights, while the island kitchen overlooks the open dining area nearby. Two first-floor family bedrooms share a hall bath. Upstairs, the master bedroom features a walk-in closet, a dressing area with a vanity, and access to a whirlpool-tub bath shared with an additional family bedroom—perfect for a nursery or home office.

Porch
12'x 9'5"

Kitchen
8'8"x 18'

Dining
11'6"x 18'

Bedroom
13'x 10'11"

Living
16'6"x 14'5"

Bedroom
13'x 10'9"

Porch
20'6"x 5'

Deck
34'x 10'

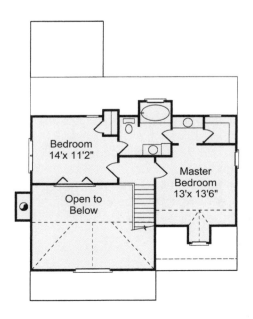

Bedroom
14'x 11'2"

Open to Below

Master Bedroom
13'x 13'6"

Plan HPT700304

First Floor: *1,122 square feet*
Second Floor: *528 square feet*
Total: *1,650 square feet*
Width: *34'-0"* **Depth:** *52'-5"*

Plan HPT700305

First Floor: *895 square feet*
Second Floor: *576 square feet*
Total: *1,471 square feet*
Width: *26'-0"* **Depth:** *36'-0"*

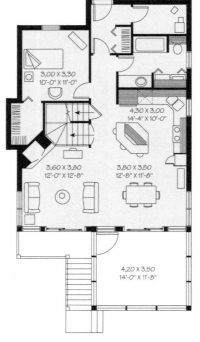

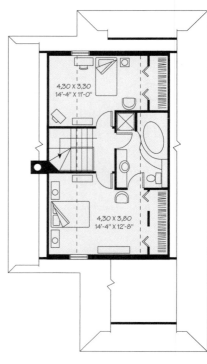

Here's a favorite waterfront home with plenty of space to kick back and relax. A lovely sun room opens from the dining room and allows great views. An angled hearth warms the living and dining areas. Three lovely windows brighten the dining space, which leads out to a stunning sun porch. The gourmet kitchen has an island counter with a snack bar. The first-floor master bedroom enjoys a walk-in closet and a nearby bath. Upstairs, a spacious bath with a whirlpool tub is thoughtfully placed between two bedrooms. A daylight basement allows a lower-level portico.

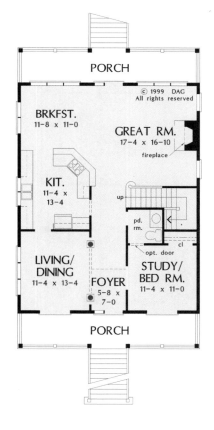

PORCH

BRKFST.
11-8 x 11-0

GREAT RM.
17-4 x 16-10

fireplace

KIT.
11-4 x
13-4

up

pd.
rm.

opt. door

cl

LIVING/
DINING
11-4 x 13-4

FOYER
5-8 x
7-0

STUDY/
BED RM.
11-4 x 11-0

PORCH

Plan HPT700306

First Floor: *1,170 square feet*
Second Floor: *1,058 square feet*
Total: *2,228 square feet*
Width: *30'-0"* **Depth:** *51'-0"*

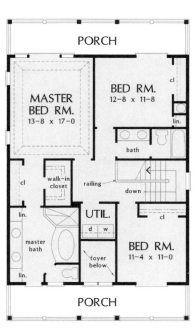

PORCH

MASTER
BED RM.
13-8 x 17-0

BED RM.
12-8 x 11-8

cl

lin.

bath

cl

walk-in
closet

railing

down

lin.

master
bath

UTIL.

d   w

foyer
below

cl

lin.

BED RM.
11-4 x 11-0

PORCH

An elevated pier foundation, narrow width, and front and rear porches make this home perfect for waterfront lots, while its squared-off design makes it easy to afford. The great room, kitchen and breakfast area are all open for a casual and spacious feeling. Flexible rooms located at the front of the home include a formal living or dining room and a study or bedroom with an optional entry to the powder room. Upstairs, every bedroom (plus the master bath) enjoys porch access. The master suite features a tray ceiling, dual closets and a sizable bath with linen cabinets.

Plan HPT700307

First Floor: *1,663 square feet*
Second Floor: *551 square feet*
Total: *2,214 square feet*
Width: *58'-10"* **Depth:** *83'-7"*

Straight from the South, this home sets a country tone. This Southern Colonial design boasts decorative two-story columns and large windows that enhance the front porch and balcony. Enter through the foyer—notice that the formal dining room on the left connects to the island kitchen. The kitchen opens to a breakfast room, which accesses a side porch that's perfect for outdoor grilling. The great room features a warming fireplace and accesses a rear porch. The master bedroom also includes a fireplace, as well as a private bath with a whirlpool tub and a walk-in closet. A home office, laundry room and carport complete the first floor. Upstairs, two additional bedrooms share a full hall bath. Please specify crawlspace or slab foundation when ordering.

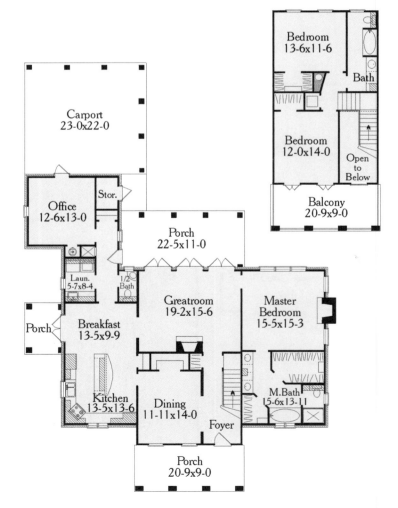

Master Bedroom
18'6"x 20'

Study
13'x 15'6"

Balcony

Plan HPT700308

First Floor: *1,623 square feet*
Second Floor: *978 square feet*
Total: *2,601 square feet*
Width: *48'-0"* **Depth:** *57'-0"*

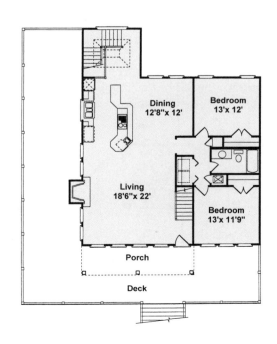

Dining
12'8"x 12'

Bedroom
13'x 12'

Living
18'6"x 22'

Bedroom
13'x 11'9"

Porch

Deck

This fine two-story pier home is filled with up-to-date amenities. The living room features a warming fireplace and plenty of windows. The galley kitchen provides a large island/peninsula overlooking the dining area. Two secondary bedrooms share a bath and easy access to the laundry. Upstairs, a lavish master suite boasts a detailed ceiling, a walk-in closet and access to a private covered porch. A secondary bedroom—or make it a study—with a large walk-in closet completes this floor.

Plan HPT700309

First Floor: *1,333 square feet*
Second Floor: *679 square feet*
Total: *2,012 square feet*
Width: *49'-4"* **Depth:** *50'-4"*

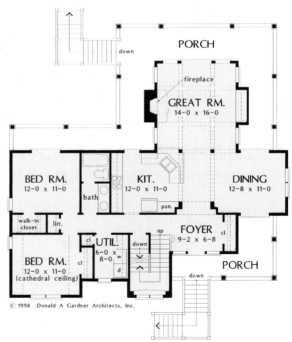

© 1998 Donald A Gardner Architects, Inc.

With an elevated pier foundation, this stunning home is perfect for waterfront properties. Magnificent porches, a balcony and a plethora of picture windows take advantage of the beach or lakeside views. The great room features a ten-foot beam ceiling, a fireplace and a space-saving built-in entertainment center. The staircase is highlighted by a grand window with an arched top, while a Palladian window accents the upstairs loft/study. The master bedroom is the essence of luxury with skylights, a fireplace, cathedral ceiling, balcony, vaulted bath and oversized walk-in closet. Family bedrooms on the first floor share a full bath.

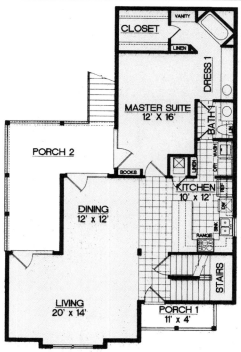

Plan HPT700310

First Floor: *1,182 square feet*
Second Floor: *838 square feet*
Total: *2,020 square feet*
Width: *34'-0"* **Depth:** *52'-0"*

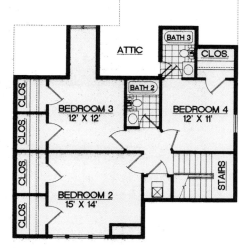

This two-story coastal home finds its inspiration in a Craftsman style that's highlighted by ornamented gables. Open planning is the key with the living and dining areas sharing the front of the first floor with the U-shaped kitchen and stairway. Both the dining room and the living room access the second porch. The master suite boasts a walk-in closet, private vanity and angled tub. The utility room is efficiently placed between the kitchen and bath.

Plan HPT700311

First Floor: *1,252 square feet*
Second Floor: *920 square feet*
Total: *2,172 square feet*
Width: *37'-0"* **Depth:** *46'-0"*

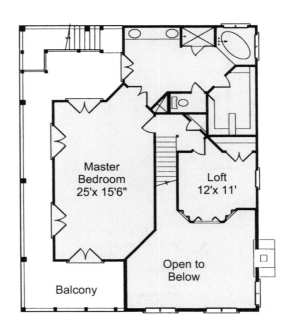

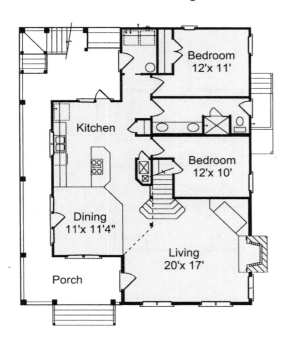

Porches and balconies are just the beginning of the amenities provided by this fine two-story home. The foyer opens to the living room, where a fireplace and built-ins warm the ambiance. The open kitchen offers a cooktop island and leads to the dining room. Upstairs, a lavish master suite boasts a private wraparound deck, a walk-in closet, a lavish bath, and an adjacent loft—perfect for a computer room or a home office. Please specify crawlspace, slab or block foundation when ordering.

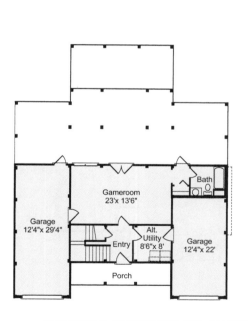

Gameroom
23'x 13'6"

Garage
12'4"x 29'4"

Bath

Alt.
Utility
8'6"x 8'

Entry

Garage
12'4"x 22'

Porch

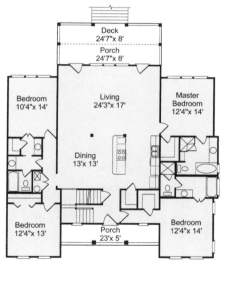

Deck
24'7"x 8'

Porch
24'7"x 8'

Bedroom
10'4"x 14'

Living
24'3"x 17'

Master
Bedroom
12'4"x 14'

Dining
13'x 13'

Bedroom
12'4"x 13'

Porch
23'x 5'

Bedroom
12'4"x 14'

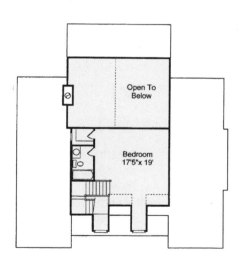

Open To
Below

Bedroom
17'5"x 19'

Plan HPT700312

Main Level: *2,061 square feet*
Upper Level: *464 square feet*
Total: *2,525 square feet*
Finished Basement: *452 square feet*
Width: *50'-0"* **Depth:** *63'-0"*

This waterfront home offers classic seaboard details with louvered shutters, covered porches and an open floor plan. The first level is comprised of two single-car garages, a game room with an accompanying full bath, and a utility room. The U-shaped staircase leads to the central living areas, where the island kitchen is open to the dining room. The living room offers a wall of windows with access to the rear porch and deck. Two bedrooms lie to the left sharing a full bath. On the right is the master suite and a fourth bedroom, each with a private bath.

Plan HPT700313

Square Footage: *1,997*
Width: *53'-0"* **Depth:** *74'-0"*

Elements of country charm adorn this lovely cottage, including shutters, keystoned lintels, a dormer window, the spire and a bay window. Inside, the open floor plan allows for comfortable living. A bayed dining area ensures well-lit entertaining near the U-shaped kitchen. A serving counter opens the kitchen to the vaulted family room and provides a view of the centerpiece corner fireplace. French doors provide access from the breakfast area to the covered patio, expanding the livable space to the outdoors. Two family bedrooms sharing a full bath reside to the right of the plan. To the left sits a luxurious master suite featuring a tray ceiling, walk-in closet and spa-style bath.

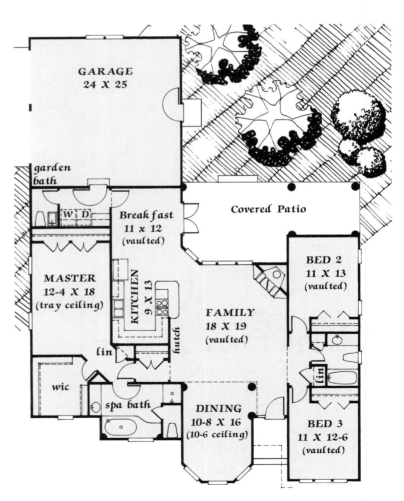

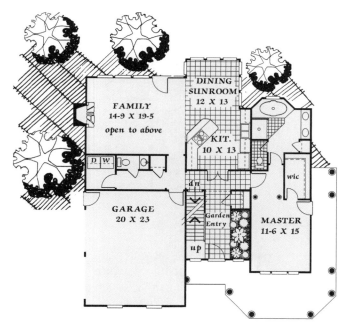

Plan HPT700314

First Floor: 1,435 square feet
Second Floor: 1,261 square feet
Total: 2,696 square feet
Width: 52'-0" **Depth:** 54'-0"

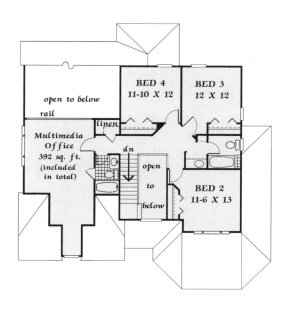

The pinnacles and corner quoins on this European cottage make this home rise above the rest. The covered porch extends around the right side of the home for maximum outdoor comfort. The master suite enjoys the ribbon of windows facing the front of the home and privately accesses the covered porch. The family room is open to the above and features a fireplace. The dining/sun room brightens the spacious kitchen. Three family bedrooms and a multimedia room are located on the second floor.

Plan HPT700315

First Floor: *792 square feet*
Second Floor: *573 square feet*
Total: *1,365 square feet*
Width: *42'-0"* **Depth:** *32'-0"*

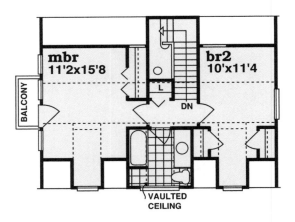

mbr
11'2x15'8

BALCONY

br2
10'x11'4

L

DN

VAULTED
CEILING

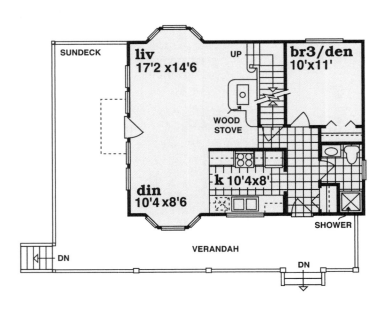

SUNDECK

liv
17'2 x14'6

UP

br3/den
10'x11'

WOOD
STOVE

k 10'4x8'

din
10'4 x8'6

SHOWER

DN

VERANDAH

DN

This distinctive vacation home is designed ideally for a gently sloping lot, which allows for a daylight basement. It can, however, accommodate a flat lot nicely. An expansive veranda sweeps around two sides of the exterior and is complemented by full-height windows. Decorative woodwork and traditional multi-pane windows belie the contemporary interior. An open living/dining room with a woodstove and two bay windows, is complemented by a galley-style kitchen. A bedroom or den, on the first floor has the use of a full bath. The second floor includes a master bedroom with a balcony, and one family bedroom. Both second-floor bedrooms have dormer windows and share a full bath that has a vaulted ceiling.

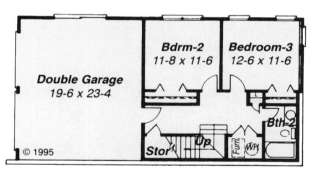

Double Garage
19-6 x 23-4

Bdrm-2
11-8 x 11-6

Bedroom-3
12-6 x 11-6

Bth-2

Stor

Up

Furn

WH

© 1995

Plan HPT700316

Main Level: *1,128 square feet*
Lower Level: *604 square feet*
Total: *1,732 square feet*
Width: *59'-0"* **Depth:** *46'-0"*

A beautiful half-circle window tops a covered front porch on this fine three-bedroom home. Inside, the main-level amenities start with the large, open great room and a warming fireplace. A uniquely shaped dining room is adjacent to the efficient kitchen, which offers a small bay window over the sink. The deluxe master suite is complete with a cathedral ceiling, sitting bay and private bath with laundry facilities. On the lower level, a two-car garage shelters the family fleet, while two bedrooms—or make one a study/home office—share a full hall bath.

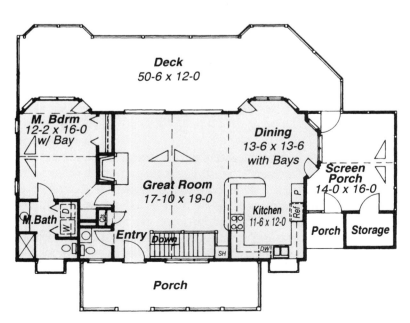

Deck
50-6 x 12-0

M. Bdrm
12-2 x 16-0
w/ Bay

M.Bath

W D

CSS

Entry

Down

Great Room
17-10 x 19-0

Kitchen
11-6 x 12-0

SH

DW

Ref.

P

Dining
13-6 x 13-6
with Bays

Screen
Porch
14-0 x 16-0

Porch

Storage

Porch

Plan HPT700317

First Floor: *1,067 square feet*
Second Floor: *464 square feet*
Total: *1,531 square feet*
Bonus Room: *207 square feet*
Width: *41'-0"* **Depth:** *44'-4"*

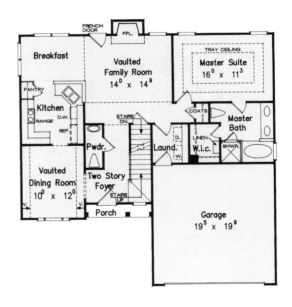

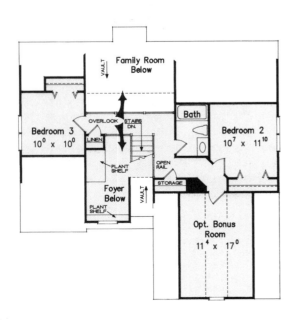

An impression of delicate elegance marks this exterior. The ambiance continues through the foyer, with the balcony above and the vaulted dining room to the left. A wider balcony overlooks the family room, which is warmed by a fireplace. The master suite offers a tray ceiling, a walk-in closet and a bath that features a double-bowl vanity. Two upstairs bedrooms share a bath, a balcony and linen and storage closets. Over the two-car garage, an optional bonus room could evolve into a recreation or hobby room. Please specify basement or crawlspace foundation when ordering.

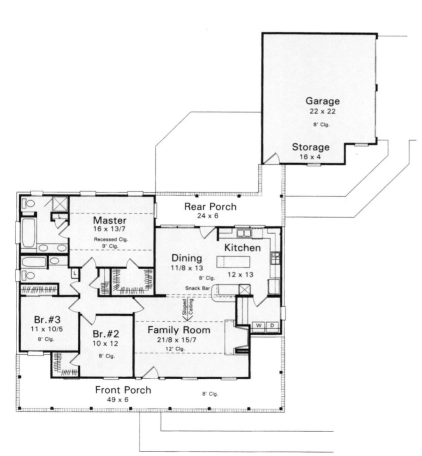

Plan HPT700318

Square Footage: *1,550*
Width: *68'-3"* **Depth:** *73'-8"*

A wide overhanging roof covers the welcoming front porch of this three-bedroom ranch home. The entrance opens directly to the family room where a sloped ceiling and a fireplace add charm to the feeling of spaciousness. A dining area is convenient to the L-shaped kitchen which offers a work island and a snack bar for casual times. The dining area also accesses the rear covered porch. A master bedroom suite features a walk-in closet, a dual-bowl vanity and a separate tub and shower. Two family bedrooms share a full hall bath and access to a hall linen closet. The two-car garage is reached via a covered walk.

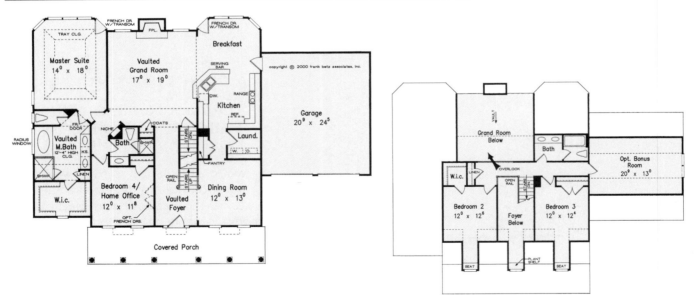

Plan HPT700319

First Floor: *1,771 square feet*
Second Floor: *627 square feet*
Total: *2,398 square feet*
Bonus Space: *285 square feet*
Width: *65'-0"* **Depth:** *49'-0"*

Three dormers and a welcoming porch greet visitors into this four-bedroom home. The foyer—note the charming plant shelf above—introduces a dining room to the right with easy access to the pantry and kitchen. This flexible design also offers an optional study with French doors opening to left of the foyer. The vaulted grand room features a fireplace and is open to the kitchen area. Two family bedrooms and an optional bonus room share a bath on the second level, while the master suite and one additional bedroom reside on the first floor. Please specify basement or crawlspace foundation when ordering.

Storage
20 x 6   8' Clg.

Carport
20 x 20

8' Clg.

Rear Porch
22 x 4

Master
15 x 13
9' Recessed Clg.

10/6 x 8

Dining
10 x 13
8' Clg.

Kitchen
9/9 x 13

B.R. #3
10 x 12
8' Clg.

B.R. #2
10 x 11
8' Clg.

Family Room
17 x 14/7
9' Clg.

Porch
40/6 x 6   8' Clg.

Plan HPT700320

Square Footage: *1,333*
Width: *55'-6"* **Depth:** *64'-3"*

The country home sports a cozy cottage look with its covered porch and chimney. The fireplace resides in the roomy family room and awaits guests. The open dining room and kitchen provide plenty of casual dining space and access the rear porch. An island offers even more counter space. Two family bedrooms and a master bedroom are located on the left of the plan. The master bedroom enjoys a spacious private bath.

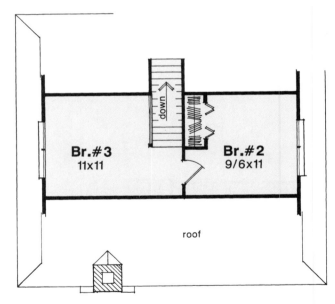

Plan HPT700321

First Floor: *728 square feet*
Second Floor: *300 square feet*
Total: *1,028 square feet*
Width: *28'-0"* **Depth:** *32'-0"*

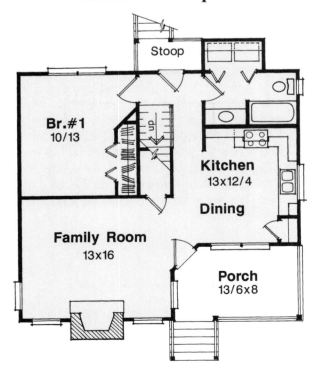

The front-facing fireplace and sloping roof create drama and privacy in this three-bedroom home. Relax on the front porch with a book or enjoy a family gathering inside. The angled front door opens to a spacious family room, complete with a cheerful fireplace. A good-sized kitchen/dining area lets the cook socialize with family or guests while preparing meals. A large bedroom and nearby full bath with an attached laundry area complete the first floor. Either of the two upstairs bedrooms could also serve as a study or recreation room.

Plan HPT700322

First Floor: *1,271 square feet*
Second Floor: *537 square feet*
Total: *1,808 square feet*
Width: *44'-4"* **Depth:** *73'-2"*

The second-floor dormer opens to the foyer of this traditional country home to fill the house with natural light. A powder room is to the left of the foyer and the family room with high ceilings and a fireplace is to the right. The open dining room and kitchen include an angled cooking area, full pantry and access to the rear patio. The master suite features a walk-in closet and a spacious bath with two separate vanities and a linen closet. Upstairs, two bedrooms—one with a walk-in closet—share a full hall bath; a study area features a built-in desk across the hall.

Plan HPT700323

First Floor: *871 square feet*
Second Floor: *1,047 square feet*
Total: *1,918 square feet*
Width: *32'-0"* **Depth:** *47'-0"*

With its shingle and siding exterior, this home has an air of oceanfront living. A large covered porch accesses a spacious gathering room, complete with a fireplace and optional shelving units. An archway leads from the gathering room to the dining room, which is highlighted with a wall of windows and boasts a doorway to the kitchen. The breakfast area overlooks a screened porch and flows smoothly into a U-shaped kitchen. The sleeping quarters reside upstairs and include two family suites, two full baths, a master suite with a tray ceiling, and a convenient laundry room.

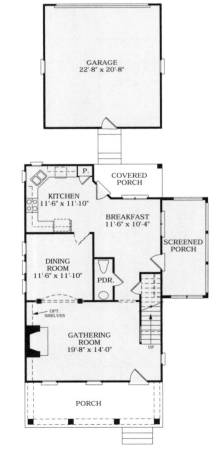

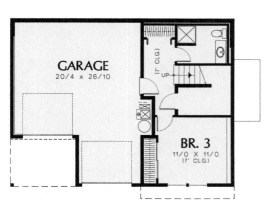

GARAGE
20/4 x 26/10

(7' CLG.)
UP

BR. 3
11/0 X 11/0
(7' CLG.)

BUILT-IN   BUILT-IN

W   D

LIVING
13/0 x 17/0
(10' CLG.)

REF.

UP   DN

DN

PAN

DINING
10/0 x 15/0
(10' CLG.)

BR. 2
14/0 x 10/0
(8' CLG.)

DN

LIN

VAULTED
BR. 1
11/8 x 13/0

Plan HPT700324

Main Level: *954 square feet*
Upper Level: *348 square feet*
Lower Level: *409 square feet*
Total: *1,711 square feet*
Width: *30'-0"* **Depth:** *40'-0"*

Just right for a sloping lot, this home places a double garage at the lower level, along with a bedroom and full bath. The main level contains living and dining space, graced by ten-foot ceilings. The living room has a fireplace surrounded by built-ins. The L-shaped kitchen is defined and separated from the living areas by its island work space. A second bedroom and full bath are on the right side of the main level. The upper level contains a private, vaulted bedroom with a long wall closet and a compartmented bath with dual sinks. Note the open deck space just off the living room and facing to the front.

Plan HPT700325

Square Footage: *1,685*
Bonus Room: *331 square feet*
Width: 62'-4" **Depth:** 57'-4"

This lovely country home provides a powerful combination of well-defined formal rooms, casual living space and flexible areas. A foyer with a convenient coat closet leads to a spacious great room packed with amenities. A cathedral ceiling soars above the heart of this home, made cozy by a massive hearth and views of the outdoors. Decorative columns announce the formal dining room, easily served by a gourmet kitchen, which boasts a breakfast area and bay window. The master suite offers a tray ceiling, a lovely triple window and a skylit bath with a garden tub and a walk-in closet. A glass door allows access to a private area of the rear porch—perfect for stargazing and quiet conversation. ©1996 Donald A. Gardner Architects, Inc.

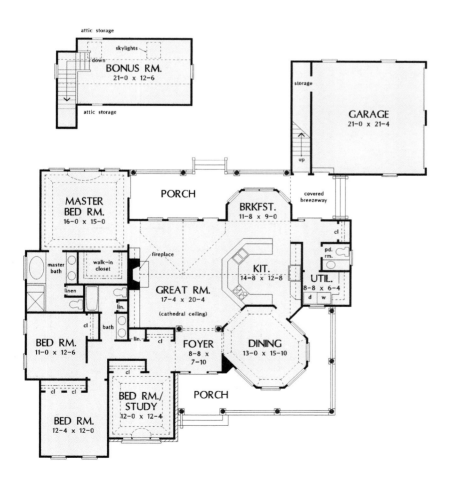

attic storage

skylights

down

BONUS RM.
21-0 x 12-6

attic storage

storage

GARAGE
21-0 x 21-4

up

MASTER
BED RM.
16-0 x 15-0

PORCH

BRKFST.
11-8 x 9-0

covered
breezeway

cl

pd.
rm.

master
bath

walk-in
closet

fireplace

KIT.
14-8 x 12-8

UTIL.
8-8 x 6-4

linen

lin.

GREAT RM.
17-4 x 20-4

d   w

lin.

(cathedral ceiling)

bath

lin.

BED RM.
11-0 x 12-6

cl

cl

FOYER
8-8 x
7-10

DINING
13-0 x 15-10

cl

cl

cl

BED RM./
STUDY
12-0 x 12-4

PORCH

BED RM.
12-4 x 12-0

Plan HPT700326

Square Footage: *2,273*
Bonus Room: *342 square feet*
Width: *74'-8"* **Depth:** *75'-10"*

With an exciting blend of styles, this home features the wrapping porch of a country farmhouse with a brick-and-siding exterior for a uniquely pleasing effect. The great room shares its cathedral ceiling with an open kitchen, while the octagonal dining room is complemented by a tray ceiling. Built-ins flank the great room's fireplace for added convenience. The master suite features a full bath, a walk-in closet and access to the rear porch. Two additional bedrooms share a full hall bath, while a third bedroom can be converted into a study. Skylit bonus space is available above the garage, which is connected to the home by a covered breezeway. ©1997 Donald A. Gardner Architects, Inc.

Plan HPT700327

First Floor: *1,743 square feet*
Second Floor: *555 square feet*
Total: *2,298 square feet*
Bonus Room: *350 square feet*
Width: *77'-11"* **Depth:** *53'-2"*

A lovely arch-top window and a wraparound porch set off this country exterior. Inside, the formal dining room opens off the foyer, which leads to a spacious great room. This living area has a fireplace and access to a screened porch with a cathedral ceiling. Bay windows allow natural light into the breakfast area and formal dining room. The master suite has a spacious bath and access to a private area of the rear porch. Two second-floor bedrooms share a bath and a balcony hall that offers an overlook to the great room.

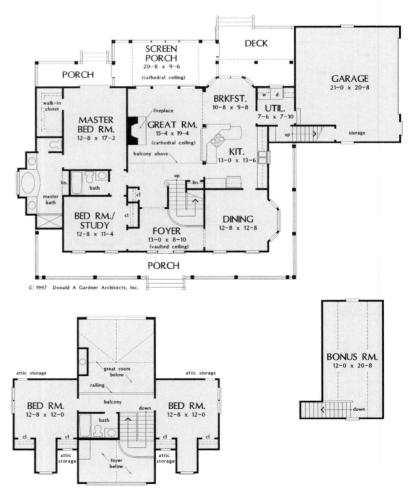

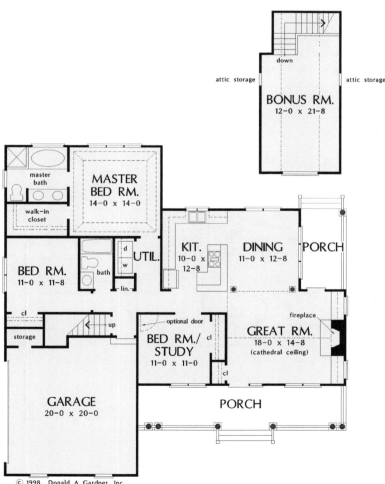

attic storage   attic storage

down

BONUS RM.
12-0 x 21-8

master bath

walk-in closet

MASTER BED RM.
14-0 x 14-0

d w   **UTIL.**

bath

lin.

KIT.
10-0 x 12-8

DINING
11-0 x 12-8

PORCH

BED RM.
11-0 x 11-8

cl

storage

up

optional door

BED RM./ STUDY
11-0 x 11-0

cl

cl

fireplace

GREAT RM.
18-0 x 14-8
(cathedral ceiling)

GARAGE
20-0 x 20-0

PORCH

© 1998 Donald A Gardner, Inc.

Plan HPT700328

Square Footage: *1,428*
Bonus Room: *313 square feet*
Width: *52'-8"* **Depth:** *52'-4"*

Stunning arched windows framed by bold front-facing gables add to the tremendous curb appeal of this modest home. Topped by a cathedral ceiling and with porches on either side, the great room is expanded further by its openness to the dining room and kitchen. Built-ins flank the fireplace for added convenience. Flexibilty, which is so important in a home this size, is found in the versatile bedroom/study as well as the bonus room over the garage. The master suite is positioned for privacy at the rear of the home, with a graceful tray ceiling, walk-in closet and private bath. An additional bedroom and a hall bath complete the plan.

This nostalgic bungalow's facade is enhanced by a charming gable, twin dormers and a wrapping front porch. Bay windows enlarge both the dining room and the master bedroom, while the vaulted great room receives additional light from a front clerestory window. The kitchen features a practical design and includes a handy pantry and ample cabinets. A nearby utility room boasts a sink and additional cabinet and countertop space. Located downstairs for convenience, the master suite enjoys a private bath and walk-in closet. Upstairs, two more bedrooms and a generous bonus room share a full bath. ©1999 Donald A. Gardner, Inc.

Plan HPT700329

First Floor: *1,293 square feet*
Second Floor: *528 square feet*
Total: *1,821 square feet*
Bonus Room: *355 square feet*
Width: *48'-8"* **Depth:** *50'-0"*

Plan HPT700330

First Floor: *1,326 square feet*
Second Floor: *1,254 square feet*
Total: *2,580 square feet*
Bonus Room: *230 square feet*
Width: *55'-4"* **Depth:** *57'-6"*

This shingle-style home is a rustic yet elegant design that does not reveal itself fully at first glance. Double French doors at the entrance lead to a magnificent gallery hall and winding staircase. Stunning columns define the formal dining room, while French doors open to the front porch. The central hall leads to a quiet study and to the great room, which offers a fireplace and built-in bookshelves. The dramatic staircase outside the great room leads upstairs, where a charming master bedroom includes a fireplace and a walk-in closet. This home is designed with a basement foundation.

Photo by Chris A. Little of Atlanta, courtesy of Chatham Home Planning, Inc.

This home, as shown in the photograph, may differ from the actual blueprints. For more detailed information, please check the floor plans carefully.

Plan HPT700331

First Floor: *1,552 square feet*
Second Floor: *653 square feet*
Total: *2,205 square feet*
Width: *60'-0"* **Depth:** *50'-0"*

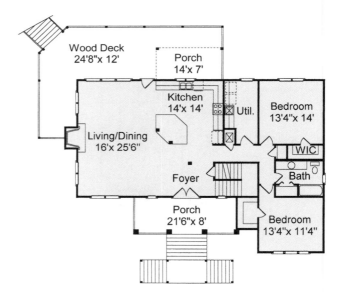

Wood Deck 24'8"x 12'
Porch 14'x 7'
Kitchen 14'x 14'
Util.
Bedroom 13'4"x 14'
Living/Dining 16'x 25'6"
WIC
Foyer
Bath
Porch 21'6"x 8'
Bedroom 13'4"x 11'4"

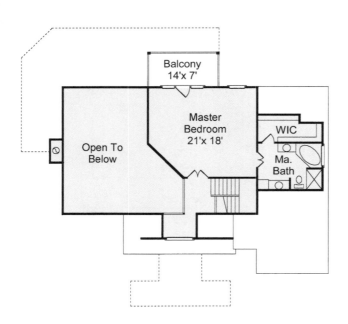

Balcony 14'x 7'
Master Bedroom 21'x 18'
WIC
Open To Below
Ma. Bath

A split staircase adds flair to this European-styled coastal home where a fireplace brings warmth on chilly evenings. The foyer opens to the expansive living/dining area and island kitchen. A multitude of windows fill the interior with sunlight and ocean breezes. The wraparound rear deck allows access from the kitchen. The utility room is conveniently tucked between the kitchen and the two first-floor bedrooms. The second-floor master suite offers a private deck and a luxurious bath with a garden tub, shower and walk-in closet.

Del Sol

mediterranean and mission styles

Plan HPT700332

Square Footage: *1,550*
Width: *43'-0"* **Depth:** *59'-0"*

Enjoy resort-style living in this striking Sun Country home. Guests will always feel welcome when entertained in the formal living and dining areas, and the eat-in country kitchen overlooking the family room will be the center of attention. Casual living will be enjoyed in the large family room and out on the patio with the help of an optional summer kitchen and a view of the fairway. Built-in shelves and an optional media center provide decorating options. The master suite features a volume ceiling and a spacious master bath.

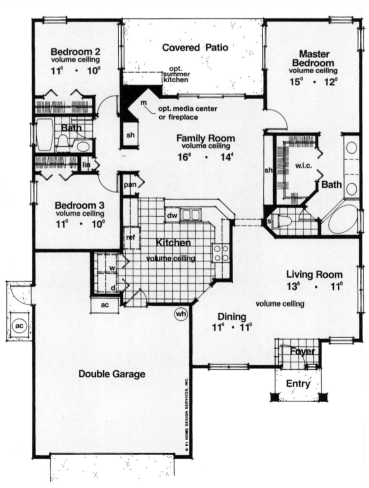

Bedroom 2
volume ceiling
11⁰ · 10⁰

Covered Patio

Master Bedroom
volume ceiling
15⁰ · 12⁰

opt. summer kitchen

Bath

sh

opt. media center or fireplace

Family Room
volume ceiling
16⁸ · 14⁴

w.i.c.

Bath

lin

pan

Bedroom 3
volume ceiling
11⁰ · 10⁰

dw

ref

Kitchen
volume ceiling

Living Room
13⁶ · 11⁰
volume ceiling

w

d

ac

wh

Dining
11⁴ · 11⁰

Foyer

Double Garage

Entry

ac

© '91 HOME DESIGN SERVICES, INC.

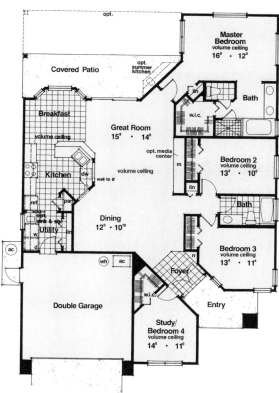

This innovative plan features an angled entry into the home, lending visual impact to the facade and giving the interior floor plan space for a fourth bedroom. A fabulous central living area with a volume ceiling includes a dining area with kitchen access, a great room with a built-in media center, and access to the rear covered patio. The bayed breakfast area with another volume ceiling shares natural light with the tiled kitchen. The kitchen and breakfast nook overlook the outdoor living space which even offers an optional summer kitchen—great for entertaining. A plush master suite opens from the great room through a privacy door and offers vistas to the rear and side grounds.

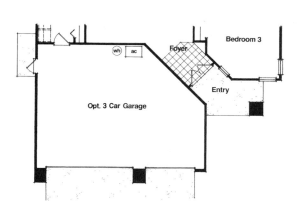

Plan HPT700333
Square Footage: *1,865*
Width: *45'-0"* **Depth:** *66'-0"*

Plan HPT700334

Square Footage: *1,284*
Width: *30'-0"* **Depth:** *60'-10"*

Stucco, muntin windows, French-style shutters and keystone lintels lend this accessible home an European air. With creative placement of the living spaces, this design allows a blending of private and public realms, with the great room leading to the master suite. Vaulted ceilings in all of the rooms bring volume to this well-designed plan, which features two additional bedrooms. The open and inviting kitchen is at the center of the living spaces, flanked by the spacious great room and the dining area.

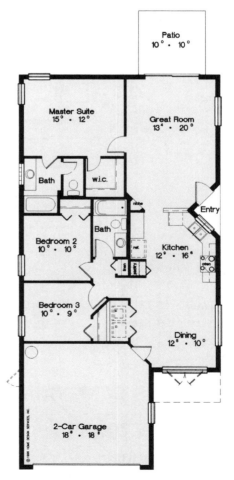

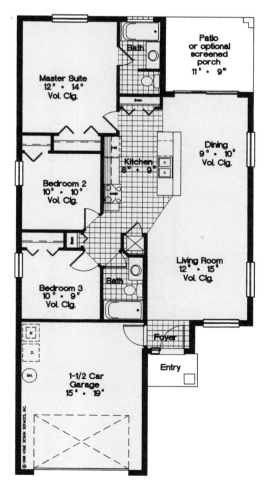

Plan HPT700335

Square Footage: *1,118*
Width: *30'-0"* **Depth:** *60'-0"*

Decorative stucco touches, an impressive entry and muntin windows grace the exterior of this home. Step inside and you will find that the open living space makes this compact home appear larger than it actually is. The living room flows easily into the dining room—both boast volume ceilings. The galley kitchen looks over to the dining room, making it perfect for serving guests. A patio or optional screened porch is accessed from the dining area. The master bath is located to the rear of the plan, away from street traffic, and sports a full bath. Bedrooms 2 and 3 share a full bath.

Plan HPT700336

Square Footage: *1,503*
Width: *59'-8"* **Depth:** *44'-4"*

Traditional lines and an elegant double-door entry give this home curb appeal. In front, a large picture window is accented by a gentle arch and keystone. The living room just to the left of the foyer is open to the dining room, which features a bumped-out bay that bathes the area with natural light and a warm ambiance. The L-shaped kitchen boasts an island and serves the dining and living rooms with ease. Two family bedrooms are down the hall. The master suite enjoys plenty of closet space. The spacious full bath features a separate tub and shower. This home is designed with a basement foundation.

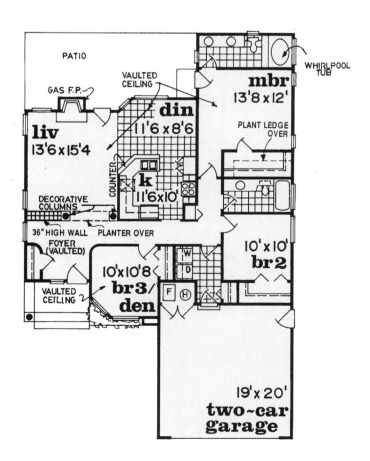

PATIO

VAULTED CEILING

GAS F.P.

liv
13'6 x 15'4

DECORATIVE COLUMNS

36" HIGH WALL   PLANTER OVER

FOYER (VAULTED)

VAULTED CEILING

din
11'6 x 8'6

COUNTER

k
11'6 x 10'

10'x 10'8
br3/ den

WHIRLPOOL TUB

mbr
13'8 x 12'

PLANT LEDGE OVER

10'x 10'
br2

W
D

F   H

19'x 20'
two-car garage

Plan HPT700337

Square Footage: *1,365*
Width: *40'-0"* **Depth:** *62'-0"*

This design offers the option of a traditional wood-sided plan or a cool stucco version. Details for both facades are included in the plans. The compact facade introduces a very comfortable floor plan. The covered entry opens to a vaulted foyer with a coat closet. Decorative columns and a three-foot wall mark the boundary of the living room, which is vaulted and warmed by a gas fireplace. The nearby dining area connects to a U-shaped kitchen with a peninsular counter. A den in the hall might be used as a third bedroom, if you choose. An additional family bedroom has a walk-in closet and a full bath nearby. A vaulted ceiling highlights the master bedroom.

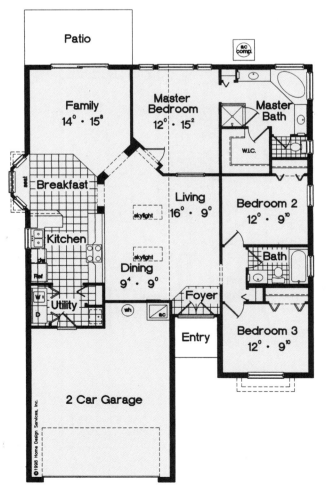

Plan HPT700338

Square Footage: *1,581*
Width: *40'-0"* **Depth:** *60'-0"*

A simple yet detailed design, the exterior of this home boasts keystone lintels, muntin windows, French-style shutters and a stucco facade. Volume ceilings, arches, plant shelves and look-over walls make this home feel much larger. A large transom above the front double doors floods the foyer with natural light. Sleeping quarters take up residence on the right side of the plan, including a large master bedroom with a full bath. The spacious dining/living room is complemented with skylights.

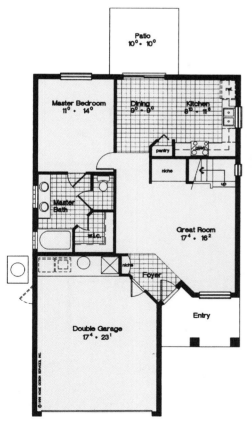

Patio
10⁰ · 10⁰

Master Bedroom
11⁰ · 14⁰

Dining
9⁰ · 9⁰

Kitchen
8⁰ · 11⁰

pantry

niche

Master Bath

w.i.c.

Great Room
17⁴ · 16²

niche

Foyer

Double Garage
17⁴ · 23¹

Entry

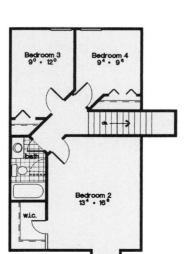

Bedroom 3
9⁰ · 12⁰

Bedroom 4
9⁴ · 9⁶

bath

Bedroom 2
13⁴ · 16⁶

w.i.c.

The exterior of this home is graced with impressive columns, distinctive eaves and decorative stucco touches. A covered entry leads to a foyer with the well-lit great room to the right. To the rear of the plan is the dining/kitchen area, which boasts a pantry and access to the rear patio. The first-floor master bedroom gives way to a lavish bath, complete with dual basins, compartmented toilet and walk-in closet. The staircase landing boasts an eight-foot window, which bathes the area in natural light. On this floor, three secondary bedrooms cluster around a hall that offers a full bath.

Plan HPT700339

First Floor: *957 square feet*
Second Floor: *612 square feet*
Total: *1,569 square feet*
Width: *30'-0"* **Depth:** *50'-8"*

© HOME DESIGN SERVICES, INC.

Plan HPT700340

Square Footage: *1,768*
Width: *40'-0"* **Depth:** *60'-0"*

All of the negatives of a narrow plan have been overcome in this ingenious design. All entrances to major spaces of this home are at an angle to give a feeling of spaciousness. The living/dining room is entered through a distinct foyer, complete with a decorative niche and low walls which define but do not restrict. An angled archway next to another niche brings you into the family center. This space brings the family room, kitchen and nook together in a new way, by allowing for a naturally lighted nook to the side of the kitchen. The master suite, with panoramic views, boasts a generous bath with a corner soaking tub, large shower, private toilet chamber with a bookshelf, and walk-in closet.

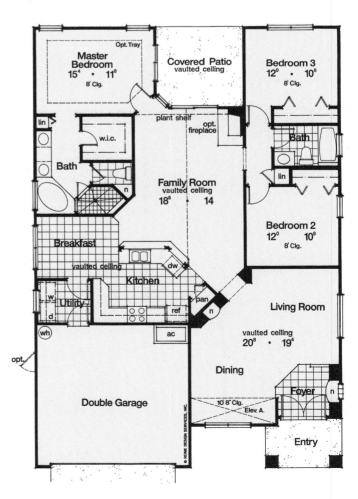

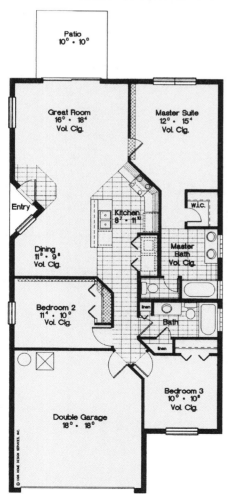

Plan HPT700341

Square Footage: *1,309*
Width: *30'-0"* **Depth:** *60'-0"*

This special design outdoes itself with the imaginative placement of living spaces that enjoy backyard views, so often unseen in other narrow footprint designs. Another design coup is the master suite, which enjoys a golf course or lake view, as well as a generously appointed master bath which can easily accommodate a soaking tub/spa. Note the private toilet chamber, usually found in more elaborate designs. Two ample secondary bedrooms, an oversized bath and a double garage complete this plan.

The choice is yours: California stucco or horizontal wood siding. Plans include details for both elevations. The floor plan places living areas to the rear of the plan to capture views and take advantage of a rear patio. A great master retreat awaits at the back of the plan. Two additional bedrooms have use of a full bath in the hall. Special amenities such as plant ledges, vaulted ceilings and a gas fireplace create an exceptional living environment with this design.

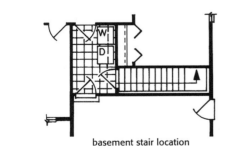

basement stair location

alternate elevation

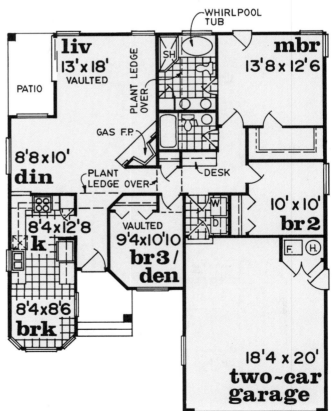

Plan HPT700342

Square Footage: *1,328*
Width: *42'-0"* **Depth:** *51'-6"*

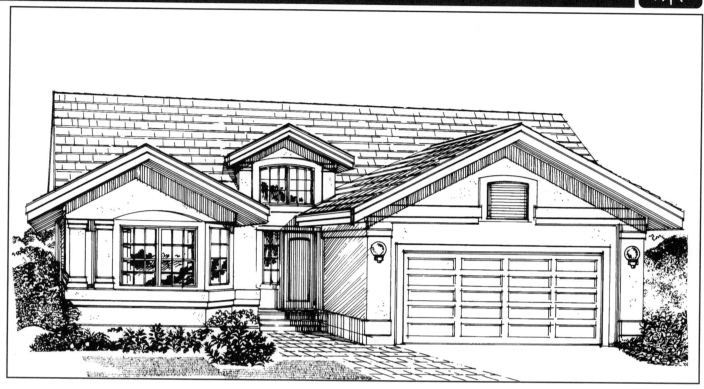

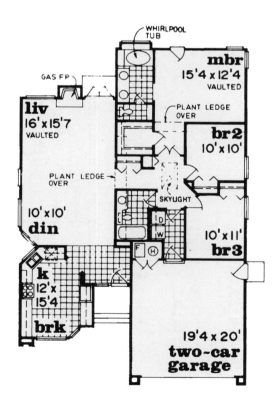

WHIRLPOOL TUB

GAS F.P.

liv
16' x 15'7
VAULTED

PLANT LEDGE OVER

mbr
15'4 x 12'4
VAULTED

PLANT LEDGE OVER

br2
10' x 10'

10' x 10'
din

SKYLIGHT

10' x 11'
br3

k
12' x 15'4

brk

19'4 x 20'
two-car garage

Plan HPT700343

Square Footage: *1,501*
Width: *39'-0"* **Depth:** *59'-0"*

Choose either the California stucco option or the version with horizontal siding and brick for the facade of this home. An interesting floor plan awaits inside. The living room has a vaulted ceiling, a fireplace and access to the rear patio. A plant ledge decorates the hall entry, which is lit by a centered skylight. Three bedrooms line the right side of the plan. Family bedrooms share a full hall bath. The master suite is to the rear and has a plant ledge at its entry, a vaulted ceiling and a bath with a whirlpool tub.

basement stair location

Plan HPT700344

First Floor: 1,583 square feet
Second Floor: 1,086 square feet
Total: 2,669 square feet
Width: 63'-8" **Depth:** 46'-8"

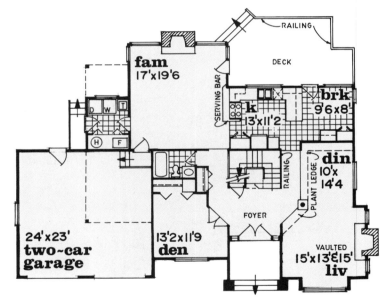

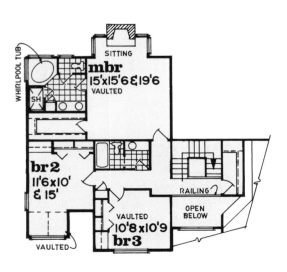

This exciting three-bedroom home can be finished in either California stucco or traditional brick with horizontal siding accents. Vaulted ceilings extend from the foyer to the living room and add a sense of spaciousness to the interior. A plant ledge lines the living and dining room and provides visual separation from the foyer. The den, with a wall closet and private access to a full bath, can double as an guest suite or bedroom. The family room features a masonry fireplace and joins the U-shaped kitchen and breakfast room in the rear of the house. Three bedrooms form the upper level of the house. The master bedroom enjoys a vaulted ceiling, a sitting room with a fireplace, and a well-appointed bath.

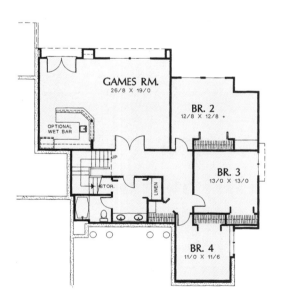

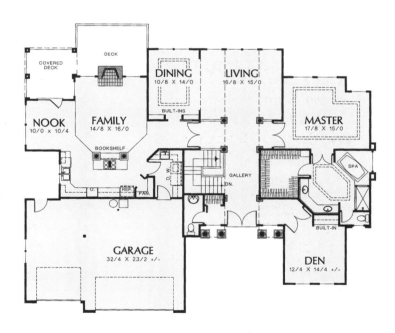

Plan HPT700345

Main Level: *2,196 square feet*
Lower Level: *1,542 square feet*
Total: *3,738 square feet*
Width: *71'-0"* **Depth:** *56'-0"*

Ⓛ

This refined hillside home is designed for lots that fall off toward the rear and works especially well with a view out the back. The kitchen and eating nook wrap around the vaulted family room where arched transom windows flank the fireplace. Formal living is graciously centered in the living room that's directly off the foyer and the adjoining dining room. A grand master suite is located on the main level for convenience and privacy. Please specify basement or crawlspace foundation when ordering.

Plan HPT700346

Square Footage: *1,771*
Width: *60'-0"* **Depth:** *54'-4"*

A home reminiscent of Mediterranean influences, this plan displays a stucco facade, a high entry and an abundance of windows. Enter through the foyer, which is flanked on the left by the library/Bedroom 4 and on the right by the spacious kitchen and breakfast area. The expansive great room is truly the *piéce de résistance* in this home—it boasts space for two optional fireplaces and looks to the rear patio through lovely muntin windows. The master suite resides on the right side of the plan for increased privacy and boasts sliding glass doors to the patio, a garden tub, separate shower and a spacious walk-in closet. The left side of the plan holds the two family bedrooms, which share a full bath.

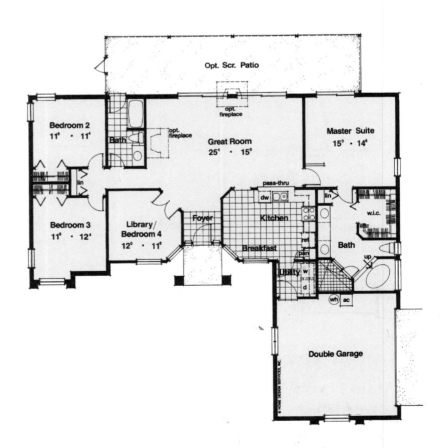

Plan HPT700347

Square Footage: *2,253*
Width: *58'-0"* **Depth:** *66'-8"*

Corner quoins combined with arch-top windows and a columned entry lend an exciting facade to this four-bedroom home. Double doors lead to the foyer, which introduces the open dining and living rooms. The master suite occupies the right side of the plan and enjoys a sun-strewn sitting room, two walk-in closets, and a luxurious bath complete with a garden tub and separate shower. The kitchen sits conveniently near the dining room and features a pantry, desk and views through the breakfast-nook windows. Two family bedrooms sharing a full bath reside near the kitchen. A third bedroom or guest suite is located by the family room and features a private bath. The family room contains a warming fireplace and a media wall.

Plan HPT700348

Square Footage: *1,833*
Width: *59'-4"* **Depth:** *48'-8"*

This home merges formal and informal spaces with the use of niches, plant shelves and attractive angles. The foyer is flanked by a living room on the left and a dining room on the right—both enjoy volume ceilings. The spacious family room also boasts a volume ceiling, as well as a fireplace and built-in shelves. The kitchen/breakfast area is graced with an abundance of windows and access to the rear covered patio. The master bedroom is generous in size and comes with a bayed vanity in the bath, a soaking tub, private toilet chamber and grand master closet. Two additional bedrooms are at the other side of the plan for privacy and share a full hall bath.

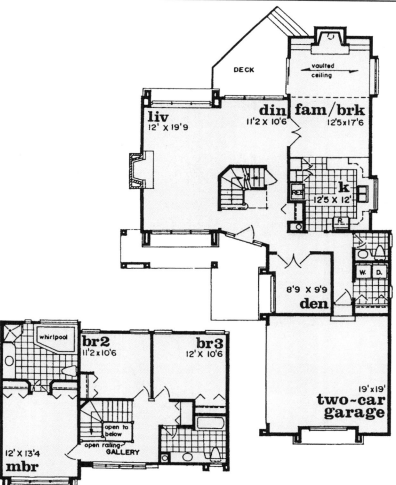

DECK

liv
12' X 19'9

din
11'2 X 10'6

fam/brk
12'5x17'6

vaulted
ceiling

k
12'5 X 12'

REF.

8'9 X 9'9
den

W. D.

whirlpool

br2
11'2 x 10'6

br3
12' X 10'6

open to
below

open railing
GALLERY

12' X 13'4
mbr

19'x19'
two~car
garage

Plan HPT700349

First Floor: *1,224 square feet*
Second Floor: *866 square feet*
Total: *2,090 square feet*
Width: *43'-3"* **Depth:** *66'-0"*

The expansive living room is the focal point of this contemporary design. The raised-hearth fireplace and free-standing staircase highlight this room. The dining area is to the back of the plan and, to the front, the den can double as a guest room or extra bedroom, with the powder room and laundry room nearby. A second fireplace, flanked by bookshelves, and a cathedral ceiling accent the family room, which accesses the rear deck through sliding glass doors and opens to the breakfast area. A box window over the kitchen sink provides abundant natural light and a view of the side yard. Upstairs, the master suite provides two closets and a bath with a whirlpool spa.

369

Plan HPT700350

Square Footage: *1,723*
Width: *45'-0"* **Depth:** *62'-6"*

A new-age contemporary touch graces the exterior of this impressive yet affordable home. The entry leads to the formal areas in the open dining room and vaulted living room. The kitchen overlooks a quaint morning room, which leads to a rear deck that's a perfect spot for outdoor activities. With a walk-in closet and private bath, homeowners will be pampered in the master suite. The second bedroom, the two-car garage and a utility room complete the plan.

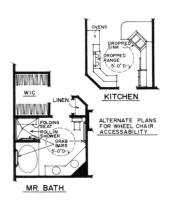

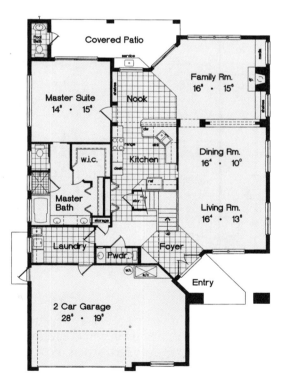

The excitement begins upon entering the foyer of this home where an impressive staircase is the focal point. Just off the nook is a sliding glass door to the covered patio with a wet bar as well as a cabana bath. The master suite is generously sized and has a wonderful wall of high transom glass, as well as sliding glass doors to the patio. A spacious loft works well as a game room, study or library—or it can be a fifth bedroom.

Plan HPT700351

First Floor: *1,844 square feet*
Second Floor: *1,017 square feet*
Total: *2,861 square feet*
Width: *45'-0"* **Depth:** *67'-8"*

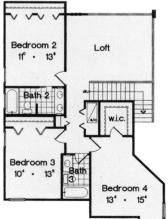

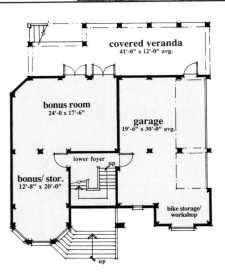

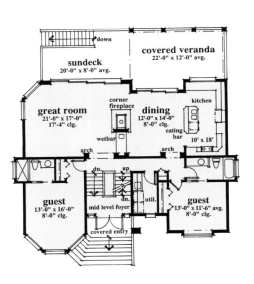

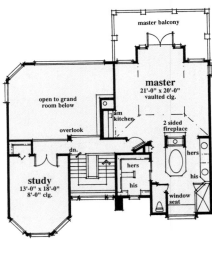

Plan HPT700352

First Floor: *1,684 square feet*
Second Floor: *1,195 square feet*
Total: *2,879 square feet*
Bonus Space: *674 square feet*
Width: *45'-0"* **Depth:** *52'-0"*

Asymmetrical rooflines set off a grand turret and a two-story bay that allow glorious views from the front of this home. Arch-top clerestory windows bring natural light into the great room, which shares a corner fireplace and a wet bar with the dining room. Two guest suites are located on this floor. A winding staircase leads to a luxurious master suite that shares a fireplace with the bath and includes a morning kitchen, French doors to the balcony, and a double walk-in closet. Down the hall, a study and a balcony overlooking the great room complete the plan.

Plan HPT700353

First Floor: *1,542 square feet*
Second Floor: *971 square feet*
Total: *2,513 square feet*
Width: *46'-0"* **Depth:** *51'-0"*

Stately and elegant, this home displays fine Tuscan columns, fanlight windows, hipped gables and a detailed balustrade that splash its facade with a subtle European flavor. Inside, a dramatic winding staircase provides a focal point to the grand entry. The foyer opens to the true a multitude of windows and French doors, the great room holds a magnificent fireplace nestled with built-in cabinetry. The formal dining room boasts a fabulous view of the outdoors as well as access to the expansive covered porch via French doors.

© 1998 Donald A Gardner Architects, Inc.

Plan HPT700425
Square Footage: *2,250*
Width: 84'-10" **Depth:** 62'-4"

A lovely courtyard precedes a grand French-door entry with an arched transom, while stone and stucco accent the exterior of this dignified French country home. The foyer, great room and dining room feature stately eleven-foot ceilings, and interior columns mark boundaries for the great room and dining room. The spacious kitchen features a pass-through to the great room, where built-in shelves flank the fireplace. Cozy side patios and a back porch add to this home's appeal. The master suite is magnificent with a double-door entry, an elegant tray ceiling, dual walk-in closets and an extravagant bath.

Plan HPT700355

Square Footage: *2,085*
Width: *82'-0"* **Depth:** *75'-0"*

Here is a home designed to pamper family members and guests alike. The spacious great room combines with an entertainment terrace to make room for a crowd; formal meals will be a pleasure in the dining room. The U-shaped kitchen offers the cook plenty of extras, such as the built-in desk, corner pantry and cooktop island. Family members and friends will enjoy quiet meals in the eating nook, which is separated from the great room by a curved glass-block wall. Spend relaxing moments in the courtyard patio and spa. The master suite offers direct access to the courtyard patio as well as to its own private covered patio. Two family bedrooms (or a bedroom and a study) complete the plan.

Plan HPT700356

Square Footage: *2,086*
Width: *82'-0"* **Depth:** *58'-4"*

A majestic facade creates magnificent curb appeal with this lovely Sun Country home. An open arrangement of the interior allows dual-use space in the wonderful sunken sitting room and media area. The kitchen has a breakfast bay and looks over the snack bar to the sunken family area. A few steps from the kitchen and functioning well with the upper patio is the formal dining room. Two family bedrooms share a full bath. The private master suite includes a sitting area and French doors that open to a private covered patio.

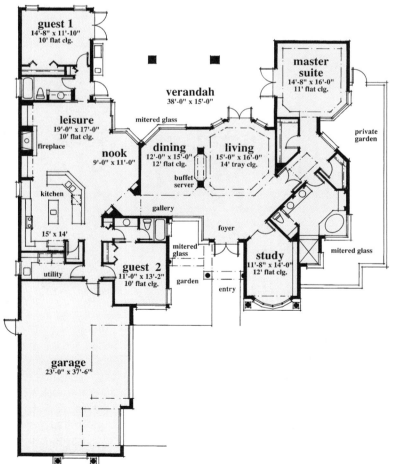

guest 1
14'-8" x 11'-10"
10' flat clg.

master
suite
14'-8" x 16'-0"
11' flat clg.

verandah
38'-0" x 15'-0"

mitered glass

leisure
19'-0" x 17'-0"
10' flat clg.

fireplace

nook
9'-0" x 11'-0"

dining
12'-0" x 15'-0"
12' flat clg.

living
15'-0" x 16'-0"
14' tray clg.

private
garden

buffet
server

kitchen

gallery

15' x 14'

foyer

guest 2
11'-0" x 13'-2"
10' flat clg.

mitered
glass

garden

study
11'-8" x 14'-0"
12' flat clg.

utility

entry

mitered glass

garage
23'-0" x 37'-6"

Plan HPT700354

Square Footage: *2,794*
Width: *70'-0"* **Depth:** *98'-0"*

L

Classic columns, circle-head windows and a bay-windowed study give this stucco home a wonderful street presence. The foyer leads to the formal living and dining areas. An arched buffet server separates these rooms and contributes an open feeling. The kitchen, nook and leisure room are grouped for informal living. A desk/message center in the island kitchen, art niches in the nook, and a fireplace with an entertainment center add custom touches. Two secondary suites have guest baths and offer full privacy from the master wing. The master suite hosts a private garden area, while the master bath features a walk-in shower that overlooks the garden, and a water-closet room with space for books.

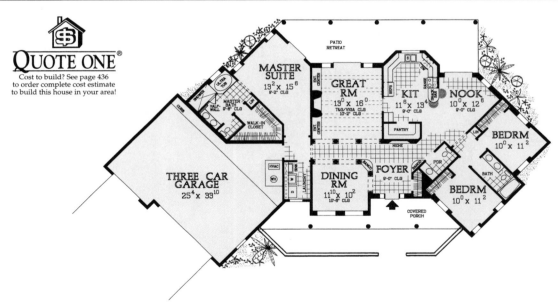

QUOTE ONE®

Cost to build? See page 436 to order complete cost estimate to build this house in your area!

Plan HPT700358

Square Footage: *2,015*
Width: *96'-5"* **Depth:** *54'-9"*

This Santa Fe-style home is as warm as a desert breeze and just as comfortable. Outside details are reminiscent of old-style adobe homes, while the interior caters to convenient living. The front covered porch leads to an open foyer. Columns define the formal dining room and the giant great room. The kitchen has an enormous pantry and a snack bar and is connected to a breakfast nook with rear-patio access. Two family bedrooms on the right side of the plan share a full bathroom that includes twin vanities. The master suite on the left side of the plan has a walk-in closet and a bath with a spa-style tub and a separate shower.

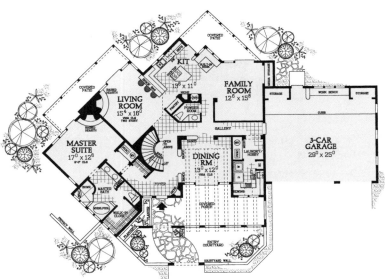

Plan HPT700357

First Floor: *1,911 square feet*
Second Floor: *828 square feet*
Total: *2,739 square feet*
Width: *87'-10"* **Depth:** *60'-8"*

L

QUOTE ONE®
Cost to build? See page 436
to order complete cost estimate
to build this house in your area!

The arched courtyard entrance is a perfect introduction to this plan's wonderful livability—indoors and out. Open spaces and interesting angles greet you at the foyer, which is elegantly intersected with a curved stairway. The formal dining room opens to the large covered patio, perfect for entertaining and outdoor meals. The living room enjoys a dramatic corner fireplace with a raised hearth and is open to the oversized kitchen through a snack bar. A built-in breakfast booth joins the kitchen to the casual family room. The master suite is a welcome retreat thanks to a raised-hearth fireplace, patio door and lavish bath. Up the grand stairway, a lovely window bench frames the hallway leading to two family bedrooms, which share a compartmented bath, and to the guest suite with a private bath.

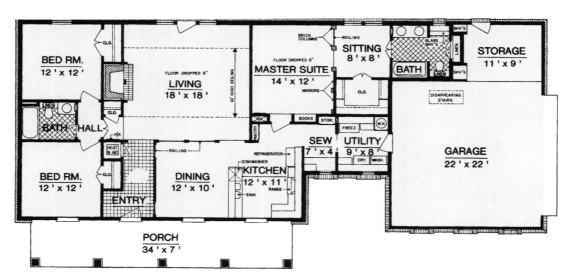

Plan HPT700359

Square Footage: *1,600*
Width: *75'-0"* **Depth:** *37'-0"*

With its side-loading garage, this three-bedroom family home fits well on a corner lot. The open front porch welcomes guests and family members into the entry foyer. A sunken living room invites comfortable conversation by its warming fireplace. Nearby, the dining room is defined by a railing and adjoins the kitchen. A sewing nook between the kitchen and utility room will please the family craft maker. To the left of the plan, two family bedrooms share a full bath. To the right of the living room, the sunken master suite enjoys a sitting area, a walk-in closet, built-in bookshelves and a private bath. Please specify basement, crawlspace or slab foundation when ordering.

Plan HPT700360

Square Footage: *2,770*
Width: *74'-0"* **Depth:** *79'-0"*

The elegance of this one-story elevation is found in the various European accents shaping the exterior and in the many lavish amenities found inside. The foyer opens to the formal dining and great rooms. Built-ins flank either side of the fireplace in the great room, which accesses the rear patio. The kitchen overlooks the casual breakfast room nearby. The master suite features a sitting room overlooking the patio that practically doubles the size of this sumptuous retreat. The luxurious master bath is impressive with a bumped-out tub and His and Hers walk-in closets. Bedrooms 2 and 3 at the front of the home share a bath and dressing area. This home is designed with a walkout basement foundation.

Plan HPT700361

Square Footage: 3,286
Width: 77'-4" **Depth:** 74'-8"

L

The hipped roof with varying planes and wide overhangs sets off this design. Meanwhile, the sheltered front entrance is both dramatic and inviting with double doors opening to the central foyer. In the sunken living room, a curved, raised-hearth fireplace acts as a focal point. Double glass doors lead to a covered terrace. The U-shaped kitchen is efficient with its island work surface, breakfast bar, pantry and broom closet. This generous, open area extends to include the family room. A careful arrangement of the sleeping arrangements provides privacy for the master suite.

QUOTE ONE®
Cost to build? See page 436
to order complete cost estimate
to build this house in your area!

patio

DINING
13-4 x 12-6

GREAT RM.
15-4 x 22-4

MASTER
BED RM.
15-4 x 16-8

fireplace

KIT.
13-4 x 10-10

(cathedral ceiling)

lin.

master
bath

UTIL.
7-4 x 7-4

skylight

walk-in
closet

d w

cl

FOYER
7-0 x 9-0

cl

bath

GARAGE
22-0 x 23-0

BED RM./
STUDY
11-8 x 11-0

BED RM.
11-8 x 12-0

covered
porch

closet

© 1994 Donald A. Gardner Architects, Inc.

Plan HPT700362

Square Footage: *1,838*
Width: *60'-0"* **Depth:** *60'-4"*

Arched windows and a dramatic arched entry enhance this exciting contemporary home. The expansive great room, highlighted by a cathedral ceiling and a fireplace, offers direct access to the rear patio and the formal dining room—a winning combination for both formal and informal get-togethers. An efficient U-shaped kitchen provides plenty of counter space and easily serves both the dining room and the great room. Sunlight fills the master bedroom through a wall of windows, which affords views of the rear grounds. The master bath invites relaxation with its soothing corner tub and separate shower. Two secondary bedrooms—one serves as an optional study—share an adjacent bath.

383

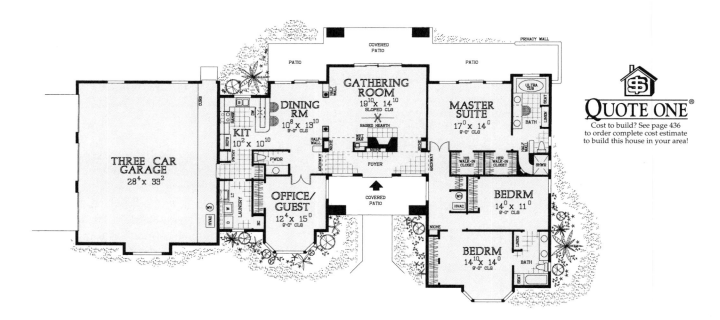

QUOTE ONE®

Cost to build? See page 436
to order complete cost estimate
to build this house in your area!

Plan HPT700363

Square Footage: *2,319*
Width: *97'-2"* **Depth:** *57'-4"*

The tiled foyer of this Sun Country design invites guests into a gathering room with a fireplace and views of the rear grounds. Half-walls define the formal dining area, which offers rear-patio access. The kitchen is equipped to serve formal and informal occasions, and includes a snack counter for meals on the go. An office or guest room has a sunny bay window and an adjacent powder room. The outstanding master suite contains twin walk-in closets, a whirlpool tub, a sit-down vanity and a stylish doorless shower. Two secondary bedrooms share a bath.

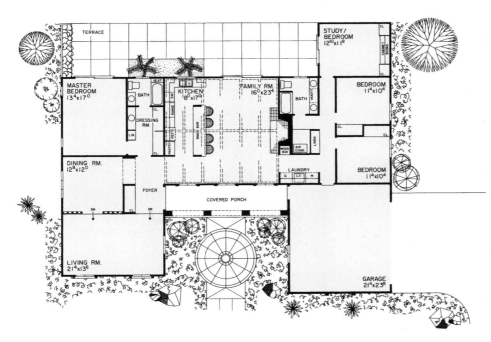

Plan HPT700364

Square Footage: *2,307*
Width: *70'-0"* **Depth:** *56'-0"*

This delightful Spanish design will fit in well, regardless of your building location: mountains, endless prairie, farmland or suburbs. The hub of the plan is the kitchen/family room area. The beam ceiling and the raised-hearth fireplace contribute to the cozy, informal atmosphere. The separate dining room and the sunken living room function together formally. The master bedroom provides privacy from the three family bedrooms located at the opposite end of the plan.

Plan HPT700365

Square Footage: *2,407*
Width: *72'-0"* **Depth:** *72'-0"*

With clean lines, a tiled roof and a multi-windowed portico, this one-story contemporary home possesses plenty of curb appeal. Inside, the living/dining area is flooded with light from two walls of windows and French-door access to the spacious courtyard. Located in the left wing, the living area includes a U-shaped kitchen with a huge walk-in pantry, breakfast area and large great room with a fireplace. To the right of the foyer is the sleeping wing. Here, a deluxe master bedroom features two walk-in closets, a round tub and access to the courtyard. Two secondary bedrooms share a hall bath.

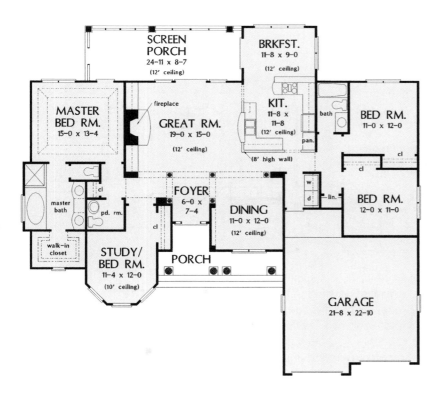

SCREEN PORCH
24-11 x 8-7
(12' ceiling)

BRKFST.
11-8 x 9-0
(12' ceiling)

fireplace

MASTER BED RM.
15-0 x 13-4

GREAT RM.
19-0 x 15-0
(12' ceiling)

KIT.
11-8 x 11-8
(12' ceiling)

bath

BED RM.
11-0 x 12-0

pan.

(8' high wall)

cl

cl

master bath

pd. rm.

cl

FOYER
6-0 x 7-4

DINING
11-0 x 12-0
(12' ceiling)

w
d

lin.

BED RM.
12-0 x 11-0

walk-in closet

cl

STUDY/ BED RM.
11-4 x 12-0
(10' ceiling)

PORCH

GARAGE
21-8 x 22-10

Plan HPT700366

Square Footage: *1,954*
Width: *64'-10"* **Depth:** *58'-10"*

Direct from the Mediterranean, this Spanish-style, one-story home offers a practical floor plan. The facade features arch-top, multi-pane windows, a columned front porch, a tall chimney and a tiled roof. The interior has a wealth of livability. What you'll appreciate first is the placement of the great room and the formal dining room—both defined by columns. A casual eating area is attached to the L-shaped kitchen and accesses a screened porch, as does the great room. Three bedrooms mean abundant sleeping space. The study could be a fourth bedroom— choose the full bath option in this case. A tray ceiling decorates the master suite, which is further enhanced by a bath with a separate shower and tub, walk-in closet and double sinks. ©1997 Donald A. Gardner Architects, Inc.

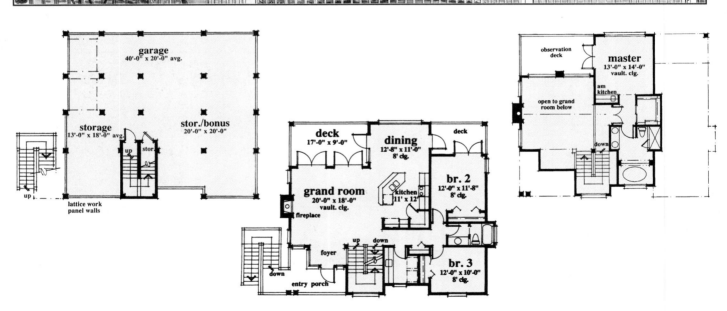

Plan HPT700367

First Floor: *1,342 square feet*
Second Floor: *511 square feet*
Total: *1,853 square feet*
Width: *44'-0"* **Depth:** *40'-0"*

Amenities abound in this delightful two-story home. The foyer opens directly into the fantastic grand room, which offers a warming fireplace and two sets of double doors to the rear deck. The dining room also accesses this deck and a second deck shared with Bedroom 2. A convenient kitchen and another bedroom also reside on this level. Upstairs, the master bedroom reigns supreme. Entered through double doors, the suite pampers with a luxurious bath, walk-in closet, morning kitchen and private observation deck. This home is designed with a pier foundation.

3,80 X 4,90
12'-8" X 16'-4"

3,40 X 2,20
11'-4" X 7'-4"

3,40 X 5,20
11'-4" X 17'-4"

3,40 X 3,60
11'-4" X 12'-0"

3,40 X 6,00
11'-4" X 20'-0"

3,90 X 1,50
13',-0" X 5'-0"

Plan HPT700368

First Floor: *1,065 square feet*
Second Floor: *1,032 square feet*
Total: *2,097 square feet*
Width: *38'-0"* **Depth:** *38'-0"*

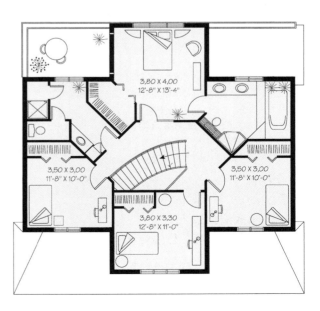

3,80 X 4,00
12'-8" X 13'-4"

3,50 X 3,00
11'-8" X 10'-0"

3,50 X 3,00
11'-8" X 10'-0"

3,80 X 3,30
12'-8" X 11'-0"

This Mediterranean home offers a dreamy living-by-the-water lifestyle, but it's ready to build in any region. A lovely arch-top entry announces an exquisite foyer with a curved staircase. The family room provides a fireplace and opens to the outdoors on both sides of the plan. An L-shaped kitchen serves a cozy morning area as well as a stunning formal dining room, which offers a bay window. Second-floor sleeping quarters include four bedrooms and two bathrooms. The master suite opens to a balcony and offers a bath with a double-bowl vanity. This home is designed with a basement foundation.

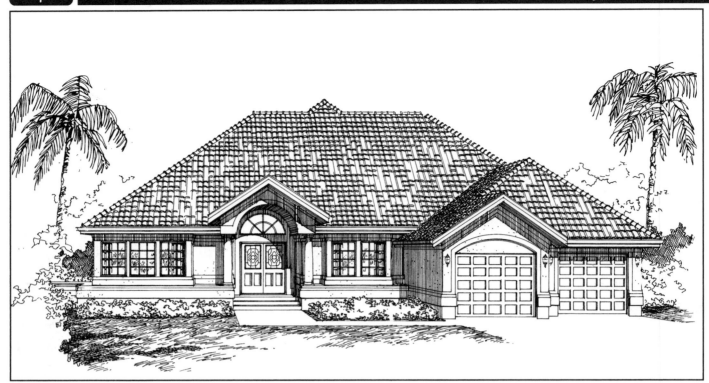

Plan HPT700369

Square Footage: *2,471*
Width: *60'-0"* **Depth:** *63'-6"*

Decorative columns with a plant ledge entablature define the living room and dining room entrances. The den, tucked off the foyer, can double as a guest room or home office. The well-planned kitchen serves the eating bar and skylit breakfast room. Large walk-in and wall closets, a luxurious ensuite with a double vanity, whirlpool tub and oversized shower, and patio access are just some of the master suite features. Two additional bedrooms share a main bath that includes a twin vanity. The large laundry area holds extra storage and a folding counter.

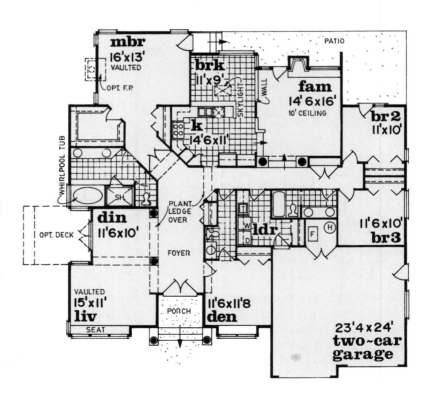

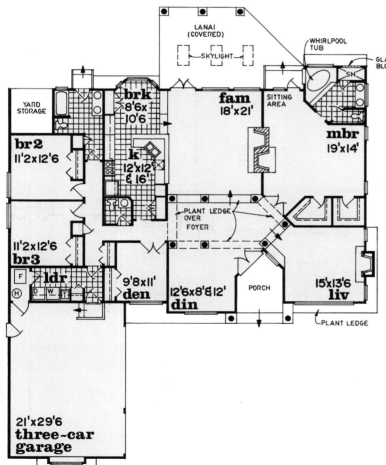

Plan HPT700370

Square Footage: *2,804*
Width: *68'-0"* **Depth:** *88'-0"*

An angled entry on this home allows privacy and adds a touch of drama. Low-slung and spacious, this one-story home begins with double doors to a columned entry foyer that's framed by a formal dining room and a sunken living room. The family room leads to a rear covered lanai with skylights. The master bedroom also accesses this lanai, just beyond its sitting area. Note the twin walk-in closets in the master bedroom. A breakfast room attaches to the kitchen and features a bay window. There are three fireplaces in the plan: in the master bedroom, the living room and the family room.

Plan HPT700371

Square Footage: *1,380*
Width: *46'-0"* **Depth:** *56'-0"*

A Palladian window set in a stucco facade under a hipped roof lends a gracious charm to this three-bedroom home. The welcoming front porch opens to a living room featuring a corner fireplace. The U-shaped kitchen opens directly to the dining room and its patio access. A utility/storage room connects the two-car garage to the kitchen. This plan splits the master suite from the two family bedrooms on the left for added privacy. Note the dual vanity sinks in the master bath. Please specify crawlspace or slab foundation when ordering.

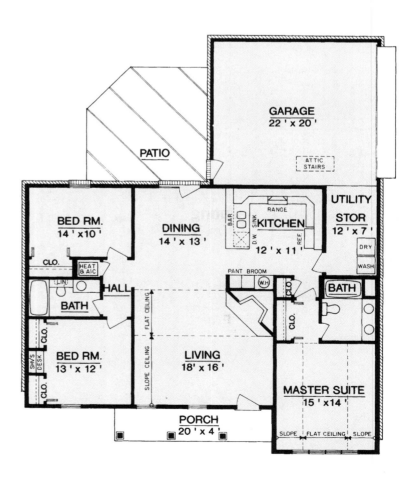

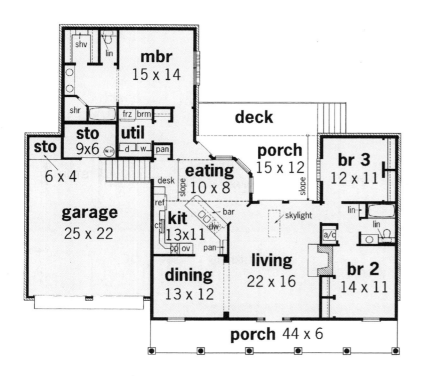

Plan HPT700372

Square Footage: *1,800*
Width: *66'-0"* **Depth:** *60'-0"*

Two arched dormers and a wide-open porch welcome guests into this charming home. The entry opens to a skylit and hearth-warmed living room, with two French doors opening to the rear porch. Two family bedrooms reside to the right, sharing a full hall bath. The dining room views the front porch. Nearby, the kitchen features a built-in desk and a snack bar angled to complement the adjoining bayed breakfast nook. Secluded to the rear of the plan, the comforting master suite provides a luxurious bath. Please specify crawlspace or slab foundation when ordering.

Plan HPT700373

Square Footage: *1,828*
Width: *64'-0"* **Depth:** *62'-0"*

With hipped roofs and muntin windows, this attractive facade brings curb appeal to this European-style home. The dining room sits just left of the entry, which leads to the living room with a fireplace. The spacious kitchen's angled counter overlooks the breakfast room, which leads to the utility room and the master bedroom. The master bedroom contains a vast walk-in closet, a vanity with a sink in the dressing room, and a full bath. Please specify basement, crawlspace of slab foundation when ordering.

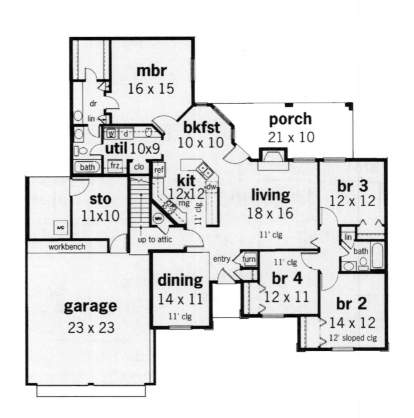

Plan HPT700374

Square Footage: *2,090*
Width: *67'-0"* **Depth:** *59'-0"*

This exciting Southwestern design is enhanced by the use of arched windows and an inviting arched entrance. The large foyer opens to a massive great room with a fireplace and built-in cabinets. The kitchen features an island cooktop and a skylit breakfast area. The master suite has an impressive cathedral ceiling and a walk-in closet as well as a luxurious bath that boasts separate vanities, a corner whirlpool tub and a separate shower. Two additional bedrooms are located at the opposite end of the home for privacy and share a full bath. ©1994 Donald A. Gardner Architects, Inc.

395

Plan HPT700375

Square Footage: *1,707*
Width: *56'-6"* **Depth:** *45'-8"*

Here's a sensational Mediterannean cottage that's well suited for a coastal environment—yet it's ready for any place on earth. The covered front porch and arch-top windows lend great curb appeal and complement a spacious rear deck. An open formal dining room provides a place for memorable events. A coffered ceiling highlights the great room, anchored by a massive fireplace. Triple-window views enhance the rear of the plan and bring in natural light to the great room, breakfast area and master suite. To the front of the plan, two secondary bedrooms surround a full bath. ©2000 Donald A. Gardner, Inc.

Plan HPT700376

First Floor: *1,679 square feet*
Second Floor: *921 square feet*
Total: *2,600 square feet*
Width: *58'-0"* **Depth:** *58'-10"*

This Mediterranean-style beauty is not just a fresh face—its well-planned interior provides all of the flexibility that the new age requires. An open two-story great room boasts a fireplace and access to the rear covered porch. The U-shaped kitchen provides a convenient pass-through shared with the great room. A triple window brightens the breakfast area, which also features access to the rear porch. Gorgeous amenities enhance the master suite, including a coffered ceiling and a bay window. Upstairs, three secondary bedrooms share a balcony hall that leads to a full bath. ©2000 Donald A. Gardner, Inc.

397

Plan HPT700377

First Floor: *1,735 square feet*
Second Floor: *841 square feet*
Total: *2,576 square feet*
Width: *58'-8"* **Depth:** *54'-0"*

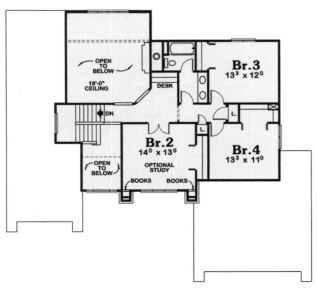

A discreet Prairie style is celebrated on the facade of this lovely design. A see-through fireplace connects the great room and the breakfast area. The formal dining room offers fabulous interior vistas that extend to the rear propery. A central staircase leads up to a landing that leads to the master suite. This suite features barrel-vaulted ceilings and an oval whirlpool tub. On the second floor, a computer loft with a built-in desk overlooks the stunning great room. Three family bedrooms share a full bath.

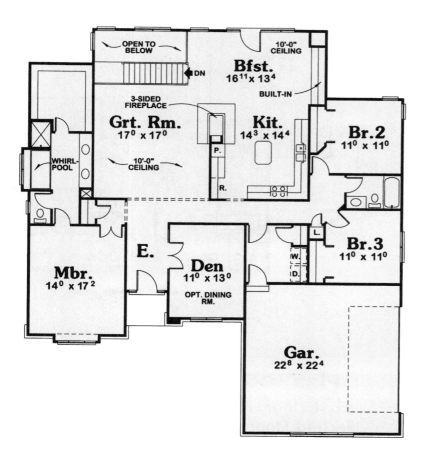

Plan HPT700378

Square Footage: *2,167*
Width: *55'-4"* **Depth:** *61'-4"*

This three-bedroom bungalow shows a definite Prairie influence. Perfect for a sloping lot, this design provides an optional stairway near the great room that can lead to a lower level. A three-sided stone fireplace brings warmth and light to the spacious island kitchen, breakfast area and great room. Depending on the need, a den or dining room is located just to the right of the entry-way. The master suite provides ample closet space and a whirlpool tub. Separated from the master wing for privacy, two secondary bedrooms share a full bath.

The unique rooflines of this home will capture the attention of passersby and provide great curb appeal. The foyer is open to the dining room on the left and the living room on the right. A large family room features a built-in bookshelf and a fireplace. The efficient kitchen offers plenty of counter space in a compact and well-planned area. A wall of windows in the eating room allows plenty of natural light into this space. The master suite includes a bath and walk-in closet. Large front and rear porches provide opportunities for outdoor entertaining. Please specify basement, crawlspace or slab foundation when ordering.

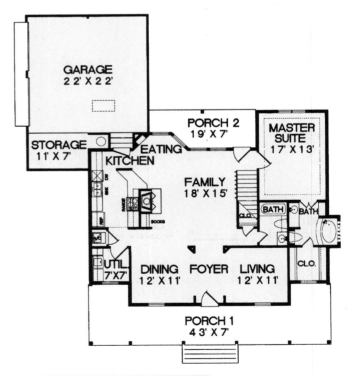

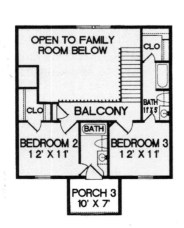

Plan HPT700379

First Floor: *1,320 square feet*
Second Floor: *552 square feet*
Total: *1,872 square feet*
Width: *56'-0"* **Depth:** *61'-0"*

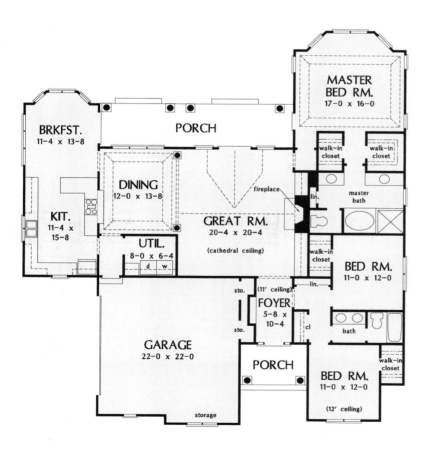

Plan HPT700380

Square Footage: *2,098*
Width: *60'-0"* **Depth:** *63'-8"*

This charming chalet is much more than just a pretty face. With tall arched windows and a hipped roof, the exceptional beauty of the facade is a mere introduction to the amenity-packed interior. The heart of the home allows wide views and provides access to an inviting rear porch—large enough for a crowd. The formal dining room achieves a casual ambiance with views and archways that connect it with the living space and the kitchen. A grand master suite provides two walk-in closets, separate vanities and a whirlpool tub. Two secondary bedrooms cluster around a full bath with a dual vanity. ©2000 Donald A. Gardner, Inc.

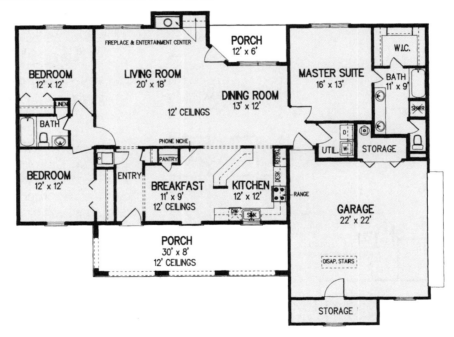

Plan HPT700381

Square Footage: *1,770*
Width: *64'-0"* **Depth:** *48'-0"*

Keystones and segmental arches draw attention to the beautifully covered porch on this French-style home. Quoins accent the stucco, along with shutters that outline the windows to make a versatile facade. A conveniently placed kitchen and breakfast nook greet the homeowner or guest upon entry—no more carrying groceries through the house! The living room and dining room are open to each other. A fireplace and entertainment center are built-in, creating a focal point. The well-lit master suite includes dual vanities and a spacious walk-in closet. Please specify crawlspace or slab foundation when ordering.

olumns, shutters and French doors give this New Orleans-style home great appeal. The living room features plenty of windows and French-door access to the rear porch. The modified galley kitchen easily serves the bay-windowed informal dining area and the formal dining room. Access to the garage is available from the kitchen through the utility area. The master suite enjoys seclusion on the first level and privately accesses the beautiful atrium. Two bedrooms sharing a full bath are tucked upstairs. Please specify basement, crawlspace or slab foundation when ordering.

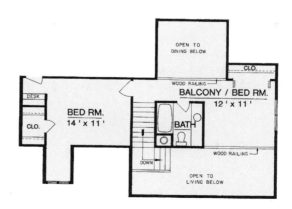

Plan HPT700382

First Floor: *1,546 square feet*
Second Floor: *512 square feet*
Total: *2,058 square feet*
Width: *46'-0"* **Depth:** *65'-0"*

Plan HPT700383

Square Footage: *984*
Width: *33'-9"* **Depth:** *43'-0"*

This snug home uses its square footage efficiently, with no wasted space. Brightened by a clerestory window, the living room features a sloped ceiling and a warming fireplace. The kitchen adjoins the dining room and opens to a back porch with a handy storage closet nearby. A spacious master suite boasts a garden tub set in a bay and a walk-in closet. Wood trim and eye-catching windows make this home charming as well as practical. Please specify crawlspace or slab foundation when ordering.

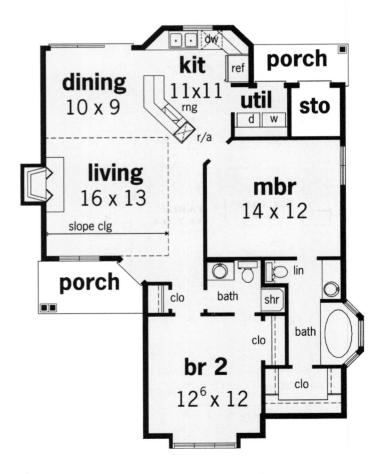

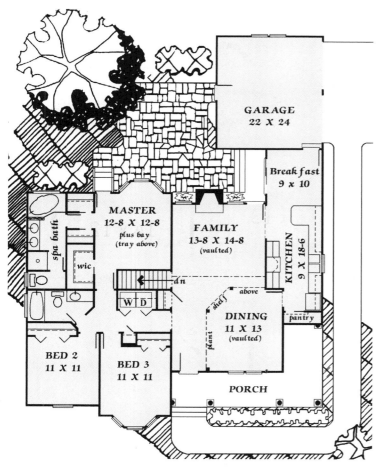

GARAGE
22 X 24

Breakfast
9 x 10

MASTER
12-8 X 12-8
plus bay
(tray above)

FAMILY
13-8 X 14-8
(vaulted)

spa bath

wic

KITCHEN
9 X 18-6

W D

dn

shelf

above

pantry

DINING
11 X 13
(vaulted)

plant

BED 2
11 X 11

BED 3
11 X 11

PORCH

Plan HPT700384

Square Footage: *1,507*
Width: *47'-0"* **Depth:** *70'-0"*

This country home enjoys a covered front porch that's great for relaxation. A gallery foyer opens to the formal dining room, which features a vaulted ceiling. To the rear of the plan, a massive fireplace highlights the spacious family room. The ample kitchen to the right of the house provides a built-in pantry and a breakfast area, which conveniently accesses the garage. To the left, two family bedrooms and a master bedroom are nicely secluded for extra privacy. The master bath boasts a walk-in closet, dual vanities and a spa-style tub.

Plan HPT700385

Main Level: *2,385 square feet*
Lower–Level Entry: *80 square feet*
Total: *2,465 square feet*
Bonus Room: *1,271 square feet*
Width: *60'-4"* **Depth:** *59'-4"*

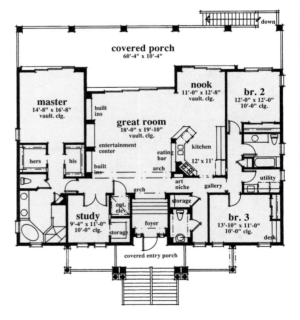

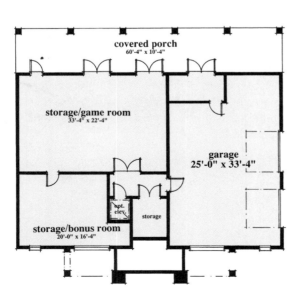

A classic pediment and low-pitched roof are topped by a cupola on this gorgeous coastal design, influenced by 19th-Century Caribbean plantation houses. Savory style blended with a contemporary seaside spirit invites entertaining as well as year-round living—plus room to grow. The beauty and warmth of natural light splash the spacious living area with a sense of the outdoors and a touch of *joie de vivre*. The great room features a wall of built-ins designed for even the most technology-savvy entertainment buff. Dazzling views through walls of glass are enlivened by the presence of a breezy porch. Please specify pier or block foundation when ordering.

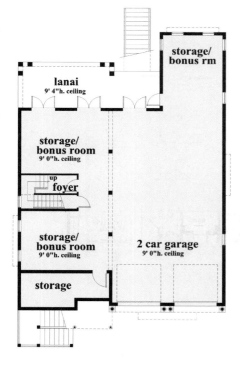

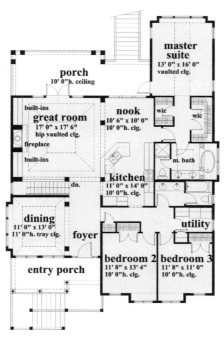

Plan HPT700386

Square Footage: *2,137*
Width: *44'-0"* **Depth:** *61'-0"*

The grand balustrade and recessed entry are just the beginning of this truly spectacular home. A hip vaulted ceiling highlights the great room—a perfect place to entertain, made cozy by a massive fireplace and built-in cabinetry. An angled snack counter provides an uninterrupted interior vista of the living area from the gourmet kitchen. To the rear of the plan, French doors open to a spacious porch—a beautiful spot for enjoying the harmonious sounds of the sea. On the lower level, separate bonus spaces easily convert to hobby rooms or can be used for additional storage.

Plan HPT700387

First Floor: *1,252 square feet*
Second Floor: *972 square feet*
Total: *2,224 square feet*
Width: *48'-0"* **Depth:** *58'-0"*

L

QUOTE ONE®
Cost to build? See page 436
to order complete cost estimate
to build this house in your area!

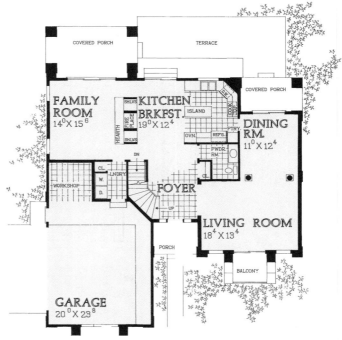

For family living, this delightful three-bedroom plan scores big. The family room focuses on a fireplace and enjoys direct access to a covered porch. The breakfast room allows plenty of space for friendly meals—the island kitchen remains open to this room, providing ease in serving meals and, of course, conversations with the cook. From the two-car garage, a utility area opens to the main-floor living areas. Upstairs, the master suite affords a quiet retreat with its private bath; here you'll find a whirlpool tub set in a sunny nook.

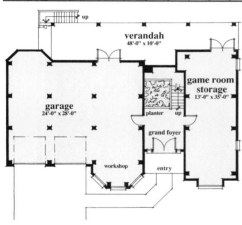

verandah
48'-0" x 10'-0"

game room storage
13'-0" x 35'-0"

garage
24'-0" x 28'-0"

planter up

grand foyer

workshop

entry

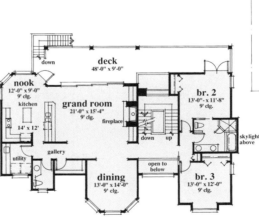

down

deck
48'-0" x 9'-0"

nook
12'-0" x 9'-0"
9' clg.

kitchen

grand room
21'-0" x 15'-4"
9' clg.

14' x 12'

fireplace

br. 2
13'-0" x 11'-8"
9' clg.

gallery

down up

skylight above

utility

dining
13'-0" x 14'-0"
9' clg.

open to below

br. 3
13'-0" x 12'-0"
9' clg.

deck
28'-0" x 8'-0"

2 view fireplace

master suite
22'-0" x 15'-0"
vault. clg.

down

loft

am kitchen

deck

open to below

reading
13'-0" x 15'-0"
vault. clg.

Quote One®

Cost to build? See page 436
to order complete cost estimate
to build this house in your area!

Plan HPT700388

First Floor: *1,642 square feet*
Second Floor: *927 square feet*
Total: *2,569 square feet*
Game Room: *849 square feet*
Width: *60'-0'''* **Depth:** *44'-6"*

L

Luxury abounds in this Floridian home. A recreation room greets you on the garage level. Up the stairs, an open grand room, a bayed nook and a deck stretch across the back of the plan. Two bedrooms occupy the right side of this level and share a full hall bath that includes dual lavatories and a separate tub and shower. The master retreat on the upper level pleases with its own reading room, a morning kitchen, a walk-in closet and a bath with a double-bowl vanity, a whirlpool tub and a shower that leads to the outdoors.

Plan HPT700389

Square Footage: *2,430*
Width: *70'-2"* **Depth:** *53'-0"*

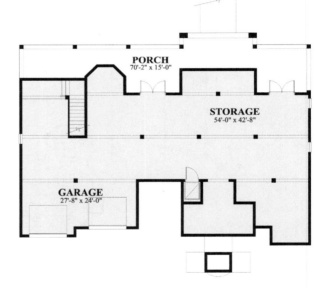

With a row of pretty windows, this gentle Mediterranean home offers plenty of views and outdoor spaces for mingling with nature. A sunburst transom creates a gorgeous entry that will be the envy of the neighborhood. Pilasters announce a grand sense of the past and offer a warm welcome to an ultra-plush interior. These inner vistas, plus the outdoor views, mix it up with fresh air and breezes stirring from open doors to the veranda. High ceilings in the great room and dining room extend the sense of spaciousness and propose planned events that spill out to the outdoor spaces. The formal dining room opens through a colonnade from the central gallery hall and shares the comfort of the central fireplace.

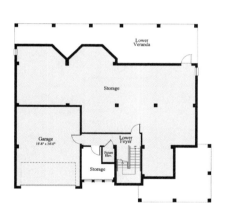

Plan HPT700390

Main Level: *2,096 square feet*
Upper Level: *892 square feet*
Total: *2,988 square feet*
Width: *56'-0"* **Depth:** *54'-0"*

Multiple windows bring natural light to this beautiful home, which offers a floor plan filled with special amenities. Arches provide a grand entry to the beam-ceilinged great room, where built-ins flank the fireplace and three sets of French doors open to a veranda. Step ceilings grace the master suite and the dining room. The master suite provides two walk-in closets and a resplendent bath, while dazzling windows in the dining room allow enjoyment of the outdoors. Two second-floor bedrooms, one with a sun deck, feature walk-in closets and private baths.

Plan HPT700391

Main Level: *2,385 square feet*
Lower–Level Entry: *109 square feet*
Total: *2,494 square feet*
Width: *60'-0"* **Depth:** *52'-0"*

This enticing European Villa boasts an Italian charm and a distinct Mediterranean feel. Stucco and columns dramatically enhance the exterior facade. Once inside, the foyer steps lead up to the formal living areas. To the left, a study is expanded by a vaulted ceiling and double doors that open to the front balcony. Vaulted ceilings create a spacious feel throughout the home, especially in the central great room, which overlooks the rear deck. The island kitchen is conveniently open to a breakfast nook. The guest quarters reside on the right side of the plan—one boasts a private bath, while the second suite uses a full hall bath.

Plan HPT700392

Square Footage: *1,932*
Width: *53'-5"* **Depth:** *65'-10"*

Enter this beautiful home through graceful archways and columns. The foyer, dining room and living room are one open space, defined by a creative room arrangement. The living room opens to the breakfast room and porch. The bedrooms are off a small hall reached through an archway. Two family bedrooms share a bath, while the master bedroom enjoys a private bath with a double-bowl vanity. A garage with storage, and a utility room complete the floor plan. Please specify slab or crawlspace foundation when ordering.

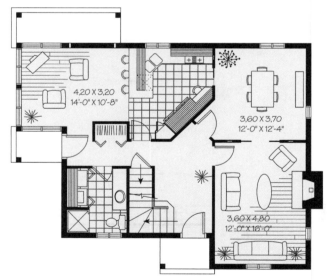

Plan HPT700393

First Floor: *957 square feet*
Second Floor: *885 square feet*
Total: *1,842 square feet*
Width: *38'-0"* **Depth:** *30'-0"*

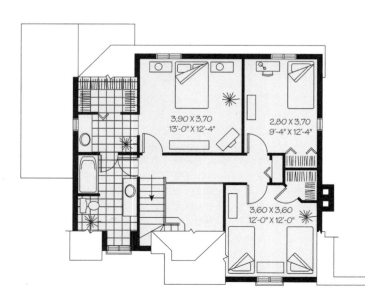

This small stucco home would go equally well in the French countryside or in your new neighborhood. A covered front entrance leads straight ahead to the kitchen, where an interesting angled counter is flanked by a writing desk and a pantry. A snack bar separates the kitchen from the family room, which receives natural light from large windows and sliding glass doors to the rear covered porch. Everyone will appreciate the fireplace in the living room and the pocket door between the kitchen and the dining room. This home is designed with a basement foundation.

Plan HPT700394

Square Footage: *1,572*
Width: *54'-0"* **Depth:** *52'-0"*

The rooflines, Palladian window and turreted bay window blend seductively to create a delightful facade that brightens every neighborhood. The private office to the left of the foyer offers a wonderful view. The dining/living room, to the right of the foyer, boasts a warming fireplace. Privacy is offered with pocket doors to the family/kitchen area and double doors to the foyer. The kitchen delights with a second bay window and a dramatically curved snack bar. The master bedroom privately accesses the shared full bath. This home is designed with a basement foundation.

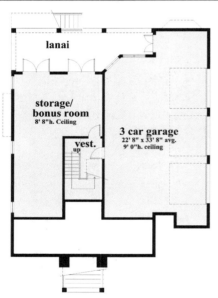

lanai

storage/
bonus room
8' 8"h. Ceiling

3 car garage
22' 8" x 33' 8" avg.
9' 0"h. ceiling

vest.
up

dn.

veranda

window seat

bedroom 3
11' 8" x 12' 4"
9' 4"h. clg.

nook
11' 0" x 8' 0"
9' 4"h. clg.

built-in
cabinetry
great room
19' 6" x 19' 0"
2-story ceiling
fireplace

kitchen

linen   ut.

up

study
11' 0" x 13' 6"
14' 0"h. clg.

foyer

up

dining
11' 0" x 13' 6"
14' 0"h. clg.

bedroom 2
11' 8" x 10' 6"
9' 4"h. clg.

entry porch
32' 0" x 8' 6"
14' 0"h. ceiling

dn.

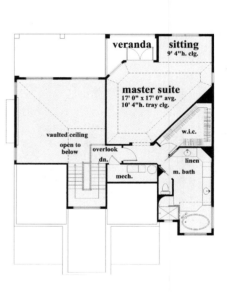

veranda   sitting
9' 4"h. clg.

master suite
17' 0" x 17' 0" avg.
10' 4"h. tray clg.

vaulted ceiling
open to
below

w.i.c.

overlook
dn.

mech.

linen
m. bath

Plan HPT700395

Main Level: *1,671 square feet*
Upper Level: *846 square feet*
Lower–Level Entry: *140 square feet*
Total: *2,657 square feet*
Width: *44'-0"* **Depth:** *55'-0"*

This magnificent villa boasts a beautiful stucco exterior, Spanish-tiled roof and Old World details such as arches and accent columns framing the spectacular entry. The striking appeal of the home introduces an interior that revisits the past in glorious style and sets a new standard for comfort and luxury. Open rooms, French doors and vaulted ceilings add an air of spaciousness throughout the home. The heart of the home is served by a well-crafted kitchen with wrapping counter space and an island counter. The breakfast nook enjoys a view of the veranda and beyond, and brings natural light to the casual eating space. To the right of the foyer, an open formal dining room provides dazzling views and an ambiance of elegance and comfort.

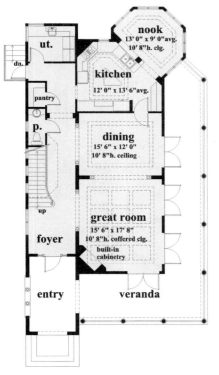

nook
13' 0" x 9' 0"avg.
10' 8"h. ceiling

ut.

dn.

kitchen
12' 0" x 13' 6"avg.

pantry

p.

dining
15' 6" x 12' 0"
10' 8"h. ceiling

up

great room
15' 6" x 17' 8"
10' 8"h. coffered clg.
built-in cabinetry

foyer

entry

veranda

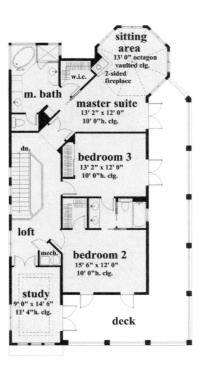

sitting area
13' 0" octagon vaulted clg.
2-sided fireplace

w.i.c.

m. bath

master suite
13' 2" x 12' 0"
10' 0"h. clg.

dn.

bedroom 3
13' 2" x 12' 0"
10' 0"h. clg.

loft

mech.

bedroom 2
15' 6" x 12' 0"
10' 0"h. clg.

study
9' 0" x 14' 6"
11' 4"h. clg.

deck

Plan HPT700396

First Floor: *1,266 square feet*
Second Floor: *1,324 square feet*
Total: *2,590 square feet*
Width: *34'-0"* **Depth:** *63'-2"*

This Casa Bellissima is pure Italian-fashioned elegance. Four double doors wrapping around the great room and dining area open to the stunning veranda. The great room is enhanced by a coffered ceiling and built-in cabinetry, while the entire first floor is bathed in sunlight from a wall of glass doors overlooking the veranda. The dining room connects to a gourmet island kitchen. Upstairs, a beautiful deck wraps gracefully around the family bedrooms. The master suite is a skylit haven enhanced by a bayed sitting area, which features a vaulted octagonal ceiling and a cozy two-sided fireplace. Private double doors access the sun deck from the master suite, Bedrooms 2 and 3 and the study.

Plan HPT700398

Square Footage: *1,907*
Width: *61'-6"* **Depth:** *67'-4"*

Graceful curves welcome you into the court-yard of this Santa Fe home. Inside, a gallery directs traffic to the work zone on the left or the sleeping zone on the right. A pantry offers storage space for kitchen items. The wide covered rear porch is accessible from the dining room, gathering room (with fireplace) and secluded master bedroom. The master bath features a whirlpool tub, separate shower, double vanity and a spacious walk-in closet. Two additional bed-rooms share a full bath, with separate vanities. Extra storage space is provided in the two-car garage.

Quote One®
Cost to build? See page 436
to order complete cost estimate
to build this house in your area!

Outer Space

cabanas and pavilions

Plan HPT700399

Main Floor: *896 square feet*
Lower Floor: *100 square feet*
Total: *996 square feet*
Width: *28'-0"* **Depth:** *32'-0"*

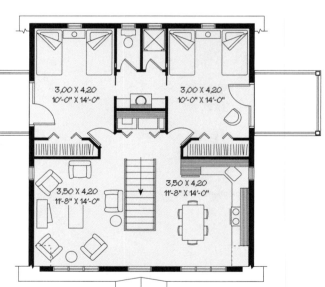

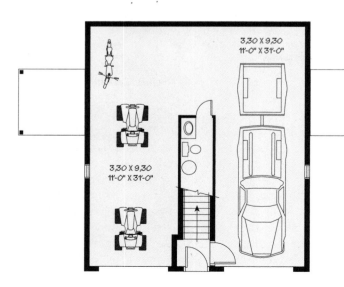

This home is a study in symmetry and perfection. The facade is unique with its siding, octagon-shaped window and two symmetrical side porches on either end of the plan. The first floor is devoted to garage and storage space; steps lead upstairs to the main living quarters. Flanking the stairway on the left is a living room and on the right is an informal dining room and kitchen area, complete with plenty of counter space. Two bedrooms of equal size provide ample closet space, share a full bath and have their own private decks and outdoor access.

Plan HPT700400

Square Footage: *633*
Width: *28'-0"* **Depth:** *26'-0"*

BR.
12/0 X 10/0

DN

W
D

LIVING
16/6 X 12/4

SHELVES

GARAGE
23/0 X 25/0

UP

Designed to fit on Any Street, USA, this garage features Craftsman-style architecture, evident by the exposed rafter tails, shingle siding and four-over-one windows. At ground level are two garage doors and an interior stairway leading to the living area upstairs. The interior stairs lead to the 16'-6" x 12'-4" living area consisting of a U-shaped kitchen and a living room with built-in shelves. Note the storage closet at the top of the stairs. The bedroom is located past the full bath and offers a wall of closets.

Plan HPT700401

Square Footage: *128*
Width: *16'-0"* **Depth:** *8'-0"*

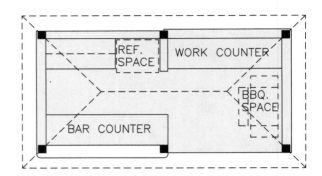

This stylish pavilion is an attractive outdoor retreat. A hipped roof shades the inner area—keep a picnic table close by for outdoor barbecues and entertaining. The barbecue area is provided for outdoor grilling next to a convenient work counter. A refrigerator space is also provided, next to another counter, for keeping cool foods fresh. A bar counter, large enough to host a wide variety of refreshments, completes the pavilion.

Plan HPT700402

Square Footage: *64*
Width: *8'-0"* **Depth:** *8'-0"*

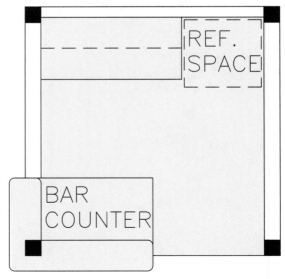

This petite pavilion design is perfect for private and refreshing entertaining. Build this structure close to a pool area to save trips in and out of the home kitchen. Summer leisure time can be more comfortably spent with this convenience close at hand. A refrigerator space is generously provided alongside a counter preparation area. Above, built-in shelves may be added for extra storage. On the opposite side, a bar counter resides for accessible convenience.

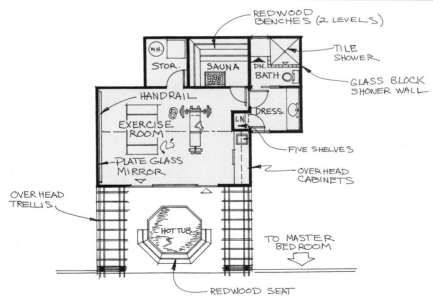

REDWOOD BENCHES (2 LEVELS)

TILE SHOWER

GLASS BLOCK SHOWER WALL

W.H.

STOR.

SAUNA

DN.

BATH

HANDRAIL

EXERCISE ROOM

DRESS.

LN.

FIVE SHELVES

OVER HEAD CABINETS

PLATE GLASS MIRROR

OVER HEAD TRELLIS

HOT TUB

TO MASTER BEDROOM

REDWOOD SEAT

Plan HPT700403

Square Footage: *588*

If you're serious about maintaining optimum personal fitness, don't turn the page until you check out this free-standing exercise cottage. A wall of mirrors, double-decked windows and sliding doors provide a great atmosphere for your workouts. High ceilings accommodate the largest equipment, and features include plenty of storage, a mini-kitchen and bathroom facilities with a glass-block shower wall. Add a sauna inside and a hot tub outside, and who could ask for anything more? A separate dressing room and linen closet are also included in this design. A ballet bar against the mirrored wall, two-level redwood benches in the sauna and ample storage are additional amenities in this inviting personal gym.

Plan HPT700406

Square Footage: *306*
Width: *36'-0"* **Depth:** *25'-0"*

Greet your clients in the business side of this multi-use structure. There's room enough for a reception/waiting room area in front with an impressive entryway through a four-column porch. Decorative recessed windows flanking the door and two more in the side wall allow for plenty of natural light. In the back is ample space for an office with a storage closet and file space. Add a half-bath for maximum convenience. Choose from four different elevations to fit your particular style.

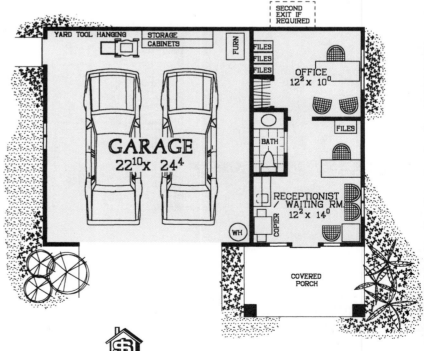

Quote One®
Cost to build? See page 436
to order complete cost estimate
to build this house in your area!

424

Plan HPT700405

Plan HPT700407

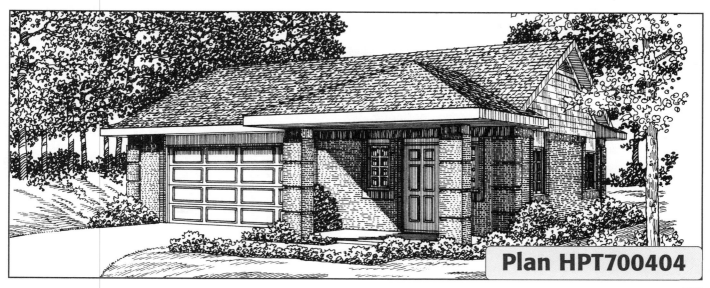

Plan HPT700404

Plan HPT700409
Square Footage: *383*
Width: *21'-4"* **Depth:** *18'-0"*

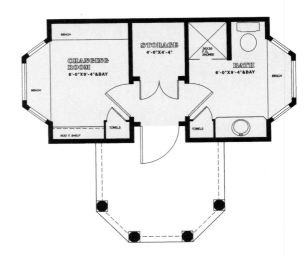

This pool pavilion offers a changing room, a summer kitchen and an elegant porch. Add the convenience of bathroom facilities and you're set for outdoor living all summer long. The design functions perfectly in a small area and features built-in benches, shelves, hanging rods and a separate linen closet.

Plan HPT700408
Square Footage: *352*
Width: *16'-0"* **Depth:** *22'-0"*

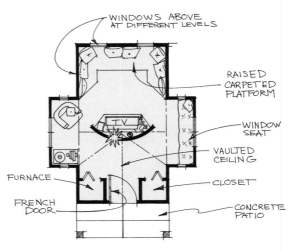

Lucky are the teenagers who have the option of staking claim to this private retreat! The overall dimensions of 16' x 22' provide plenty of space for study, TV or just hangin' out. Special features include a raised, carpeted platform in the TV lounge; a comfy window seat for reading or a catnap; a separate niche for electronic games; and a unique, brightly painted graffiti wall in the entryway.

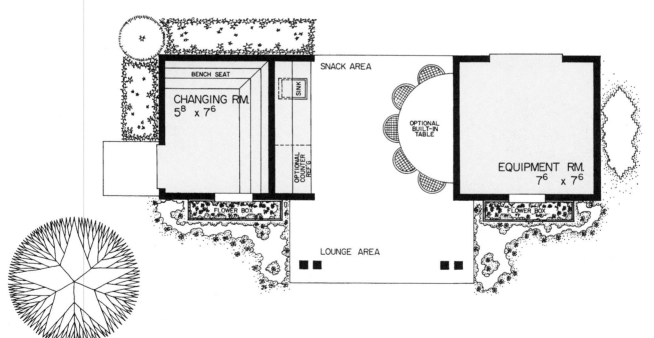

BENCH SEAT

CHANGING RM.
5^8 x 7^6

SINK

OPTIONAL
COUNTER
REF'G

SNACK AREA

OPTIONAL
BUILT-IN
TABLE

EQUIPMENT RM.
7^6 x 7^6

FLOWER BOX

FLOWER BOX

LOUNGE AREA

Plan HPT700410
Width: *24'-0"* **Depth:** *12'-8"*

You can enhance both the beauty and the function of any pool area with this charming structure. A mini-kitchen and an optional built-in table are tucked in the breezeway of this double-room; you'll have shelter for poolside repasts no matter what the weather. The two rooms on either side of the breezeway provide a changing area, with built-in seating and space for the convenient storage of pool supplies.

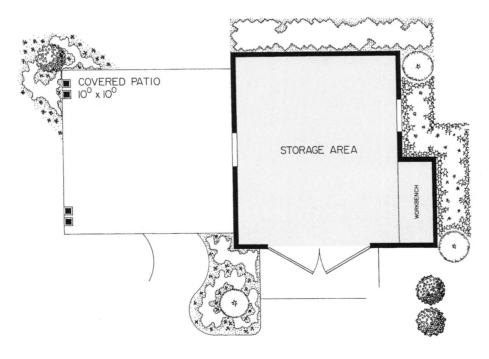

Plan HPT700411

Square Footage: *120*
Width: *10'-0"* **Depth:** *12'-0"*

No words quite convey everything this storage shed/covered patio combination has to offer. The 120 square feet of storage area presents a delightful facade that belies its practical function. Grooved plywood siding and a shingled double roof are accented by double doors, shutters at the window, a birdhouse tucked in the eaves and a trellis for your favorite climbers. Use the storage area as a potting shed, storage shed or workshop.

Plan HPT700413
Square Footage: *168*
Width: *14'-0"* **Depth:** *12'-0"*

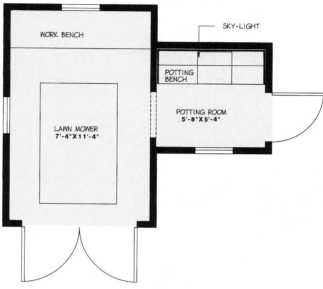

O pen the double doors of this multi-purpose structure and it's a mini-garage for garden tools. The tool-shed section is large enough to house the largest lawn tractor, with room to spare for other garden equipment such as shovels, rakes, lawn trimmers and hoses. With windows on all sides and a skylight above the potting bench, the interior has plenty of natural light; the addition of electrical wiring would make this structure even more practical.

Plan HPT700412
Square Footage: *72*
Width: *12'-0"* **Depth:** *6'-0"*

D esigned to blend into the garden surroundings, this cozy little building keeps all your garden tools and supplies at your fingertips. You can vary the materials to create the appearance best suited to your site. This 72-square-foot structure is large enough to accommodate a potting bench, shelves and an area for garden tools.

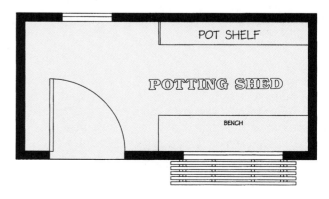

This cleverly designed structure is filled with amenities that make a small space seem huge. The ceiling of the main part of the building is vaulted and features clerestory windows. Bumped-out areas on both sides are perfect for desks and work areas. The built-in bookshelf is complemented by a walk-in storage closet. A half-bath and wet bar round out the plan. The entry is graced by a columned porch and double French doors.

For a bare-essentials outdoor structure, this weekend cottage offers a wealth of options for its use. Choose it for handy home office space, extra room for visitors, a playhouse or a game room. It features a covered front porch and offers two lovely rustic exteriors for you to choose. The interior features built-in bunk beds, a closet and a bumped-out window.

Plan HPT700414

Square Footage: *432*
Width: *20'-0"* **Depth:** *30'-0"*

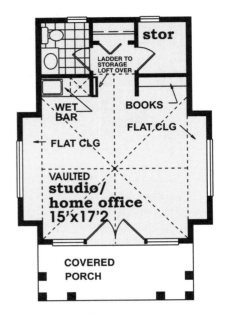

Plan HPT700415

Square Footage: *144*
Width: *12'-0"* **Depth:** *16'-0"*

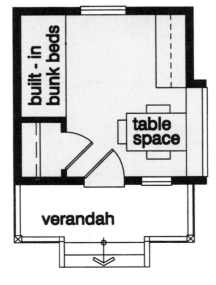

Quote One®

Cost to build? See page 436
to order complete cost estimate
to build this house in your area!

Plan HPT700417
Width: *24'-0"* **Depth:** *32'-0"*

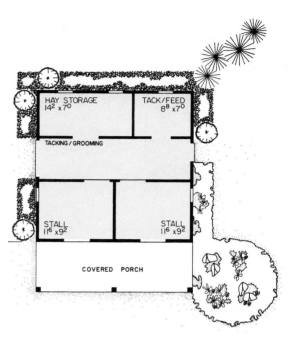

Right out of Kentucky horse country comes this all-in-one design for a two-horse stable, plus tack room and covered hay storage. Two generous 11'-6" x 9'-2" stalls provide shelter and security for your best stock, with easy access through Dutch doors. Against the far wall is a 14'-2" x 7' hay "loft" and next to it, an 8'-8" x 7' tack room.

Plan HPT700416
Square Footage: *114*
Width: *12'-0"* **Depth:** *12'-0"*

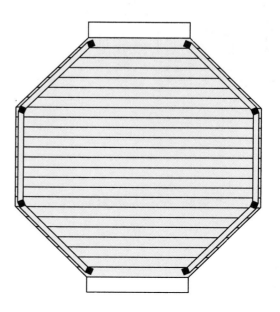

Victorian on a small scale, this gazebo will be the highlight of any yard. With a cupola topped by a weathervane, a railed perimeter and double steps up, it's the essence of historic design. Small enough to fit on just about any size lot, yet large enough to accommodate a small crowd, it is perfect for outdoor entertaining. Choose standard gingerbread details from your local supplier to make it your own.

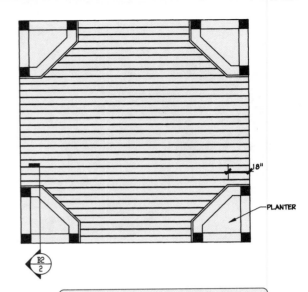

The built-in planters and open roof areas of this multiple-entrance gazebo make this design a gardener's dream-come-true. The open roof allows sun and rain ample access to the planters and gives the structure a definite country-garden effect. Built with or without a cupola, the open lattice work in the walls and roof will complement a wide variety of landscapes and home designs.

Plan HPT700428
Square Footage: *256*
Width: *16'-0"* **Depth:** *16'-0"*

Shining copper on the cupola and shimmering glass windows all around enhance this double-entrance gazebo with dancing light and color. The many windows allow natural light to engulf the interior, making it a perfect studio. Easy to heat and cool, this gazebo contains operable louvers in the cupola to increase the flow of air. An exhaust fan could be added to the cupola to further maximize air flow. The masonry base with brick steps gives the structure a definite feeling of both elegance and permanence. The roof structure is made from standard framing materials with the cupola adorned with a copper cover.

Plan HPT700429
Square Footage: *585*
Width: *19'-10"* **Depth:** *29'-6"*

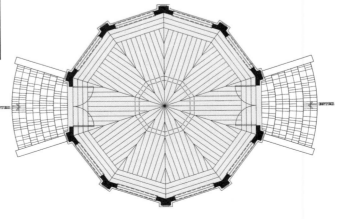

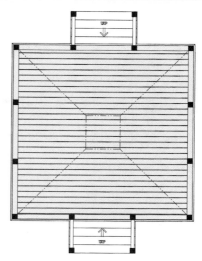

Dance the night away in this double-entrance, pass-through-style gazebo. By day, the open-air construction provides a clear view in all directions. The large floor area of 256 square feet seats twelve to sixteen people comfortably or nicely accommodates musicians or entertainers for a lawn party. The decorative cupola can be lowered, louvered, or removed to create just the appearance you want. Or, add an antique weathervane just for fun. This gazebo has five steps up, which give it a large crawlspace for access to any added utilities. Its square shape allows for simple cutting and floor framing, plus easy assembly of the roof frame.

Plan HPT700430
Width: *16'-0"* **Depth:** *22'-4"*

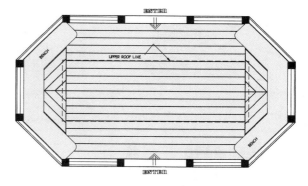

Plan HPT700431
Square Footage: *162*
Width: *18'-0"* **Depth:** *10'-0"*

Designed for serious entertaining, the size alone—162 square feet—ensures you that this gazebo is unique. The star-lattice railing design, built-in benches and raised center roof with accent trim make this structure as practical as it is attractive. Large enough for small parties, there is built-in seating for about twenty people and enough floor area for another ten to twenty. Ideal for entertaining, the addition of lights and a wet bar make this design an important extension of any home. The rooflines and overhang can be modified to give an Oriental effect, or removed completely to give a carousel-like appearance.

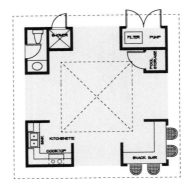

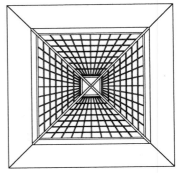

trellis roof

Plan HPT700432

Square Footage: *576*
Width: *24'-0"* **Depth:** *24'-0"*

Cost to build? See page 436
to order complete cost estimate
to build this house in your area!

E ntertain the possibilities for poolside parties with this smart, multi-functional ramada. Four corner units are united by open-air walkways and are almost literally tied together by a trellis roof. Pull up a chair to the outside bar in one corner for a refreshing drink or snack. Across the walkway is an efficiency kitchenette to make the goodies. In the next corner is a restroom and a shower, each with a separate entrance. The final corner hides all the pool essentials with double doors leading to the filter and pump room and a separate storage room for other pool equipment and toys.

I f you run a large operation, consider this expanded floor plan for your stable requirements. Six 12'-2" x 12' livestock pens with dirt floors feature built-in feed and water troughs and Dutch doors leading either to a fenced exercise area or into either of two conveniently located grooming areas. Both grooming areas have grooved cement floors, sloped for easy hosing and draining. A convenient connecting hall between the grooming areas also has sloped concrete floors for easy maintenance. A central secured tack room with built-in saddle racks and grain bins, a bath with a toilet and sink and a 10' x 17' inside storage area for hay complete the available features. Seven skylights throughout the structure provide an abundance of natural light.

Cost to build? See page 436
to order complete cost estimate
to build this house in your area!

Plan HPT700433

Square Footage: *1,918*
Width: *56'-0"* **Depth:** *53'-0"*

LET US SHOW YOU OUR HOME BLUEPRINT PACKAGE.

BUILDING A HOME? PLANNING A HOME?

OUR BLUEPRINT PACKAGE HAS NEARLY EVERYTHING YOU NEED TO GET THE JOB DONE RIGHT,

whether you're working on your own or with help from an architect, designer, builder or subcontractors. Each Blueprint Package is the result of many hours of work by licensed architects or professional designers.

QUALITY

Hundreds of hours of painstaking effort have gone into the development of your blueprint plan. Each home has been quality-checked by professionals to insure accuracy and buildability.

VALUE

Because we sell in volume, you can buy professional quality blueprints at a fraction of their development cost. With our plans, your dream home design costs substantially less than the fees charged by architects.

SERVICE

Once you've chosen your favorite home plan, you'll receive fast, efficient service whether you choose to mail or fax your order to us or call us toll free at 1-800-521-6797. After you have received your order, call for customer service toll free 1-888-690-1116.

SATISFACTION

Over 50 years of service to satisfied home plan buyers provide us unparalleled experience and knowledge in producing quality blueprints.

ORDER TOLL FREE 1-800-521-6797

After you've looked over our Blueprint Package and Important Extras, call toll free on our Blueprint Hotline: 1-800-521-6797, for current pricing and availability prior to mailing the order form on page 445. We're ready and eager to serve you. After you have received your order, call for customer service toll free 1-888-690-1116.

Each set of blueprints is an interrelated collection of detail sheets which includes components such as floor plans, interior and exterior elevations, dimensions, cross-sections, diagrams and notations. These sheets show exactly how your house is to be built.

SETS MAY INCLUDE:

FRONTAL SHEET

This artist's sketch of the exterior of the house gives you an idea of how the house will look when built and landscaped. Large floor plans show all levels of the house and provide an overview of your new home's livability, as well as a handy reference for deciding on furniture placement.

FOUNDATION PLANS

This sheet shows the foundation layout including support walls, excavated and unexcavated areas, if any, and foundation notes. If slab construction rather than basement, the plan shows footings and details for a monolithic slab. This page, or another in the set, may include a sample plot plan for locating your house on a building site.

DETAILED FLOOR PLANS

These plans show the layout of each floor of the house. Rooms and interior spaces are carefully dimensioned and keys are given for cross-section details provided later in the plans. The positions of electrical outlets and switches are shown.

HOUSE CROSS-SECTIONS

Large-scale views show sections or cut-aways of the foundation, interior walls, exterior walls, floors, stairways and roof details. Additional cross-sections may show important changes in floor, ceiling or roof heights or the relationship of one level to another. Extremely valuable for construction, these sections show exactly how the various parts of the house fit together.

INTERIOR ELEVATIONS

Many of our drawings show the design and placement of kitchen and bathroom cabinets, laundry areas, fireplaces, bookcases and other built-ins. Little "extras," such as mantelpiece and wainscoting drawings, plus molding sections, provide details that give your home that custom touch.

EXTERIOR ELEVATIONS

These drawings show the front, rear and sides of your house and give necessary notes on exterior materials and finishes. Particular attention is given to cornice detail, brick and stone accents or other finish items that make your home unique.

*INTRODUCING IMPORTANT PLANNING AND CONSTRUCTION
AIDS DEVELOPED BY OUR PROFESSIONALS TO HELP YOU
SUCCEED IN YOUR HOME-BUILDING PROJECT*

MATERIALS LIST

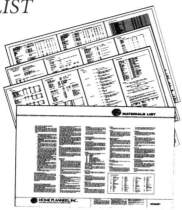

*(Note: Because of the diversity
of local building codes, our
Materials List does not include
mechanical materials.)*

For many of the designs in our portfolio, we offer a customized materials take-off that is invaluable in planning and estimating the cost of your new home. This Materials List outlines the quantity, type and size of materials needed to build your house (with the exception of mechanical system items). Included are framing lumber, windows and doors, kitchen and bath cabinetry, rough and finish hardware, and much more. This handy list helps you or your builder cost out materials and serves as a reference sheet when you're compiling bids. Some Materials Lists may be ordered before blueprints are ordered, call for information.

SPECIFICATION OUTLINE

This valuable 16-page document is critical to building your house correctly. Designed to be filled in by you or your builder, this book lists 166 stages or items crucial to the building process. It provides a comprehensive review of the construction process and helps in choosing materials. When combined with the blueprints, a signed contract, and a schedule, it becomes a legal document and record for the building of your home.

QUOTE ONE®

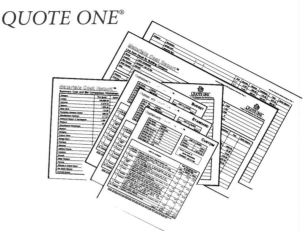

SUMMARY COST REPORT **MATERIAL COST REPORT**

A product for estimating the cost of building select designs, the Quote One® system is available in two separate stages: The Summary Cost Report and the Material Cost Report.

The **Summary Cost Report** is the first stage in the package and shows the total cost per square foot for your chosen home in your zip-code area and then breaks that cost down into various categories showing the costs for building materials, labor and installation. The report includes three grades: Budget, Standard and Custom. These reports allow you to evaluate your building budget and compare the costs of building a variety of homes in your area.

Make even more informed decisions about your home-building project with the second phase of our package, our **Material Cost Report.** This tool is invaluable in planning and estimating the cost of your new home. The material and installation (labor and equipment) cost is shown for each of over 1,000 line items provided in the Materials List (Standard grade), which is included when you purchase this estimating tool. It allows you to determine building costs for your specific zip-code area and for your chosen home design. Space is allowed for additional estimates from contractors and subcontractors, such as for mechanical materials, which are not included in our packages. This invaluable tool includes a Materials List. A Material Cost Report cannot be ordered before blueprints are ordered. Call for details. In addition, ask about our Home Planners Estimating Package.

If you are interested in a plan that is not indicated as Quote One®, please call and ask our sales reps. They will be happy to verify the status for you. To order these invaluable reports, use the order form.

CONSTRUCTION INFORMATION

If you want to know more about techniques— and deal more confidently with subcontractors — we offer these useful sheets. Each set is an excellent tool that will add to your understanding of these technical subjects. These helpful details provide general construction information and are not specific to any single plan.

PLUMBING

The Blueprint Package includes locations for all the plumbing fixtures, including sinks, lavatories, tubs, showers, toilets, laundry trays and water heaters. However, if you want to know more about the complete plumbing system, these Plumbing Details will prove very useful. Prepared to meet requirements of the National Plumbing Code, these fact-filled sheets give general information on pipe schedules, fittings, sump-pump details, water-softener hookups, septic system details and much more. Sheets also include a glossary of terms.

ELECTRICAL

The locations for every electrical switch, plug and outlet are shown in your Blueprint Package. However, these Electrical Details go further to take the mystery out of household electrical systems. Prepared to meet requirements of the National Electrical Code, these comprehensive drawings come packed with helpful information, including wire sizing, switch-installation schematics, cable-routing details, appliance wattage, doorbell hook-ups, typical service panel circuitry and much more. A glossary of terms is also included.

CONSTRUCTION

The Blueprint Package contains information an experienced builder needs to construct a particular house. However, it doesn't show all the ways that houses can be built, nor does it explain alternate construction methods. To help you understand how your house will be built—and offer additional techniques—this set of Construction Details depicts the materials and methods used to build foundations, fireplaces, walls, floors and roofs. Where appropriate, the drawings show acceptable alternatives.

MECHANICAL

These Mechanical Details contain fundamental principles and useful data that will help you make informed decisions and communicate with subcontractors about heating and cooling systems. Drawings contain instructions and samples that allow you to make simple load calculations, and preliminary sizing and costing analysis. Covered are the most commonly used systems from heat pumps to solar fuel systems. The package is filled with illustrations and diagrams to help you visualize components and how they relate to one another.

THE HANDS-ON HOME FURNITURE PLANNER

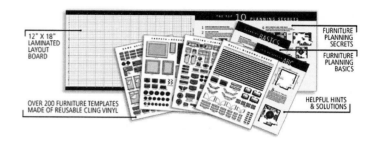

Effectively plan the space in your home using The **Hands-On Home Furniture Planner**. It's fun and easy—no more moving heavy pieces of furniture to see how the room will go together. And you can try different layouts, moving furniture at a whim.

The kit includes reusable peel and stick furniture templates that fit onto a 12" x 18" laminated layout board—space enough to layout every room in your home.

Also included in the package are a number of helpful planning tools. You'll receive:

- ✓ Helpful hints and solutions for difficult situations.
- ✓ Furniture planning basics to get you started.
- ✓ Furniture planning secrets that let you in on some of the tricks of professional designers.

The **Hands-On Home Furniture Planner** is the one tool that no new homeowner or home remodeler should be without. It's also a perfect housewarming gift!

To Order, Call Toll Free
1-800-521-6797

After you've looked over our Blueprint Package and Important Extras on these pages, call for current pricing and availability prior to mailing the order form. We're ready and eager to serve you. After you have received your order, call for customer service toll free 1-888-690-1116.

THE DECK BLUEPRINT PACKAGE

Many of the homes in this book can be enhanced with a professionally designed Home Planners Deck Plan. Those homes marked with a **D** have a complementary Deck Plan, sold separately, which includes a Deck Plan Frontal Sheet, Deck Framing and Floor Plans, Deck Elevations and a Deck Materials List. A Standard Deck Details Package, also available, provides all the how-to information necessary for building *any* deck. Our Complete Deck Building Package contains one set of Custom Deck Plans of your choice, plus one set of Standard Deck Building Details, all for one low price. Our plans and details are carefully prepared in an easy-to-understand format that will guide you through every stage of your deck-building project. This page shows a sample Deck layout to match your favorite house. See Blueprint Price Schedule for ordering information.

THE LANDSCAPE BLUEPRINT PACKAGE

For the homes marked with an **L** in this book, Home Planners has created a front-yard Landscape Plan that is complementary in design to the house plan. These comprehensive blueprint packages include a Frontal Sheet, Plan View, Regionalized Plant & Materials List, a sheet on Planting and Maintaining Your Landscape, Zone Maps and Plant Size and Description Guide. These plans will help you achieve professional results, adding value and enjoyment to your property for years to come. Each set of blueprints is a full 18" x 24" in size with clear, complete instructions and easy-to-read type. A sample Landscape Plan is shown below. See Blueprint Price Schedule for ordering information.

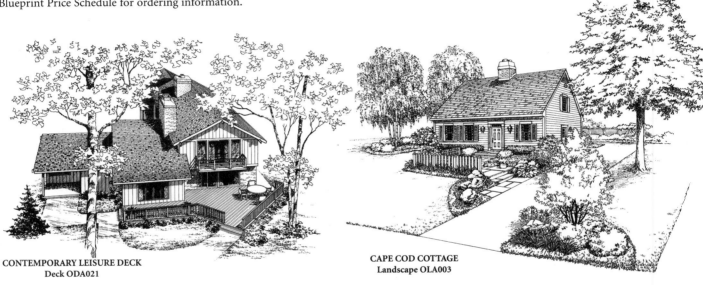

CONTEMPORARY LEISURE DECK
Deck ODA021

CAPE COD COTTAGE
Landscape OLA003

REGIONAL ORDER MAP

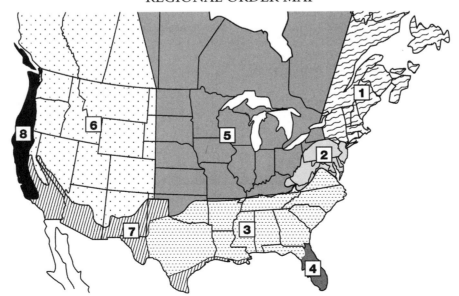

Most Landscape Plans are available with a Plant & Materials List adapted by horticultural experts to 8 different regions of the country. Please specify the Geographic Region when ordering your plan. See Blueprint Price Schedule for ordering information and regional availability.

Region	1	Northeast
Region	2	Mid-Atlantic
Region	3	Deep South
Region	4	Florida & Gulf Coast
Region	5	Midwest
Region	6	Rocky Mountains
Region	7	Southern California & Desert Southwest
Region	8	Northern California & Pacific Northwest

BLUEPRINT PRICE SCHEDULE

Prices guaranteed through December 31, 2002

TIERS	1-SET STUDY PACKAGE	4-SET BUILDING PACKAGE	8-SET BUILDING PACKAGE	1-SET REPRODUCIBLE*
P1	$20	$50	$90	$140
P2	$40	$70	$110	$160
P3	$70	$100	$140	$190
P4	$100	$130	$170	$220
P5	$140	$170	$210	$270
P6	$180	$210	$250	$310
A1	$440	$480	$520	$660
A2	$480	$520	$560	$720
A3	$520	$560	$600	$780
A4	$565	$605	$645	$850
C1	$610	$655	$700	$915
C2	$655	$700	$745	$980
C3	$700	$745	$790	$1050
C4	$750	$795	$840	$1125
L1	$825	$875	$925	$1240
L2	$900	$950	$1000	$1350
L3	$1000	$1050	$1100	$1500
L4	$1100	$1150	$1200	$1650

* Requires a fax number

OPTIONS FOR PLANS IN TIERS A1–L4

Additional Identical Blueprints
in same order for "A1–L4" price plans ....$50 per set
Reverse Blueprints (mirror image)
with 4- or 8-set order for "A1–L4" plans...$50 fee per order
Specification Outlines...$10 each
Materials Lists for "A1–C3" plans ....$60 each
Materials Lists for "C4–L4" plans...$70 each

OPTIONS FOR PLANS IN TIERS P1–P6

Additional Identical Blueprints
in same order for "P1–P6" price plans..$10 per set
Reverse Blueprints (mirror image) for "P1–P6" price plans ....$10 fee per order
1 Set of Deck Construction Details ....$14.95 each
Deck Construction Package ....**add $10 to Building Package price**
(includes 1 set of "P1–P6" plans, plus 1 set Standard Deck Construction Details)

IMPORTANT NOTES

• The 1-set study package is marked "not for construction."
• Prices for 4- or 8-set Building Packages honored only at time of original order.
• Some foundations carry a $225 surcharge.
• Right-reading reverse blueprints, if available, will incur a $165 surcharge.
• Additional identical blueprints may be purchased within 60 days of original order.

TO USE THE INDEX, refer to the design number listed in numerical order (a helpful page reference is also given). Note the price tier and refer to the Blueprint Price Schedule above for the cost of one, four or eight sets of blueprints or the cost of a reproducible drawing. Additional prices are shown for identical and reverse blueprint sets, as well as a very useful Materials List for some of the plans. Also note in the Plan Index those plans that have Deck Plans or Landscape Plans. Refer to the schedules above for prices of these plans. The letter "Y" identifies plans that are part of our Quote One® estimating service and those that offer Materials Lists.

TO ORDER, Call toll free 1-800-521-6797 for current pricing and availability prior to mailing the order form. FAX: 1-800-224-6699 or 520-544-3086.

PLAN INDEX

DESIGN	PRICE	PAGE	MATERIALS LIST	QUOTE ONE®	DECK	DECK PRICE	LANDSCAPE	LANDSCAPE PRICE	REGIONS
HPT700001	A4	14							
HPT700002	C1	15							
HPT700003	A4	16	Y						
HPT700004	C1	17							
HPT700005	C4	18							
HPT700006	C1	19							
HPT700007	C3	20							
HPT700008	A4	21							
HPT700009	C2	22	Y						
HPT700010	A3	23							
HPT700011	A3	24							
HPT700012	C3	26							
HPT700013	C2	27							
HPT700014	C1	28	Y						
HPT700015	C2	29	Y						
HPT700016	C2	30	Y						
HPT700017	C2	31	Y						
HPT700018	A4	32	Y	Y					
HPT700019	A3	34	Y	Y					
HPT700020	A3	35	Y	Y	ODA018	P3	OLA026	P3	123568
HPT700021	A2	36	Y						
HPT700022	A2	37	Y						
HPT700023	A2	38	Y						
HPT700024	A4	39	Y						
HPT700025	A3	40	Y	Y			OLA010	P3	1234568
HPT700026	A1	41	Y						
HPT700027	A4	72							
HPT700028	A2	42	Y						
HPT700029	A1	43	Y	Y					
HPT700030	A3	44							
HPT700031	A4	45	Y						
HPT700032	A3	46							
HPT700033	A3	47							
HPT700034	A2	48	Y						
HPT700035	A2	49	Y						
HPT700036	A2	50							
HPT700037	A2	51							
HPT700038	A4	52							
HPT700039	A3	53							
HPT700040	A4	54	Y						
HPT700041	A4	55	Y						
HPT700042	A4	56							
HPT700043	A3	57							
HPT700044	A3	58	Y						
HPT700045	A4	59	Y						
HPT700046	A4	60	Y	Y					
HPT700047	A4	61	Y	Y			OLA012	P3	12345678
HPT700048	A3	62							
HPT700049	A3	63	Y						
HPT700050	A4	64							

PLAN INDEX

DESIGN	PRICE	PAGE	MATERIALS LIST	QUOTE ONE®	DECK	DECK PRICE	LANDSCAPE	LANDSCAPE PRICE	REGIONS
HPT700051	A4	65							
HPT700052	A3	66							
HPT700053	A4	67							
HPT700054	A3	68							
HPT700055	A4	69							
HPT700056	A4	70	Y	Y	ODA013	P2	OLA021	P3	123568
HPT700057	A4	71	Y	Y			OLA010	P3	1234568
HPT700058	A3	73	Y						
HPT700059	A4	74	Y						
HPT700060	A3	75							
HPT700061	A2	76	Y						
HPT700062	A2	77							
HPT700063	A2	78							
HPT700064	A2	79	Y						
HPT700065	A4	80	Y						
HPT700066	A2	81							
HPT700067	A3	82	Y						
HPT700068	A3	83	Y	Y	ODA015	P2	OLA006	P3	123568
HPT700069	A4	84							
HPT700070	A3	85							
HPT700071	A2	86							
HPT700072	C1	87							
HPT700073	C1	88	Y						
HPT700074	A4	89	Y	Y					
HPT700075	A2	90							
HPT700076	A4	91							
HPT700077	A4	92	Y						
HPT700078	A3	93							
HPT700079	A4	94							
HPT700080	A3	95							
HPT700081	A4	96	Y						
HPT700082	C1	97	Y						
HPT700083	C2	98	Y						
HPT700084	C1	99							
HPT700085	A4	100							
HPT700086	A3	101	Y	Y					
HPT700087	A4	102							
HPT700088	C1	104	Y						
HPT700089	A3	105	Y						
HPT700090	A4	106							
HPT700091	C1	107							
HPT700092	C3	108							
HPT700093	C3	109							
HPT700094	A2	110	Y						
HPT700095	A2	111							
HPT700096	C1	112	Y						
HPT700097	A3	113	Y						
HPT700098	A1	114							
HPT700099	A2	115	Y						
HPT700100	A2	116							
HPT700101	A2	117	Y						
HPT700102	A2	118	Y						
HPT700103	A3	119							
HPT700104	A1	120	Y						
HPT700105	C1	121	Y						
HPT700106	A3	122	Y	Y	ODA003	P2	OLA003	P3	123568
HPT700107	A2	123	Y						
HPT700108	A3	124	Y						
HPT700109	A2	125	Y						
HPT700110	A3	126	Y						
HPT700111	A4	127	Y						
HPT700112	A2	128	Y						
HPT700113	A1	129	Y						
HPT700114	A4	130	Y	Y					
HPT700115	A3	131	Y						
HPT700116	C3	132	Y						
HPT700117	A3	133	Y	Y	ODA016	P2			
HPT700118	C1	134							
HPT700119	C1	135							
HPT700120	C2	136							
HPT700121	A3	137	Y						
HPT700122	A4	138	Y						
HPT700123	A4	139							
HPT700124	A4	140							
HPT700125	A4	141	Y						
HPT700126	A4	142	Y						
HPT700127	C2	143	Y						
HPT700128	C3	144							
HPT700129	C2	145							
HPT700130	C2	146	Y						
HPT700131	C1	147							
HPT700132	A4	148							
HPT700133	A4	149	Y						
HPT700134	C3	150							
HPT700135	L2	151							
HPT700136	C1	152							
HPT700137	A3	153							
HPT700138	C2	154							
HPT700139	C2	155							
HPT700140	C4	156							
HPT700141	C4	157							
HPT700142	L1	158							
HPT700143	L1	159							
HPT700144	A4	160							
HPT700145	C2	161							
HPT700146	C1	162							
HPT700147	A2	163	Y						
HPT700148	A4	164							
HPT700149	A3	165							
HPT700150	A4	166							

Before filling out

the order form,

please call us on

our Toll-Free

Blueprint Hotline

1-800-521-6797.

You may want to

learn more about

our services and

products. Here's

some information

you will find helpful.

OUR EXCHANGE POLICY

With the exception of reproducible plan orders, we will exchange your entire first order for an equal or greater number of blueprints within our plan collection within 90 days of the original order. The entire content of your original order must be returned before an exchange will be processed. Please call our customer service department for your return authorization number and shipping instructions. If the returned blueprints look used, redlined or copied, we will not honor your exchange. Fees for exchanging your blueprints are as follows: 20% of the amount of the original order...plus the difference in cost if exchanging for a design in a higher price bracket or less the difference in cost if exchanging for a design in a lower price bracket. **(Reproducible blueprints are not exchangeable or refundable.)** Please call for current postage and handling prices. Shipping and handling charges are not refundable.

ABOUT REPRODUCIBLES

When purchasing a reproducible you may be required to furnish a fax number. The designer will fax documents that you must sign and return to them before shipping will take place.

ABOUT REVERSE BLUEPRINTS

Although lettering and dimensions will appear backward, reverses will be a useful aid if you decide to flop the plan. See Price Schedule and Plans Index for pricing.

REVISING, MODIFYING AND CUSTOMIZING PLANS

Like many homeowners who buy these plans, you and your builder, architect or engineer may want to make changes to them. We recommend purchase of a reproducible plan for any changes made by your builder, licensed architect or engineer. As set forth below, we cannot assume any responsibility for blueprints which have been changed, whether by you, your builder or by professionals selected by you or referred to you by us, because such individuals are outside our supervision and control.

ARCHITECTURAL AND ENGINEERING SEALS

Some cities and states are now requiring that a licensed architect or engineer review and "seal" a blueprint, or officially approve it, prior to construction due to concerns over energy costs, safety and other factors. Prior to application for a building permit or the start of actual construction, we strongly advise that you consult your local building official who can tell you if such a review is required.

ABOUT THE DESIGNS

The architects and designers whose work appears in this publication are among America's leading residential designers. Each plan was designed to meet the requirements of a nationally recognized model building code in effect at the time and place the plan was drawn. Because national building codes change from time to time, plans may not comply with any such code at the time they are sold to a customer. In addition, building officials may not accept these plans as final construction documents of record as the plans may need to be modified and additional drawings and details added to suit local conditions and requirements. We strongly advise that purchasers consult a licensed architect or engineer, and their local building official, before starting any construction related to these plans.

LOCAL BUILDING CODES AND ZONING REQUIREMENTS

At the time of creation, our plans are drawn to specifications published by the Building Officials and Code Administrators (BOCA) International, Inc.; the Southern Building Code Congress (SBCCI) International, Inc.; the International Conference of Building Officials (ICBO); or the Council of American Building Officials (CABO). Our plans are designed to meet or exceed national building standards. Because of the great differences in geography and climate throughout the United States and Canada, each state, county and municipality has its own building codes, zone requirements, ordinances and building regulations. Your plan may need to be modified to comply with local requirements regarding snow loads, energy codes, soil and seismic conditions and a wide range of other matters. In addition, you may need to obtain permits or inspections from local governments before and in the course of construction. Prior to using blueprints ordered from us, we strongly advise that you consult a licensed architect or engineer—and speak with your local building official—before applying for any permit or beginning construction. We authorize the use of our blueprints on the express condition that you strictly comply with all local building codes, zoning requirements and other applicable laws, regulations, ordinances and requirements. Notice: Plans for homes to be built in Nevada must be re-drawn by a Nevada-registered professional. Consult your building official for more information on this subject.

TOLL FREE 1-800-521-6797

REGULAR OFFICE HOURS:
8:00 a.m.-9:00 p.m. EST, Monday-Friday

If we receive your order by 3:00 p.m. EST, Monday-Friday, we'll process it and ship within **two business days**. When ordering by phone, please have your credit card or check information ready. We'll also ask you for the Order Form Key Number at the bottom of the order form.

By FAX: Copy the Order Form on the next page and send it on our FAX line: 1-800-224-6699 or 520-544-3086.

Canadian Customers Order Toll Free 1-877-223-6389

DISCLAIMER

The designers we work with have put substantial care and effort into the creation of their blueprints. However, because they cannot provide on-site consultation, supervision and control over actual construction, and because of the great variance in local building requirements, building practices and soil, seismic, weather and other conditions, WE CANNOT MAKE ANY WARRANTY, EXPRESS OR IMPLIED, WITH RESPECT TO THE CONTENT OR USE OF THE BLUEPRINTS, INCLUDING BUT NOT LIMITED TO ANY WARRANTY OF MERCHANTABILITY OR OF FITNESS FOR A PARTICULAR PURPOSE. ITEMS, PRICES, TERMS AND CONDITIONS ARE SUBJECT TO CHANGE WITHOUT NOTICE. REPRODUCIBLE PLAN ORDERS MAY REQUIRE A CUSTOMER'S SIGNED RELEASE BEFORE SHIPPING.

TERMS AND CONDITIONS

These designs are protected under the terms of United States Copyright Law and may not be copied or reproduced in any way, by any means, unless you have purchased Reproducibles which clearly indicate your right to copy or reproduce. We authorize the use of your chosen design as an aid in the construction of one single family home only. You may not use this design to build a second or multiple dwellings without purchasing another blueprint or blueprints or paying additional design fees.

HOW MANY BLUEPRINTS DO YOU NEED?

Although a standard building package may satisfy many states, cities and counties, some plans may require certain changes. For your convenience, we have developed a Reproducible plan which allows a local professional to modify and make up to 10 copies of your revised plan. As our plans are all copyright protected, with your purchase of the Reproducible, we will supply you with a Copyright release letter. The number of copies you may need: 1 for owner; 3 for builder; 2 for local building department and 1-3 sets for your mortgage lender.

ORDER TOLL FREE!

For information about any of our services or to order call 1-800-521-6797

Browse our website: www.eplans.com

BLUEPRINTS ARE NOT REFUNDABLE EXCHANGES ONLY

For Customer Service, call toll free 1-888-690-1116.

HOME PLANNERS, LLC wholly owned by Hanley-Wood, LLC
3275 WEST INA ROAD, SUITE 110 • TUCSON, ARIZONA • 85741

THE BASIC BLUEPRINT PACKAGE

Rush me the following (please refer to the Plans Index and Price Schedule in this section):

___Set(s) of reproducibles*, plan number(s) _____ $_____
    indicate foundation type _____ surcharge (if applicable): $_____
___Set(s) of blueprints, plan number(s) _____ $_____
    indicate foundation type _____ surcharge (if applicable): $_____
___Additional identical blueprints (standard or reverse) in same order @ $50 per set $_____
___Reverse blueprints @ $50 fee per order. Right-reading reverse @ $165 surcharge $_____

IMPORTANT EXTRAS

Rush me the following:

___Materials List: $60 (Must be purchased with Blueprint set.) Add $10 for Schedule C4–L4 plans $_____
___**Quote One**® Summary Cost Report @ $29.95 for one, $14.95 for each additional,
    for plans _____ $_____
    Building location: City _____ Zip Code _____
___**Quote One**® Material Cost Report @ $120 Schedules P1–C3; $130 Schedules C4–L4,
    for plan _____(Must be purchased with Blueprints set.) $_____
    Building location: City _____ Zip Code _____
___Specification Outlines @ $10 each $_____
___Detail Sets @ $14.95 each; any two $22.95; any three $29.95; all four for $39.95 (save $19.85) $_____
    ❑ Plumbing ❑ Electrical ❑ Construction ❑ Mechanical
___Home Furniture Planner @ $15.95 each $_____

DECK BLUEPRINTS

(Please refer to the Plans Index and Price Schedule in this section)

___Set(s) of Deck Plan _____. $_____
___Additional identical blueprints in same order @ $10 per set. $_____
___Reverse blueprints @ $10 fee per order. $_____
___Set of Standard Deck Details @ $14.95 per set. $_____
___Set of Complete Deck Construction Package (Best Buy!) Add $10 to Building Package.
    Includes Custom Deck Plan _____ Plus Standard Deck Details

LANDSCAPE BLUEPRINTS

(Please refer to the Plans Index and Price Schedule in this section.)

___Set(s) of Landscape Plan _____ $_____
___Additional identical blueprints in same order @ $10 per set $_____
___Reverse blueprints @ $10 fee per order $_____
Please indicate appropriate region of the country for Plant & Material List. Region _____

POSTAGE AND HANDLING *SIGNATURE IS REQUIRED FOR ALL DELIVERIES.*	1–3 sets	4+ sets
DELIVERY No CODs (Requires street address—No P.O. Boxes)		
•Regular Service (Allow 7–10 business days delivery)	❑ $20.00	❑ $25.00
•Priority (Allow 4–5 business days delivery)	❑ $25.00	❑ $35.00
•Express (Allow 3 business days delivery)	❑ $35.00	❑ $45.00
OVERSEAS DELIVERY	fax, phone or mail for quote	

Note: All delivery times are from date Blueprint Package is shipped.

POSTAGE (From box above) $_____
SUBTOTAL $_____
SALES TAX (AZ & MI residents, please add appropriate state and local sales tax.) $_____
TOTAL (Subtotal and tax) $_____

YOUR ADDRESS (please print legibly)

Name _____

Street_____

City _____State_____Zip _____

Daytime telephone number (required) (_____) _____

* Fax number (required for reproducible orders) _____
TeleCheck® Checks By Phone℠ available

FOR CREDIT CARD ORDERS ONLY

Credit card number _____ Exp. Date: (M/Y) _____

Check one ❑ Visa ❑ MasterCard ❑ Discover Card ❑ American Express

Order Form Key

Signature (required) _____

| HPT70 |

Please check appropriate box: ❑ Licensed Builder-Contractor ❑ Homeowner

ORDER TOLL FREE!
1-800-521-6797

BY FAX: Copy the order form above and send it on our FAXLINE: 1-800-224-6699 OR 520-544-3086

1 BIGGEST & BEST

1001 of our best-selling plans in one volume. 1,074 to 7,275 square feet. 704 pgs $12.95 1K1

2 ONE-STORY

450 designs for all lifestyles. 800 to 4,900 square feet. 384 pgs $9.95 OS

3 MORE ONE-STORY

475 superb one-level plans from 800 to 5,000 square feet. 448 pgs $9.95 MO2

4 TWO-STORY

443 designs for one-and-a-half and two stories. 1,500 to 6,000 square feet. 448 pgs $9.95 TS

5 VACATION

430 designs for recreation, retirement and leisure. 448 pgs $9.95 VS3

6 HILLSIDE

208 designs for split-levels, bi-levels, multi-levels and walkouts. 224 pgs $9.95 HH

7 FARMHOUSE

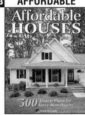

300 Fresh Designs from Classic to Modern. 320 pgs. $10.95 FCP

8 COUNTRY HOUSES

208 unique home plans that combine traditional style and modern livability. 224 pgs $9.95 CN

9 BUDGET-SMART

200 efficient plans from 7 top designers, that you can really afford to build! 224 pgs $8.95 BS

10 BARRIER-FREE

Over 1,700 products and 51 plans for accessible living. 128 pgs $15.95 UH

11 ENCYCLOPEDIA

500 exceptional plans for all styles and budgets—the best book of its kind! 528 pgs $9.95 ENC

12 ENCYCLOPEDIA II

500 completely new plans. Spacious and stylish designs for every budget and taste. 352 pgs $9.95 E2

13 AFFORDABLE

300 Modest plans for savvy homebuyers. 256 pgs. $9.95 AH2

14 VICTORIAN

210 striking Victorian and Farmhouse designs from today's top designers. 224 pgs $15.95 VDH2

15 ESTATE

Dream big! Eighteen designers showcase their biggest and best plans. 224 pgs $16.95 EDH3

16 LUXURY

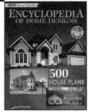

170 lavish designs, over 50% brand-new plans added to a most elegant collection. 192 pgs $12.95 LD3

17 EUROPEAN STYLES

200 homes with a unique flair of the Old World. 224 pgs $15.95 EURO

18 COUNTRY CLASSICS

Donald Gardner's 101 best Country and Traditional home plans. 192 pgs $17.95 DAG

19 COUNTRY

85 Charming Designs from American Home Gallery. 160 pgs. $17.95 CTY

20 TRADITIONAL

85 timeless designs from the Design Traditions Library. 160 pgs $17.95 TRA

21 COTTAGES

245 Delightful retreats from 825 to 3,500 square feet. 256 pgs. $10.95 COOL

22 CABINS TO VILLAS

Enchanting Homes for Mountain Sea or Sun, from the Sater collection. 144 pgs $19.95 CCV

23 CONTEMPORARY

The most complete and imaginative collection of contemporary designs available anywhere. 256 pgs. $10.95 CM2

24 FRENCH COUNTRY

Live every day in the French countryside using these plans, landscapes and interiors. 192 pgs. $14.95 PN

25 SOUTHERN

207 homes rich in Southern styling and comfort. 240 pgs $8.95 SH

26 SOUTHWESTERN

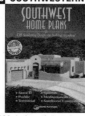

138 designs that capture the spirit of the Southwest. 144 pgs $10.95 SW

27 SHINGLE-STYLE

155 Home plans from Classic Colonials to Breezy Bungalows. 192 pgs. $12.95 SNG

28 NEIGHBORHOOD

170 designs with the feel of main street America. 192 pgs $12.95 TND

29 CRAFTSMAN

170 Home plans in the Craftsman and Bungalow style. 192 pgs $12.95 CC

30 GRAND VISTAS

200 Homes with a View. 224 pgs. $10.95 GV

31 DUPLEX & TOWNHOMES

115 Duplex, Multiplex &
Townhome Designs. 128 pgs.
$17.95 MFH

32 WATERFRONT

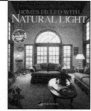

200 designs perfect for your
waterside wonderland.
208 pgs $10.95 WF

33 NATURAL LIGHT

223 Sunny home plans for all
regions. 240 pgs. $8.95 NA

34 NOSTALGIA

100 Time-Honored designs
updated with today's features.
224 pgs. $14.95 NOS

35 STREET OF DREAMS

Over 300 photos showcase
54 prestigious homes.
256 pgs $19.95 SOD

36 NARROW-LOT

250 Designs for houses
17' to 50' wide. 256 pgs.
$9.95 NL2

---

37 SMALL HOUSES

Innovative plans for
sensible lifestyles.
224 pgs. $8.95 SM2

38 GARDENS & MORE

225 gardens, landscapes,
decks and more to
enhance every home.
320 pgs. $19.95 GLP

39 EASY-CARE

41 special landscapes
designed for beauty and
low maintenance.
160 pgs $14.95 ECL

40 BACKYARDS

40 designs focused solely on
creating your own specially
themed backyard oasis. 160
pgs $14.95 BYL

41 BEDS & BORDERS

40 Professional designs
for do-it-yourselfers
160 pgs. $14.95 BB

42 BUYER'S GUIDE

A comprehensive look at 2700
products for all aspects of
landscaping & gardening.
128 pgs $19.95 LPBG

LANDSCAPE DESIGNS

---

43 OUTDOOR

74 easy-to-build designs,
lets you create and build
your own backyard oasis.
128 pgs $9.95 YG2

44 GARAGES

145 exciting projects from
64 to 1,900 square feet.
160 pgs. $9.95 GG2

45 DECKS

A brand new collection
of 120 beautiful and
practical decks. 144 pgs.
$9.95 DP2

46 HOME BUILDING

Everything you need to know
to work with contractors and
subcontractors. 212 pgs
$14.95 HBP

47 RURAL BUILDING

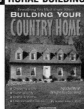

Everything you need to know
to build your home in the
country. 232 pgs.
$14.95 BYC

48 VACATION HOMES

Your complete guide to
building your vacation
home. 224 pgs.
$14.95 BYV

PROJECT GUIDES

Book Order Form

To order your books, just check the box of the book numbered below and complete the coupon. We will process
your order and ship it from our office within two business days. Send coupon and check (in U.S. funds).

YES! Please send me the books I've indicated:

❑ **1:1K1** $12.95	❑ **17:EURO** ...$15.95	❑ **33:NA** $8.95
❑ **2:OS** $9.95	❑ **18:DAG** $17.95	❑ **34:NOS** $14.95
❑ **3:MO2** $9.95	❑ **19:CTY** $17.95	❑ **35:SOD** $19.95
❑ **4:TS** $9.95	❑ **20:TRA** $17.95	❑ **36:NL2** $9.95
❑ **5:VS3** $9.95	❑ **21:COOL** ...$10.95	❑ **37:SM2** $8.95
❑ **6:HH** $9.95	❑ **22:CCV** $19.95	❑ **38:GLP** $19.95
❑ **7:FCP** $10.95	❑ **23:CM2** $10.95	❑ **39:ECL** $14.95
❑ **8:CN** $9.95	❑ **24:PN** $14.95	❑ **40:BYL** $14.95
❑ **9:BS** $8.95	❑ **25:SH** $8.95	❑ **41:BB** $14.95
❑ **10:UH** $15.95	❑ **26:SW** $10.95	❑ **42:LPBG** ...$19.95
❑ **11:ENC** $9.95	❑ **27:SNG** $12.95	❑ **43:YG2** $9.95
❑ **12:E2** $9.95	❑ **28:TND** $12.95	❑ **44:GG2** $9.95
❑ **13:AH2** $9.95	❑ **29:CC** $12.95	❑ **45:DP2** $9.95
❑ **14:VDH2** ...$15.95	❑ **30:GV** $10.95	❑ **46:HBP** $14.95
❑ **15:EDH3** ...$16.95	❑ **31:MFH** $17.95	❑ **47:BYC** $14.95
❑ **16:LD3** ...$12.95	❑ **32:WF** $10.95	❑ **48:BYV** $14.95

Books Subtotal $ _____
ADD Postage and Handling (allow 4–6 weeks for delivery) $ 4.00
Sales Tax: (AZ & MI residents, add state and local sales tax.) $ _____
YOUR TOTAL (Subtotal, Postage/Handling, Tax) $ _____

YOUR ADDRESS (PLEASE PRINT)

Name _____

Street _____

City _____State _____Zip _____

Phone (_____) _____—_____

YOUR PAYMENT

TeleCheck® Checks By Phone℠ available
Check one: ❑ Check ❑ Visa ❑ MasterCard ❑ Discover ❑ American Express
Required credit card information:

Credit Card Number _____

Expiration Date (Month/Year)_____ / _____

Signature Required _____

Canadian Customers Order Toll Free 1-877-223-6389

Home Planners, LLC
3275 W. Ina Road, Suite 110, Dept. BK, Tucson, AZ 85741

HPT70

447

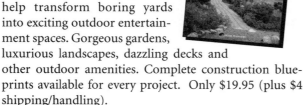